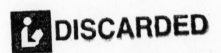

China and the World War

CHINA AND THE WORLD WAR

———

By

THOMAS EDWARD LA FARGUE

New York · HOWARD FERTIG · 1973

Library of Congress Cataloging in Publication Data
La Fargue, Thomas Edward, 1900-
    China and the World War.
    Reprint of the ed. published by Stanford University
Press, Stanford University, Calif., which was issued
as no. 12 of Hoover War Library publications.
    Bibliography: p.
    1. European War, 1914-1918—China. I. Title.
II. Series: Stanford University. Hoover Institution
on War, Revolution, and Peace. Publications, no. 12.
D621.C6L3   1973   940.3'51   79-80563

Printed in the United States of America
by Noble Offset Printers, Inc.

PREFACE

ONE of the most important questions which arose in the Far East as a direct result of the outbreak of war in Europe in August 1914 was the so-called Shantung question. This question was primarily concerned with disposal of the leasehold and economic rights formerly enjoyed by Germany in the Chinese province of Shantung.

The presence of a fortified German base on the coast of China inevitably drew the Far East into the area of hostilities. Japan entered the war with the primary and almost exclusive aim of eliminating the German foothold on the China coast. The capture of Tsingtao early in the war by Japanese naval and military forces, aided by a small and unimportant contingent of British troops, raised the question of the eventual disposition of the German leasehold of Kiaochow and of the valuable economic rights held by Germany in connection with the leasehold. Japan's desire to bind China to transfer to her the German leasehold and rights was partially, but by no means wholly, responsible for the "Twenty-one Demands" which Japan presented to China early in 1915. The nature and extent of these demands and the method by which they were presented to China brought into sharp contrast the conflicting policies of the United States and Japan in China.

Finally, the entrance of the United States into the war gave President Wilson the opportunity to bring forward his conception of a new world order. The methods by which Japan had secured the consent of China and the support of the Entente Powers to her claims to the former German rights in Shantung became, in the eyes of President Wilson and of a large part of the American people, an outstanding example of the evils of the old diplomacy which President Wilson's new world order was designed to overcome. In consequence, the Shantung question assumed at the Peace Conference a significance altogether out of keeping with its intrinsic importance. It came to be regarded in America as a test case of the strength of President Wilson's idealism. Ironically enough, his subsequent inability at Paris to overcome the secret treaties with which Japan had come armed to the Peace Conference and his failure to secure "justice" for China were among the chief

v

arguments used by his political opponents to defeat the acceptance of the Treaty of Versailles by the United States.

It is largely because of this latter consideration that the Shantung question assumes any importance at all in international affairs. It had little permanent effect upon the subsequent history of China except to deepen the already deep distrust of the Chinese people for Japan. In fact, the World War had only a remote and passing interest for the Chinese people. At no time did they exhibit other than a mild interest in the fact of its existence. It was not until the Chinese Delegation at Paris came out in unqualified defiance of Japan that the enthusiastic interest of the Chinese people in the victory of the Allies was aroused. The hope of being able successfully to defy Japan, however, proved to be illusory and ended in bitter disappointment.

The complete subservience of the many important questions which arose concerning China's relations with the powers at war with Germany to the vicissitudes of the factional strife which characterized Chinese domestic politics during this period has continually impressed itself upon the author. Accordingly, he has made every effort to show the intimate connection between such important questions as China's entrance into the war and the formulation of the Chinese program at Paris, and the internal political situation prevailing at the time these questions arose.

No attempt has been made to cover exhaustively all phases of China's relations with the various belligerents during the war. Certain phases of China's relations with Russia and Japan, for instance, have been passed over. What has been attempted, however, is to give an adequate account of the main events which occurred in China because of the war and thus to correct the errors and distortions with which a too facile journalism has surrounded these events.

The author wishes to express his appreciation to those who have aided and encouraged him in the preparation of this contribution to the history of the Far East. He wishes to thank the staff of the Hoover War Library of Stanford University who have made accessible to him the extensive collection of documents pertaining to the Peace Conference, and especially to thank Professor Ralph H. Lutz, who, in his capacity as Director of the Hoover War Library, has been very generous in placing the facilities of that Library at his disposal. Thanks are due also to Professor Payson J. Treat, whose penetrating suggestions and high standards of criticism have acted as an ever present tonic in times both of enthusiasm and of discouragement; to Professor Yamato Ichihashi, of Stanford University; to Dr. E. T. Williams, of the University of California, and to the staff of Stanford University Press, for valuable criticism and suggestions; and also to Mr. David Hunter Miller for permission to reproduce certain documents from *My Diary at the Conference of Paris.* Finally, the author reserves his ultimate and final gratitude for that traditional and indispensable "best friend and severest critic," his wife, who has lived up to the highest traditions of her calling.

THOMAS E. LA FARGUE

NEW HAVEN, CONNECTICUT
May 1, 1937

TABLE OF CONTENTS

China and the World War

Map of Shantung Province and China Coast

CHAPTER I

THE OUTBREAK OF THE WAR

The outbreak of the World War came at a time when the affairs of China were in a particularly precarious condition. The young republic was less than three years old, yet already in its short history ominous signs of the civil strife which were to mark the first two decades of its existence had appeared. By August 1914, at least on the surface, the worst of the disturbances caused by the Revolution of 1911 had subsided. It seemed as if internal order was well on its way to be restored. The reorganized Salt Gabelle was beginning to bring urgently needed additional revenues to the Central Government. Contributions from the provinces, which had entirely ceased during the Revolution, were beginning to trickle toward Peking once again.

On the political side of affairs, however, the situation was far from reassuring. Gradually the more liberal aims of the Revolution were being sacrificed to the personal ambitions of Yuan Shih-k'ai, the president of the Republic. Through a series of arbitrary acts Yuan had seized control of the Central Government, and by the advent of the World War he had succeeded in making himself dictator of the political affairs of China. But he had obtained this position at the expense of embittering such men as Sun Yat-sen and other leaders of the Revolution and of setting the Revolutionary party (the Kuomintang or National People's party) in uncompromising opposition to his regime.

In 1912 Sun Yat-sen and his fellow revolutionists, because of their military weakness, had been forced to make a deal with Yuan Shih-k'ai in order to bring the revolution to a successful termination. By this deal Yuan, who was in command of the Imperial forces, agreed to persuade the Manchu imperial family to abdicate, and he was to become president of the Republic in place of Sun Yat-sen, who had already been elected to that office. Accordingly Yuan took the oath of office on March 10, 1912, and the Provisional Constitution was proclaimed on the same day.

However, a bitter quarrel soon broke out between him and the National Assembly in which the Kuomintang held a large majority.[1] The leaders of this party were largely composed of the men who had carried through the Revolution of 1911. They wished to set up a conventional parliamentary type of government in which the president would be subordinated to the parliament, and had provided for such a form of government in the Provisional Constitution. Yuan had no intention of subordinating his authority to that of the Assembly and immediately began to act in defiance of that body. There ensued a struggle between Yuan and the Assembly. This struggle finally culminated in the so-called Nanking Rebellion, in which Sun Yat-sen and his associates attempted to overthrow Yuan Shih-k'ai by force. With his superior troops Yuan easily defeated his opponents, and most of them were forced to flee from China. Shortly thereafter he dissolved the Kuomintang, and a few months later he abolished the Assembly and threw into discard the Kuomintang Provisional Constitution.

The result of these acts was to place Yuan in a position of supreme authority. Opposition to Yuan, however, was driven underground rather than eliminated. It was ready to break out anew at the earliest opportunity and it gradually became centered at Canton, where Yuan's opponent's set themselves up as champions of parliamentary procedure against his dictatorship and later, after his death in June 1916, against the military domination of the *tuchuns,* or provincial military governors, who succeeded to his power. The struggle between the parliamentarians of the south and the military leaders of the north continued all through the years of the World War. It colored all of China's foreign relations during this period, and it forms the background to which such events as the entrance of China into the war and the stand taken by the Chinese Delegation at the Paris Peace Conference of 1919 must be related in order to be properly understood.

The immediate effect of the war upon China was to cause an almost complete cessation of China's foreign trade, which was accompanied by a temporary financial stringency. Shanghai harbor was deserted by all shipping with the exception of native coastwise boats. The government's plans for a second large foreign loan,

---

[1] See T'ang Leang-Li, *The Inner History of the Chinese Revolution,* chapters viii and xi, for a detailed, although anti-Yuan and somewhat anti-foreign, account of the struggle between the Kuomintang and Yuan.

negotiations for which had almost been completed, had to be given up, and for the first time the republican government turned to its own citizens for a public loan. Shortly after the outbreak of the war, the Chinese government floated a domestic loan for the sum of M$16,000,000.[2] The foreign communities in China, the international character of which was a marked feature of life in the treaty ports, suddenly became alive to the import of the war for them. Nationals of the Allies began to be called home for military service, and German and Austrian reservists from all over China began to move toward Kiaochow, the German fortified base in the province of Shantung. Both the German and the British naval forces were withdrawn from the Yangtze, leaving the protection of foreign interests in that region to American and Japanese forces.

In view of China's position with regard to the belligerents of both sides, her situation was most delicate. Germany possessed a strongly fortified base on the Shantung coast within the leased area of Kiaochow and excellent accommodations for the outfitting and supplying of her warships at the leasehold's port of Tsingtao. Great Britain had her base of operations at Hong Kong, which, although British territory, nevertheless threatened to make the preservation of neutrality by China difficult. In addition, Great Britain held leaseholds at Weihaiwei and Kowloon, and France possessed the leasehold of Kwangchowan. All of the belligerents held trade and resident settlements in various Chinese ports and also maintained bodies of troops within territory nominally under Chinese sovereignty.

In view of this situation any attempt of the Chinese government to preserve its neutrality from violation was certain to meet with great difficulties. The simplest solution from the viewpoint of the Chinese government would be to get the belligerents to agree to exclude Chinese territory from the area of hostilities. This it attempted to do by enlisting the good offices of the United States government. On August 3, MacMurray, the American chargé d'affaires in Peking, reported that he had "been approached on behalf of the Minister for Foreign Affairs with an inquiry as to the consideration the American Government would give to a request that it endeavor to obtain the consent of the belligerent European nations to an undertaking not to engage in hostilities either

[2] Later increased to M$26,000,000 (Mexican dollars).

in Chinese territory and marginal waters or in adjacent leased territories."[3]

The inclusion of "leased areas" in this proposal was very important, as it meant, if accepted, that the German fortified base at Kiaochow would be excluded from the area of hostilities and therefore would remain in the hands of Germany at the conclusion of the war. As the situation developed, it became apparent that this was not at all in harmony with the views of Japan, who wanted to seize the opportunity afforded by the war to remove permanently the German base, which she considered not alone to be a menace to the safety of Japan but to be a factor disturbing to the entire Far East.

Secretary of State Bryan acted somewhat cautiously upon the request of the Chinese government. On August 7, he authorized MacMurray "to participate in proposed arrangements to neutralize all foreign settlements in China not including leased areas."[4] In answer to the more sweeping request of the Chinese government to exclude all of the Chinese territory and marginal waters, including leased areas from the area of hostilities, he replied that "the Department is giving the matter careful consideration."[5]

In the meantime the situation in the Far East was becoming a little clearer. The German commandant at Kiaochow was giving every evidence of his intention to prepare for a siege. On August 1 martial law was declared within the leased area.[6] On the same date, Sir John Jordan, the British Minister at Peking, reported that "all German reservists throughout China are ordered to proceed to Tsingtao where German, Austrian and Italian ships of war are concentrating."[7] It was evident that Germany was going to defend her stronghold at Kiaochow against any attempts on the part of the Allies to force its surrender.

The United States government, instead of attempting formally to suggest to the belligerents that China might be excluded from the area of hostilities, began to make discreet inquiries among the belligerent powers as to their views about preserving the status quo in

---

[3] MacMurray to Bryan, August 3, 1914, *Papers Relating to the Foreign Relations of the United States, 1914, Supp.*, p. 162. Hereafter cited as *Foreign Relations*.

[4] Bryan to MacMurray, August 7, 1:00 P.M., 1914, *ibid.*, p. 163.

[5] Bryan to MacMurray, August 7, 5:00 P.M., 1914, *ibid.*, p. 163.

[6] G. P. Gooch and H. W. V. Temperley, *British Documents on the Origins of the War, 1898–1914*, Vol. XI, p. 322. Hereafter cited as *British Documents*.

[7] Jordan to Grey, August 1, 1914, *ibid.*, p. 248.

the Far East. The American Ambassador in London, Mr. Page, reported to the Department on August 11:

Sir Edward Grey has conferred with me about suggestions that he says you have made through the British Embassy at Washington concerning the possible neutralization of the Pacific Ocean. He fears that so sweeping an arrangement could hardly be made. But suggestion from the United States to England and Germany to agree that *status quo* in China be maintained by each of them would be a great advantage if agreed to. Grey must consult British Cabinet before committing himself but there is little doubt in my mind about the Cabinet's acceptance. Please consider whether our Government will make such a suggestion and inform me. . . . .

Grey's concern is to prevent fighting in China or in Chinese waters for fear of causing disturbance in China.[8]

On the same day, August 11, Bryan telegraphed instructions to the American Ambassador in Germany, Gerard, to "discreetly ascertain the views of the German Government as to the possibility of circumscribing the area of hostilities and maintaining the status quo in the Far East."[9] But these discreet feelers on the part of the United States were to come to nought in accomplishing the desired aim. It was not the European powers who were to determine whether the Far East should or should not be involved in the hostilities of the World War; Japan was to be the determining factor, and her attitude was rapidly becoming defined.

The Japanese government had followed the situation in Europe very closely, and as soon as it became apparent that Great Britain might be involved in the conflict the two allies had communicated with each other under the terms of the Anglo-Japanese Alliance.

Following the declaration of war by Great Britain against Germany, on August 4, the German government made no announcement of its intentions with regard to the leased territory of Kiaochow. Japan, therefore, had no clue to the course Germany was going to follow in the Far East. A factor which complicated the situation was that the German representatives in Peking and Tokyo were cut off from communication with their government and consequently were without instructions.[10] Despite lack of instructions,

---

[8] Page to Bryan, August 11, 1914, *Foreign Relations, 1914, Supp.*, p. 165.

[9] Bryan to Gerard, August 11, 1914, *ibid.*, p. 167. See *infra*, pp. 8–16, for the discussions which were going on simultaneously with the American efforts at neutralization of the Far East between Great Britain and Japan relative to action of the latter against Kiaochow.

[10] On August 11, the German Ambassador in Tokyo, through the American Ambassador, requested the American State Department to inform his government

the German authorities in Kiaochow were making every preparation for hostilities. German warships were being outfitted in the
harbor at Tsingtao and made ready for action. Most of the regular
German troops in China had been drawn within the leased territory, and their number was being rapidly supplemented by German
reservists from all over China, who poured daily into Kiaochow
over the Tsingtao-Tsinan Railway.

These warlike preparations within the leased area and the failure
of the German government to bring forward any suggestion as to
the possibility of neutralizing the fortified bases of the belligerents
in the Orient precipitated Japan's demand that Germany either surrender Kiaochow peaceably or suffer the consequences of a military
and naval attack upon the stronghold. On August 11, just twelve
hours after he had optimistically reported his conversation with
Sir Edward Grey with regard to the possibility of maintaining the
status quo in China, Ambassador Page in London had to report:
"Sir Edward Grey informs me that Japan finds herself unable to
refrain from war with Germany."[11]

Several days elapsed, however, before the Japanese government
gave effect to this decision by delivering to Germany an ultimatum
demanding the unconditional surrender of Kiaochow. This delay
is in part explainable by certain differences of opinion which had
arisen between Great Britain and Japan as to the scope which
Japan's belligerent operations should take. Japan's decision to enter
the conflict had been preceded by several communications with the
British government indicating that Japan was coming to her support
under the terms of the Anglo-Japanese Alliance. An examination
of the correspondence between the two governments leads one to
the conclusion, however, that Japan's final decision was taken only
in part because of Great Britain's call under the Alliance.

As early as August 1 Sir Edward Grey informed the Japanese
Ambassador in London that "under certain conditions we might
find it necessary to intervene," but he "did not see that we were
likely to have to apply to Japan under our alliance, or that the inter-

---

that he advised neutralization of the Orient in order to prevent an attack upon
German possessions by Japan. The State Department doubted the propriety of
becoming the medium through which such a proposal should be transmitted but
continued to make inquiries on its own account. Guthrie to Bryan, August 11,
1914, *Foreign Relations, 1914, Supp.*, p. 166, and Bryan to Guthrie, August 11,
1914, *ibid.*, p. 167.

[11] Page to Bryan, August 11, 1914, *ibid.*, p. 167.

ests dealt with by the alliance would be involved . . . ."[12] To this
the Japanese government replied, through Sir Conyngham Greene,
the British Ambassador at Tokyo: "His Majesty's Government may
count upon Japan at once coming to assistance of her ally with all
her strength, if called on to do so, leaving it entirely to His Majesty's
Government to formulate the reason for, and the nature of the
assistance required . . . ."[13]

Evidently there was some doubt in the mind of Sir Edward
Grey whether or not Great Britain, under the terms of the Alliance,
could as yet rightfully call upon Japan for assistance. He therefore asked Sir William Tyrell, of the British Foreign Office, for
his opinion as to "whether the present situation in any way affects
the Japanese under the 1911 Agreement and whether we have anything to ask them." In response to this request, Sir William Tyrell
prepared the following minute:

> The only ways in which the Japanese could be brought in would be if
> hostilities spread to the Far East, e.g., an attack upon Hong Kong by the
> Germans, or if a rising in India were to take place.
>
> There seems no reason to say anything about India, but it might be as well
> to warn the Japanese Government that in event of a war with Germany there
> might be a possibility of an attack upon Hong Kong or Wei-hai-Wei when
> we should look to them for support.
>
> The Japanese are no doubt quite alive to this possibility, but perhaps
> under Article 1 of the agreement we should communicate with them. [signed]
> W.T. [date] 3. 8. 14.[14]

To this minute Sir Edward Grey appended the following note:
"Do so by telegraph without further reference to me. E. G."

Accordingly, on August 3, Sir Conyngham Greene was instructed to inform the Japanese government that "if hostilities
spread to Far East, and an attack on Hong Kong or Wei-hai-Wei
were to take place, we should rely on their support."[15] On August 4
the Japanese government replied, through Sir Conyngham Greene:

> . . . . in the special eventualities referred to, namely;—an attack on Hong
> Kong or Wei-hai-Wei or a similar concrete act of aggression the Imperial
> Government will be ready at once to support His Majesty's Government if
> called upon, as explained in my telegram No. 58 [refers to his telegram of
> August 3, quoted above]. In the hypothetical cases, such as a capture of a

---

12 Grey to Greene, August 1, 1914, *British Documents,* Vol. XI, p. 256.

13 Greene to Grey, August 3, 1914, *ibid.,* p. 305.

14 Note by Sir Wm. Tyrell, August 3, 1914, *ibid.,* p. 292.

15 Grey to Greene, August 3, 1914, *ibid.,* p. 298.

British merchant ship or a case involving, perhaps, a question of Chinese or Russian territorial waters, the Imperial Government would wish to have the opportunity of considering it and consulting with His Majesty's Government before taking definite action.[16]

Sir Edward Grey evidently decided, for the time at least, not to call upon Japan for assistance, and on the following day, August 4, he replied to Japan's offer as follows:

I asked the Japanese Ambassador today to thank Baron Kato most cordially for his generous offer of assistance.

I told the Ambassador how much I had been impressed by the way in which Japan, during the Russo-Japanese War, demanded nothing of us under our alliance with her except what was strictly in accord with the Treaty of Alliance . . . . I had thought that a fine attitude of good faith and restraint; and now we in turn should avoid, if we could, drawing Japan into any trouble.[17]

This communication is the last in this series of exchanges of views between the two governments which appear in the *British Documents on the Origins of the War*. There is sufficient additional evidence, however, to indicate that between August 4, the date of the last communication, and August 15, the day upon which Japan dispatched her ultimatum to Germany demanding the surrender of Kiaochow, the British and Japanese governments were not entirely in accord as to how far Japan's belligerent activities should extend.

In this initial correspondence the British Foreign Office made no mention of the fact that an attack upon the German naval and military base at Kiaochow might possibly constitute a reason for Japan's entrance into the war. Japan now suggested this possibility, together with the question of Japanese naval operations against the German islands in the Pacific. Sir Edward Grey indicates that it was the latter question which caused a difference in views to arise between the two allies. Baron Kato, the Japanese Foreign Minister at this time, according to his semiofficial biography, claims that it was the reluctance of Sir Edward Grey to agree to a Japanese attack upon Kiaochow which caused the difference of opinion.

The following statement is made by Sir Edward Grey in his memoirs:

Let me now deal specifically with some of the questions which arose between us and America as the war proceeded.

[16] Greene to Grey, August 4, 1914, *British Documents*, Vol. XI, p. 327.
[17] Grey to Greene, August 1914, *ibid.*, p. 329.

In the early days the Japanese Alliance was a matter of some embarrassment and even anxiety. Japan was ready to take her part in the war as our Ally; the Far East and the whole of the Pacific Ocean lay open to her and were her natural sphere of operations. But the prospect of unlimited Japanese action was repugnant to Australia and New Zealand. They already regarded Germany, her position, and transactions in the Pacific with misgivings; they would have viewed the substitution of Japan for Germany with positive alarm. Equally important, the effect of Japanese action on public opinion in the United States might be disastrous; it might even make American sentiment definitely antagonistic to us. It was unthinkable that we should not have the most scrupulous care for the interest and the feelings of British Dominions that were taking their part in the war, ready to face danger and to make sacrifices with so much patriotism. We dared not risk offending the United States. We had, therefore, to explain to Japan that her help would be welcome, but that her action must be limited and her prospective acquisition of German territory must not extend beyond certain bounds. To explain to an Ally that her help will be welcome, but that you hope it will not be made inconvenient, is a proceeding that is neither agreeable nor gracious. It was, however, not only politic, but essential for us and the Allies.[18]

The biography of Baron Kato, which is based largely on official Japanese government sources, quite definitely reveals that it was the question of an attack on Kiaochow that caused the differences between Great Britain and Japan to arise at this juncture.[19] It also reveals that the Okuma cabinet and the Genro, the four Elder Statesmen whose advice was traditionally sought upon questions of grave national import, did not come to the final decision to enter the war without certain misgivings and that an effort was made to get Germany to surrender her base on the China coast without actually going to war.

Three days after Grey's message of August 4, in which he had stated that "we in turn should avoid, if we could, drawing Japan into any trouble," Great Britain definitely requested the assistance of Japan. The request, however, confined the belligerent activities of Japan within limits which the Japanese government felt unable to accept. Sir Edward Grey proposed:

As some time will be needed in order that our ships of war may find and destroy German ships in Chinese waters, it is most important that the Japanese fleet should, if possible, hunt out and destroy the armed German merchant cruisers who are now attacking our commerce.

If the Imperial Government would be good enough to employ some of

[18] Viscount Grey, *Twenty-Five Years, 1892–1916*, Vol. II, pp. 103–4.

[19] Masunori Ito, *Kato Takaaki Den* (a biography of Count Takaaki Kato); see especially Vol. II, Part xiv. Hereafter cited as *Kato Biography*.

their men-of-war thus, it would be of the greatest advantage to his Majesty's Government. This, of course, means an act of war against Germany but this is, in our opinion, unavoidable.[20]

Kato's immediate response to the invitation of Great Britain to attack German war vessels in Chinese waters was that this did not constitute an adequate reason for Japan to move against Germany. Furthermore, he did not believe that mere attacks on the high seas upon British merchant vessels by German warships brought the Anglo-Japanese Alliance into operation. His idea was that if Japan were to enter the war, it would be for the chief purpose of permanently eliminating the German base upon the China coast. He, therefore, did not consider Great Britain's proposal at all satisfactory.[21] Immediately upon receiving the message cited, on August 7, he held a consultation with Count Okuma, the Premier. As a result of this conference three points were agreed upon. It was decided: first, to enter the war; second, that Japan's belligerent actions were not to be limited to the destruction of German war vessels; and, third, that negotiations should be carried on with Great Britain to establish a satisfactory reason for entering the war, namely, the elimination of the German base of Kiaochow.[22]

On that same evening the cabinet met at the private residence of Baron Kato to discuss what action should be taken. At this meeting Kato led the discussion; and although he did not urge that Japan join the Allies, he pointed out the advantages which would accrue to Japan if such a course were followed.[23]

On the following day the most important members of the cabinet met with the four Genro. Some of the Genro were uncertain as to the wisdom of actually declaring war; and, therefore, the possibility of causing Germany to surrender Kiaochow without Japan becoming a belligerent was discussed.[24]

In the evening of this same day, August 8, Kato held a secret meeting with three members of the cabinet. The object of this meeting was to evolve a plan whereby Japan could accomplish her aim of removing Germany from Kiaochow Bay without actually going to war.[25] It was decided to send an ultimatum demanding the surrender of the German base. If Germany surrendered it peaceably there would be no necessity of going to war. It was also decided that it would be necessary to have Kiaochow surrendered

---

[20] *Kato Biography*, Vol. II, p. 78.   [21] *Ibid.*, p. 77.

[22] *Ibid.*, pp. 78–79.   [23] *Ibid.*   [24] *Ibid.*, p. 80.   [25] *Ibid.*, pp. 82–83.

directly to Japan in order to prevent Germany from entering into a secret agreement with China whereby the leasehold would be temporarily retroceded to China with the expectation of Germany's recovering it at the end of the war.[26] The plan evolved at this meeting explains why Japan's ultimatum to Germany allowed one week for Germany's reply instead of the customary twenty-four or, at the most, forty-eight hours. After the decision to adopt the course described above had been reached, negotiations with Great Britain were reopened. On August 9, Baron Kato informed the British government that Japan could go to war only on the basis of the Anglo-Japanese Alliance and that the task of destroying the German base at Kiaochow would provide the *casus belli* to bring the Alliance into active operation.[27]

The British government did not find Kato's proposal to its liking. The Japanese Ambassador in London, Inouyé, was informed:

> There is a danger of causing a disturbance throughout Asia as a result of Japan entering the war and as a consequence to vitally disturb the trade of Great Britain. Therefore, the British Government asks that Japan will postpone her war activities until advices are received from the Commander of the British fleet in Chinese waters and from the British Minister in China and the Cabinet comes to a decision.[28]

Ambassador Greene, in Tokyo, was instructed to deliver to Kato an even more explicit message. He was instructed to inform the Japanese government that:

> Since a declaration of war by Japan will create the impression that the war is being extended to the Chinese mainland and will cause anxiety in China, Great Britain asks Japan to limit its activities to the protection of commerce on the sea, and asks that a declaration of war be postponed until further consideration by the Cabinet.[29]

Kato seems to have been quite surprised at the unfavorable reception of his plan for an attack upon Kiaochow. He immediately dispatched a long memorandum to London in which he again asked Great Britain to agree to the destruction of the German base as the reason for Japan's entrance in the war under the terms of the Anglo-Japanese Alliance.[30]

Grey replied to this request of Kato on August 11. He reiterated the desire of Great Britain to keep hostilies from being extended

<hr />

[26] *Ibid.*   [27] *Ibid.*, p. 86.
[28] *Ibid.*, p. 88.   [29] *Ibid.*   [30] *Ibid.*

to the Chinese mainland and again requested that Japan "postpone for the time being hostile activities under the Anglo-Japanese Alliance."[31]

Kato, however, insisted that public opinion in Japan would not now permit Japan to draw back. Grey finally agreed to an attack on Kiaochow. He, however, remained reluctant to have Japan declare war without at the same time announcing that its sphere of naval operations would be confined in such a way as not to arouse criticism in Australia and New Zealand. Kato continued to insist that no restrictions be placed on Japan's activities. Finally, on August 14, Grey agreed to the extent that no limitation of Japan's actions need be incorporated in the ultimatum to Germany, but he did not withdraw his ideas as to the restrictions which should be set upon Japan's naval operations in the Pacific. Baron Kato refused to agree to any restrictions upon Japan's warlike activities.[32]

Meanwhile, the American government had received a reply from the German government as to the possibility of circumscribing the area of hostilities in the Pacific and maintaining the status quo in the Far East. The German proposal included the following:

1. Germany does not seek war with Japan.

2. If Japan, on account of the treaty with England, asks that Germany do nothing against English colonies, warships, or commerce in the East, Germany will assent in return for corresponding promise from England.

3. England and Germany to reciprocally agree that either all warships of both in East leave eastern waters or remain inactive as against the other, if remaining there.

4. Japan, England, and Germany to agree that none of these three shall attack warships, colonies, territory, or commerce of any of the others in the East.

5. The East to mean all lands and seas between parallels London 90° east and all Pacific to Cape Horn.[33]

[31] *Kato Biography*, Vol. II, p. 90.

[32] *Ibid.*, pp. 92–93. When Viscount Grey attempted to limit Japan's action in the South Seas, Kato pointed out that Japan had to protect its merchant vessels wherever they should go and therefore Japan's actions could not be limited to capturing German islands in the South Pacific (*ibid.*, p. 93). The two governments seemed not to have arrived at a clear understanding, as Great Britain, on August 18, released an official statement in which she stated: "It is understood that the action of Japan will not extend to the Pacific Ocean beyond the China Seas except in so far as it may be necessary to protect Japanese shipping lines in the Pacific, nor beyond Asiatic waters westward of the China Seas, nor to any foreign territory except territory in German occupation on the Continent of Eastern Asia" (*The Times* [London], August 18, 1914).

[33] Gerard to Bryan, August 13, 1914, *Foreign Relations, 1914, Supp.*, p. 169. Parallel 90° East runs just east of Calcutta.

This proposal was received by the American government on August 14 and was repeated to its Ambassador in Tokyo on August 15.[34] The proposal, however, came too late to have any bearing upon the situation. On the same day, the Japanese government dispatched an ultimatum to Germany demanding that she remove all her men-of-war and armed ships from Chinese waters immediately and "deliver up on a date not later than September 15, 1914, to the Imperial Japanese authorities without condition or compensation the entire leased territory of Kiaochow, with a view to eventual restoration of the same to China."[35] A reply was required by noon of August 23.

The language of the ultimatum indicated that Japan was taking the action therein contemplated solely upon her own responsibility. This was confirmed some time later by Baron Kato, who definitely stated before the Imperial Diet that the Japanese government had acted independently in dispatching the ultimatum. He further asserted that neither had any promise to Great Britain been made to restore Kiaochow to China nor had there been any agreement to limit the sphere of Japanese warlike operations in any way.[36]

On August 19, Count Okuma, the Japanese Premier, gave out a statement in Tokyo as follows:

Japan's object is to eliminate from continental China the root of German influence. . . . .

Japan's warlike operations will not, therefore, extend beyond the limits necessary for the attainment of that object and for the defense of her own legitimate interests. . . . .[37]

This statement was amplified by an official statement issued by the Japanese Foreign Office, which, after commenting on the demoralization of trade caused by the German warlike activities at Kiaochow, gave more fully the reason for Japan's action in demanding from Germany the surrender of the leased territory. In part, it said:

The history of the seizure of the place [Kiaochow] by Germany and her conduct preceding and including her intervention, in conjunction with Russia and France, after the Chino-Japanese war show that it is absolutely necessary to eliminate such possession completely if Japan is to restore immediate and

---

[34] *Ibid.*   [35] Guthrie to Bryan, August 15, 1914, *ibid.*, p. 170.

[36] Replies of the Minister of Foreign Affairs to interpellations in the Diet, December 10, 1914; see "Enclosure" in dispatch, Guthrie to Bryan, December 31, 1914, *Foreign Relations, 1914, Supp.*, pp. 210–11.

[37] *The Times* (London), August 21, 1914.

complete peace in the Far East in accordance with the terms of the Anglo-Japanese Alliance. If Japan is to look far enough into the future and adopt measures to insure an abiding peace in Eastern Asia she must realize that a strong military base in the hands of a hostile militant power right in the heart of the country cannot in itself fail to be a menacing factor . . . .[38]

The German government chose to ignore Japan's ultimatum, and on August 23 the Japanese government declared war upon Germany. In the interval between the dispatch of the ultimatum and the declaration of war, the German chargé d'affaires in Peking attempted on his own authority to come to some arrangement with the Chinese government whereby Germany would immediately retrocede Kiaochow to China. Such a procedure would have left to Germany the possibility of recovering Kiaochow at the end of the war or at least would have given her the right to claim, under the "compensation clause" in the lease agreement, an equivalent leasehold from China.[39] These pourparlers were not viewed with favor by Japan, and on August 19, MacMurray, the American chargé d'affaires, reported that he had learned that "the Chinese Government has now been warned to discontinue such *pourparlers*."[40] On the next day he further reported:

. . . . In reply to informal inquiries as to the possibility of Germany's retroceding Kiaochow directly to China, British Minister informed the Chinese that his Government could not now recognize such a transfer. In view of the threatening attitude adopted by Japan and apparently acquiesced in by Great Britain, the Chinese Government dares take no official action.

Liang [Minister of Communications], however, on his own responsibility requests me to telegraph to the Department an intimation that it would be acceptable to the Chinese Government if the United States were to find it possible to undertake to bring about the immediate retrocession of the leased territory and he suggests that the purpose might be accomplished by the American Government approaching Great Britain and Germany with a proposal that, in order to avert hostilities, the German rights in Kiaochow might be ceded to the United States for immediate transfer to China. He added that the Chinese regard the occupation of Tsingtao as a menace to the independence of China. . . . .[41]

[38] *New York Times*, August 21, 1914.

[39] Section I, Article V, Kiaochow Lease Agreement of March 6, 1898. J. V. H. MacMurray, *Treaties and Agreements with and concerning China*, Vol. I, p. 114. This clause permitted Germany to claim another leasehold on the coast of China if for any reason the Kiaochow leasehold were given up prior to the maturity of the lease agreement.

[40] MacMurray to Bryan, August 19, 1914, *Foreign Relations, 1914, Supp.*, p. 172.   [41] MacMurray to Bryan, August 20, 1914, *ibid.*, p. 173.

The proposal of Liang came to nothing. Mr. Bryan replied that "the Department feels sure that such a course would do more to provoke war than to avert war."[42] As soon as the opposition of the British and Japanese governments toward any attempts on the part of Germany to retrocede Kiaochow to China became apparent, the Chinese government gave up the discussions with the German chargé d'affaires.

In view of Japan's determination to evict Germany from Kiaochow and Germany's refusal to surrender the leasehold peacefully, Japan was left with no alternative but to reduce the stronghold by force.

The German commercial and strategic base on the China coast had been acquired under the Sino-German agreement of March 6, 1898. The leasehold embraced an area of about two hundred square miles surrounding the Bay of Kiaochow. When the Germans had taken possession of it, this area was little more than a salt marsh; but, with characteristic German enterprise, they had created there a fine harbor with docks and wharves sufficient to accommodate large vessels and warships. Tsingtao was conceded to be the model town of the Far East. Its wide streets and rows of trim buildings gave it the appearance of a typical German city. In accordance with its rights under the convention of 1898, the German government had fortified the hills back of the city and had erected forts to protect the immediate entrance to the bay. The two principal forts were the Iltis and the Bismarck. They carried heavy guns, but of a type which could not hope to withstand a siege by up-to-date battleships. Only a portion of the Bismarck fort was designed to resist an attack from the land side, the rest of the fortifications having been planned to defend the base from an attack by sea.

Tsingtao was connected with the interior of China by the Tsingtao-Tsinan Railway. This railway, some 240 miles long, had been built by private German capital at a cost of 53,000,000 marks. By the agreement of 1898, German subjects were given the right to mine for fifteen miles on either side of the railway; but this was later changed in a way which gave German interests a controlling share in most of the important coal and iron mines in Shantung. Finally, German subjects were granted the privilege of having the first opportunity to supply foreign personnel, capital, or materials for all public enterprises throughout the province of Shantung. At the outbreak

42 *Ibid.,* p. 174.

of war Germany kept a regular garrison of over 3,000 troops in Tsingtao, and complete facilities were available to condition and provision Germany's cruiser fleet in the Far East at the naval dockyard. This cruiser fleet under the command of Admiral Von Spee consisted of the two armored cruisers, "Scharnhorst" and "Gneisnau," three light cruisers, and several merchant colliers for provisioning the war vessels at sea. This fleet was specifically designed to prey upon enemy commerce and to avoid as far as possible direct conflict with enemy war vessels. Surrounding the leasehold proper on the land side there was a neutralized area some thirty miles deep in which the Chinese government had agreed not to issue any ordinances without the consent of the German government and in which German troops were to be accorded free passage. Within the leasehold Germany exercised all the rights of sovereignty.

On August 27 a Japanese fleet invested the port of Tsingtao, but this action came too late to prevent the escape of the German Far Eastern squadron. This squadron, under Admiral Von Spee, had sailed for a rendezvous at Ponape in the Caroline Islands as soon as the hostile attitude of Japan had convinced Von Spee that "any idea of engaging his fleet in cruiser warfare in the East Asia areas should be given up."[43] With the investment of Tsingtao, the trade of the Far East, largely carried on in British ships, was resumed. For the three weeks prior to the investment of the German port all coastal shipping had practically ceased and ocean-going vessels had remained in port.

In the meantime there had been assembled in Tsingtao about 3,500 regular German troops and about 2,500 reservists. These reservists represented a large proportion of the German commercial community in the Far East and, regardless of the results of the war, Germany could ill afford to waste these men in the foolhardy gesture of defending Tsingtao. Yet, under these circumstances, the only message the Kaiser could find to send to the beleaguered garrison was: "God will protect you as you fight bravely on."

The Japanese plan of attack upon the fortified area of Kiaochow was based upon a bombardment from the combined British and Japanese fleets lying off Tsingtao and an approach from the land side by Japanese troops.[44] As the eventual reduction of the Kiaochow

[43] T. E. Frothingham, *The Naval History of the World War, 1914–15*, p. 99.

[44] To which later was added a small British contingent in order to give the enterprise an Allied character.

fortresses was merely a matter of time, the chief concern of the Japanese commander of the expeditionary forces was to effect the reduction with as little loss of life as possible. Any attempt on the part of the Japanese troops to land within the leased area was out of the question, as such troops would have been completely at the mercy of the fire from the German forts on the hills immediately back of Tsingtao. Most of the fortifications were built with a view to defense against an attack from the sea and did not contemplate an attack from the land side. Thus strategic considerations indicated that the assault should be made by troops landing on the Shantung coast out of the range of the German guns and marching across the province to attack the weakly protected rear of the fortified area.

This plan involved the neutrality of China, but in determining upon it and in following it out the Japanese government followed the precedent set in the Russo-Japanese War. In that war the Japanese government laid down the principle that owing to the peculiar situation which had arisen as a result of the Russian forces occupying portions of Chinese territory, the neutrality of China was not absolute but was conditional on the actions of the enemy. Acting upon this principle, the Japanese government agreed to respect the neutrality of China within a well-defined theater of war as long as Russia did likewise. But Japan reserved the right to extend her operations outside this war zone in case Russia violated China's neutrality by extending her operations outside of these accepted limits.[45]

In making preparations for the defense of the leased territory, the German authorities had continually violated China's territorial neutrality by transporting armed forces from the Legation guard in Peking and Tientsin over the German-owned Tsingtao-Tsinan Railway into Kiaochow.[46] The Chinese authorities had been unable to

---

[45] See Nagao Ariga, *La Guerre Russo-Japonaise au point de vue continental et la droit international,* chapter xix, and especially pp. 505 and 508, for a discussion of Japan and Chinese neutrality during the Russo-Japanese War. Acting on this principle, the Japanese naval forces did not hesitate to enter the harbor of Chefoo in pursuit and capture of the Russian destroyer "Rechitelny," which had taken refuge there, and when Russian cavalry crossed the neutral zone west of the Liao River in Manchuria Japanese forces occupied this region.

[46] See Nagao Ariga, *La Chine et la Grande Guerre Européenne au point de vue du droit international,* pp. 33–35 and 55–56, for instances of German violations of Chinese territorial neutrality. The Chinese government held that Great Britain, France, and Russia in transporting detachments of troops from Peking to Hong Kong, Tientsin, and Vladivostok, respectively, were not violating Chinese neutrality, as these places were not seats of war (*ibid.,* p. 59).

prevent these violations of neutrality, and as early as August 10 the civil and military governors of Shantung suggested to the Central Government that, in view of the insufficiency of the forces at their disposal for defending Chinese neutrality in case of an attack upon Kiaochow, a war zone be delimited.[47]

In consequence, when it became evident that Germany was not going to avail herself of the terms of the ultimatum, Japan felt herself free to carry out her plans for a land attack upon the German base and to occupy the line of the German railway which traversed the province from east to west.

Negotiations looking to the delimitation of a war zone in Shantung in which belligerent operations could take place without violating China's neutrality were entered into with China on August 20. The principle of the war zone was agreed upon but not its extent. Japan wished to have the zone include all Shantung east of the Yellow River. Such a zone would have included the entire line of the Shantung Railway. The Chinese authorities wished to limit the zone to east of Weihsien, a town about halfway between the port of Tsingtao and Tsinan, the western terminal of the railway.[48] The Chinese government was itself anxious to set up a war zone, as the only alternative would be to prevent by force the Germans from transporting men, munitions, and supplies into the leased area. In addition to the difficulty of carrying out such a procedure there were substantial rumors that British and French volunteers, unable to get transportation home, were forming battalions at Tientsin with the intention of crossing Shantung to attack Kiaochow.[49] In such an eventuality Chinese authorities, if they wished to preserve China's neutrality, would be under the necessity of preventing the expedi-

---

[47] Ariga, *La Chine et la Grande Guerre Européenne* . . . ., p. 30.

[48] The Japanese statement of the Sino-Japanese negotiations relative to the setting up of a war zone, given at the Paris Peace Conference, was as follows: "Prior to the landing of Japanese troops, negotiations had been entered into at Peking, as early as August 20th, with a view to the establishment of a war zone east of the Yellow River. China had asked that the war zone should be limited to the west by Weihsien. The declaration of China relative to the war zone was made on September 3rd, one day after the first landing of the Japanese troops. But an understanding in regard to the principle of the establishment of this zone, outside of the 50 kilometer radius around Tsingtao, had already preceded the declaration." "Quelques Observations sur le memorandum Chinois demandant la restitution directe du territoire cédé à Bail de Kiaotchéou . . . ." (*Paris Peace Conference, Japanese Delegation Documents*, pp. 6–7).

[49] Ariga, *La Chine et la Grande Guerre Européenne* . . . . , pp. 40–44.

tion.[50] It seemed, therefore, that any action on the part of the Chinese government looking forward to the protection of its neutrality beyond perfunctory protests would involve it in serious trouble with both sides. The Chinese government, therefore, although disagreeing as to its extent, was quite willing to enter into negotiations with Japan relative to the setting up of a war zone within which the Chinese government would not be responsible for the actions of the belligerents.

Following her declaration of war against Germany, Japan, in pursuance of her plan of attack, on September 2, landed troops at Lungkow on the northern Shantung coast. These troops started overland and on September 14 came in contact with the German outposts. On September 23, a small British contingent landed at Laoshan Bay within the fifty-kilometer neutral zone but not within the leased area.[51] They were able to do this because the Japanese forces had already succeeded in driving the German forces back within the leased area proper.

On September 3, the day following the landing of the first Japanese contingent at Lungkow, the Chinese government, pressed by the necessity of absolving itself from responsibility, although the negotiations with Japan as to the limits of the war zone were not yet concluded, notified the representatives of the foreign powers at Peking of its inability to preserve neutrality in the regions affected by the operations of the troops of Japan, Great Britain, and Germany. It cited as a precedent the similar action taken by the Chinese government in Manchuria during the Russo-Japanese War. The Chinese government declared that "so far as concerning Lungkow, Laichow and places adjacent to Kiaochow Bay within the narrowest possible limits absolutely necessary for military operations of the belligerent troops, our Government will not be wholly responsible as a neutral state."[52]

Neither Germany nor Japan, however, recognized the zone somewhat loosely defined in this proclamation. The German chargé

---

[50] *Ibid.*, pp. 40–44. The Chinese government had already entered into correspondence with the British and French Ministers in regard to these rumors. In his reply the French Minister not only did not deny these rumors but indicated that he considered that France had a right to recruit armed forces on Chinese soil.

[51] The Japanese land forces comprised about 30,000 men. The British contingent totaled approximately 1,500 men.

[52] MacMurray, *Treaties and Agreements with and concerning China*, Vol. II, p. 1154.

d'affaires immediately protested against the delimitation of a war zone as being "obviously intended to facilitate the operations of the allied force!"[53] Later, the Chinese Minister in Berlin, Dr. Yen, telegraphed that the German government had refused to consent to the delimitation of the war zone on the grounds that Germany could derive no benefit from the action of the Chinese government and that it had reserved its free action in future with regard to damages.[54]

The Japanese government, in response to the action of the Chinese government, replied that the question had already passed from the sphere of diplomacy to that of military necessity and that as the extent of military action depended entirely upon the action of the enemy it would be impossible for Japan to consent in advance to any delimitation of the sphere of military operations.[55]

While these events were taking place, rumors persisted in the Chinese press and in official circles that the United States was preparing to send considerable naval forces to the Far East to protect China from aggression by any outside power. The reply of the United States government to the note of the Japanese government informing the United States of Japan's ultimatum to Germany contained references to the Root-Takahira notes of 1908 and cited these notes as the basis for consultation between Japan and the United States "should disturbances in the interior of China seem to the Japanese Government to require measures to be taken by Japan or other powers to restore order."[56] This suggestion of consultation between the two governments seems to have been interpreted by certain Chinese circles "as indicating a determination on the part of our Government [the United States] to insist upon its approval as a condition precedent to any Japanese action in Chinese territory."[57] In this connection, the American chargé d'affaires, MacMurray, under date of September 10, reported:

On the 27th ultimo Dr. V. K. Wellington Koo, of [the] Wai Chiao Pu, called upon me . . . . to inquire as to the precise terms and purport of the

[53] MacMurray, *op. cit.,* Vol. II, p. 1367.

[54] *North China Herald,* October 17, 1914, p. 171. The German protest was made in order to hold China responsible and possibly looked to the "compensation clause" in the Kiaochow Lease Agreement as a means by which Germany could demand another leasehold from China at the end of the war (Section I, Article V, Kiaochow Lease Agreement of March 6, 1898. MacMurray, *op. cit.,* Vol. I, p. 116).

[55] Ariga, *La Chine et la Grande Guerre Européenne* . . . . , pp. 47–48.

[56] Bryan to Guthrie, August 19, 1914, *Foreign Relations, 1914, Supp.,* p. 172.

[57] MacMurray to Bryan, September 10, 1914, *ibid.,* p. 187.

American note . . . . In discussing the matter with me Dr. Koo strongly intimated the view that the Root-Takahira exchange of notes established in favor of the United States a right to be consulted with respect to any action contemplated by Japan in Chinese territories, as though to imply that such rights were held by our Government in trust for the Government of China; and he specified the possible landing of an expeditionary force in Shantung . . . . as constituting a question in regard to which the Japanese Government would thereby be required to seek the approval of the United States.[58]

The attempt of the Chinese government to involve the United States in the question of China's neutrality in this manner was unsuccessful. Mr. Lansing, the Acting Secretary of State, replied to the suggestion in a tone which very well summed up the limits of action the United States would take with regard to China. He said: ". . . . it would be quixotic in the extreme to allow the question of China's territorial integrity to entangle the United States in international difficulties."[59]

It was not, however, the movement of the Japanese forces across the Shantung peninsula which caused the Chinese government to protest most vigorously. The fact that China, by permitting Germany to fortify the leased territory of Kiaochow, had inevitably opened her territory to hostilities in the event of war occurring between Germany and any other power was too obvious for the protests of China to be any other than perfunctory. What was to cause her great concern and to lead to events of special international significance was the determination of the Japanese military authorities to occupy the entire length of the Tsingtao-Tsinan Railway. This railway had its origin in the city of Tsingtao and, after passing through the leased territory, traversed the province of Shantung for 240 miles to its terminus at Tsinan, where it connected with the Tientsin-Pukow line.

The unneutral uses to which the German authorities at Tsingtao had put this railway in transporting troops from Tientsin and Peking and reservists into the leased territory has already been mentioned. These violations of Chinese neutrality continued after Japan had declared war upon Germany, and as late as August 27 the *North China Herald* correspondent reported that "German reservists from distant parts of China are still passing Kiaochow on their way to Tsingtao."[60] On August 20 the German chargé d'affaires in Peking had

<hr />

[58] *Ibid.*
[59] Lansing to MacMurray, November 4, 1914, *ibid.*, p. 190.
[60] *North China Herald*, September 5, 1914.

warned the Chinese government of the intention of Japan to land troops on the coast of Shantung and, somewhat ironically, had requested the Chinese government to forbid the passage of foreign troops across Chinese territory.[61] In response to this request the Chinese Minister of Foreign Affairs protested against the unneutral actions of the German authorities in making preparations for war at Kiaochow. Particular attention was called to the fact that the railway had been used to transport German troops, arms, ammunitions, and provisions into Kiaochow.[62] The Japanese authorities, in view of this situation and acting upon the precedent of the Russo-Japanese War, together with the military necessity of securing their rear communications against any dangers to their position at Kiaochow, determined to occupy the entire length of the railway.

On September 26 a detachment of Japanese troops occupied the railway station at Weihsien, and on October 6 they extended their control over the entire line by occupying the railway stations at Tsinan. These movements had been preceded by negotiations with the Chinese government in which the Japanese government attempted to get the Chinese government to agree to the occupation of the entire length of the line; but the negotiations were not yet concluded when the actions mentioned took place.

The occupation of the station at Weihsien called forth a protest from the Chinese government on September 27 as being in violation of Chinese neutrality.[63] The following day the Japanese Minister notified the Chinese government that the Japanese government was compelled by military necessity to take possession of the railway as far west as Tsinan.[64] On September 30 the Chinese government more fully protested against the Japanese action on the grounds that the railway was the private property of German and Chinese capitalists and that, in any case, the German troops were isolated in Tsingtao, and therefore it was beyond their power to use the railway.[65] On October 2, the Japanese government replied to the Chinese protests by reiterating its determination to occupy the full length of the line. The reasons given were that the railway was inseparable

---

[61] Ariga, *La Chine et la Grande Guerre Européenne* . . . . . , p. 37.

[62] *Ibid.*, pp. 37–38.

[63] MacMurray, *op. cit.*, Vol. II, pp. 1154–55.

[64] MacMurray to Bryan, September 29, 1914, *Foreign Relations, 1914, Supp.*, p. 181.

[65] MacMurray, *op. cit.*, Vol. II, p. 1155.

from the leased area and was German property of a public nature; that after the outbreak of hostilities the railway had been used to facilitate and augment military operations of the Germans; and that the occupation of the line as far west as Tsinan was necessary in order not to cause a breakdown of communications. Finally, it was stated that

Although the Chinese Government holds that under the present conditions the Shantung Railway cannot be utilized by the German troops in view of its severance with China, yet from the attacking troops' point of view, the Railway being immediately behind Tsingtao, and in view of the present situation, it is a serious danger to the military operations to leave a railway owned by the enemy perfectly free. We are, therefore, compelled to secure the railway by all means.[66]

On October 9, the Chinese government again protested the occupation of the railway by Japanese troops and reiterated its belief that the military necessity for occupying the line no longer existed and, further, that the Chinese government was quite capable of protecting the line against any unneutral uses.[67]

In this exchange of notes the fundamental difference in viewpoint between the Japanese and the Chinese governments with regard to the scope and purpose of Japan's action against the German base at Tsingtao was revealed. In its note of October 2, the Japanese government repeated its declaration that "The War now declared has for its aim not only the attack on the men-of-war and forts of the enemy in the leased territory of Kiaochow Bay, but also the elimination of the base of German activities in the Far East, which aim has been repeatedly communicated to the Government of China, and, we hope, has been clearly understood."[68]

To this statement the Chinese government, in its answer of October 9, replied:

Your country has announced that its declaration of war against Germany was for the purpose of preserving the peace of the Far East. Therefore, only the disarmament of German War vessels and the restoration of Kiaochow have been proclaimed. We have never heard of the so-called elimination of the base of German activities in the East.[69]

The Japanese envisaged the permanent removal of the German base because they were convinced that its presence constantly menaced the peace of the Far East. The Japanese government had stated that

---

[66] *Ibid.*, pp. 1155–56.   [67] *Ibid.*, pp. 1156–57.
[68] *Ibid.*, pp. 1155–56.   [69] *Ibid.*, pp. 1156–57.

to accomplish this aim was the avowed purpose of Japan in entering the war and that this end would not be fully attained until Germany was finally defeated. Therefore, until this event occurred it was under the necessity of taking every measure to prevent Germany from re-establishing her foothold on the China coast. The Chinese view on the other hand seems to have been that Japan's aim should be confined to rendering powerless Germany's means of carrying on hostilities in Chinese territory and marginal waters, and that, as soon as this had been accomplished by isolating all German war vessels and troops within the German base, the action of the Japanese troops in Shantung should be restricted to the narrowest possible limits.

Yuan Shih-k'ai was much concerned over the Japanese occupation of the Tsingtao-Tsinan Railway. He feared that it would cause the ever-threatening internal disturbances to break out. He therefore attempted to get the United States and Great Britain to prevail upon Japan to restrict her operations to the minimum necessary to the reduction of the German base.[70] His prestige was at stake, and in view of his ambition to become emperor he could not afford to "lose face" at this critical juncture.

The formal surrender of Kiaochow took place on November 10, and the entire leased territory was occupied by Japanese forces a few days later. On November 19, the Japanese military authorities at Kiaochow, in accordance with the intention of the Japanese government to retain control of the leased area until the end of the war, issued regulations establishing a military administration for the occupied area.

One more incident occurred to aggravate the already strained relations which had arisen between Japan and China as a result of the situation created by the war. On January 7, 1915, the Chinese government abruptly and without previous notification canceled the war zone which it had set up by its note of September 3. In a note addressed to the British and Japanese Ministers at Peking, the Chinese government stated:

Now, as the hostilities have ceased, and all military preparations have been entirely withdrawn, it is clear that there will be no more occasion to use Lungkow or the places near Kiaochow for military actions. It is, therefore, hereby declared that all the previous communications relating to the delimitation of the war zone shall be cancelled, and that the original status of the said area be restored.

[70] Reinsch to Bryan, October 2, 1914, *Foreign Relations, 1914, Supp.*, p. 183.

Wherefore I request, through you, Your Excellency, that your Government, in order to respect the neutrality of China, withdraw all the troops, if there is still any, from the said area.

Signed: SUN PAO-CHI.[71]

To this dénouement, the Japanese government replied on January 9, charging the Chinese government by its sudden cancellation of the war zone as acting in "want of confidence in international good faith and regardless of friendly relations" and added that "the Imperial Government would not permit the movement and actions of their troops within a necessary period to be affected or restricted by such act of cancellation."[72]

The series of incidents described above was marked by an increasing tension between Japan and China. The Japanese believed that the Chinese government was intent upon obstructing Japan's plan to eject the Germans from Kiaochow and were irritated by what they considered the pin-prick policy of their neighbor. The Chinese were disturbed by the nature and extent of Japan's military operations in Shantung. The difficulties which China found herself in as a result of the war reflected the anomalous position she occupied in the family of nations. Because of her own weakness and because of the restrictions placed upon her by the powers she was unable to discharge properly her international obligations. To any unneutral usages that the belligerents cared to make of her territory she could oppose only the formal precepts of international law. But her anomalous position precluded the full application of these precepts to China. The truth of the situation was that under the circumstances none of the belligerents were willing to restrict their actions in the Far East for the sake of China's neutrality.

Japan, now in full possession of the German leasehold in Shantung, began to prepare for a diplomatic move which would, at one fell swoop, settle many of what the Japanese government described as "outstanding questions between Japan and China." These questions took the form of the Twenty-one Demands with which the Chinese government was confronted shortly after the events described above had taken place.

[71] MacMurray, *op. cit.*, Vol. II, p. 1157.
[72] *Ibid.*, p. 1158.

CHAPTER II

THE BACKGROUND OF THE TWENTY-ONE DEMANDS

On January 18, 1915, the Japanese government approached the Chinese government with a series of proposals which have become generally known as the Twenty-one Demands. This diplomatic démarche came to the press and the general public of the Occident as a surprise. In reality, however, events in the Far East had been long pointing to some such move upon the part of Japan. These events found their culmination in the situation brought about by the capture of the German leased territory in Shantung by Japanese military forces. The removal of Germany from the China coast raised the problem of the eventual disposal of the German leasehold and the important economic rights which Germany had possessed in the province of Shantung. The settlement of the so-called Shantung question, however, while greatly enhancing the necessity which the Japanese government felt of arriving at a general settlement with China, was only one of several questions outstanding between the two countries which the Japanese government believed demanded some sort of solution.

These questions were all concerned with two fundamental problems of Sino-Japanese relations. The first, and probably the most important to Japan, was the necessity which past events had revealed of placing her position in South Manchuria upon a stronger treaty basis than it up to this time had possessed. This was to be accomplished by securing from China definite treaty rights which would constitute an effective recognition of Japan's paramount interests in this region over those of any other foreign power and would place Japan's hegemony there beyond challenge. The second problem was concerned with the increasing unsatisfactoriness of Japan's position in China proper as compared to that of the other Great Powers.

It has been commonly thought that Japan's victory over Russia in 1905 inaugurated an epoch of Japanese ascendancy in the affairs of China. On the contrary, the period between 1905 and 1914 was marked by a continual struggle on the part of Japan to preserve the favored or special position she had won for herself in South Manchuria. Japan's economic domination of this great area was continually menaced by powerful American and European financial interests, who, with the diplomatic support of their respective governments, attempted to extend to Manchuria the open competition for railway, mining, and industrial concessions which, in theory, at least, prevailed in China proper. Furthermore, south of the Great Wall it had become increasingly evident that Japan, because of her comparative financial weakness, was hopelessly outmatched in the competition which was being waged among the Great Powers for preferential positions with regard to the railway and mining development of modern China.[1] The monopolistic character of most of the railway and mining concessions, which European and American financial groups had secured from the Chinese government, threatened to exclude Japan from participation in this development.[2] Added to the financial inability of Japanese interests to compete for these concessions was the marked preference which the new republican government of China had shown to grant concessions to European and American concessionaires rather than to Japanese interests.[3]

The Revolution of 1911 marked the opening of a new "battle for concessions," but in this new battle the powers were not seeking slices of Chinese territory as they had been in 1898. Rather, they were content to support their nationals who sought from the Chinese government the right to finance and construct numerous railways and to exploit the mineral resources of China. In the competition for these concessions, Japanese interests were rapidly falling behind those of the Great Powers and were even being forced to take a position inferior to such national groups as the Belgian.[4]

The terms of the Four-Power Consortium (Great Britain, France, Germany, and the United States) Agreement of April 15, 1911, whereby the Chinese government granted to banking combines of these four nations a practical monopoly of furnishing it with funds for political and currency reform and for industrial loans, had

---

[1] Mr. Wakatsuki, Minister of Finance, speaking before the federated Chambers of Commerce of Japan in June, 1914, stated that "Japan is a debtor; she has to pay at present 90,000,000 yen of interest annually for foreign loans." Quoted in *Japan Times*, weekly edition, June 20, 1914.

[2] See *infra*, note 10.

[3] E.g., in the case of the so-called Yangtze Valley Railways; see *infra*, p. 42.

[4] E.g., in the Franco-Belgian concession to construct a railway from Kansu to Haichow on the coast north of Shanghai.

threatened to exclude Japan altogether from this profitable business and to reduce her political influence with the Chinese government to a very secondary place as compared with that of the Consortium powers. Japan, in company with Russia, in order not to be entirely excluded from the China business, demanded participation in the Consortium.[5] Upon being admitted, these two powers, in turn, strove to get the terms of the Consortium agreement modified in so far as it applied to Manchuria.[6] In these efforts they were partially successful, but when, later, the Consortium decided to exercise its loan monopoly in China only in so far as political and currency reform loans were concerned, throwing open to general competition industrial loans for all of China, the financial inability of Japan to compete for such business was fully realized.[7] It led Mr. Yagyu, the president of the Bank of Formosa, to remark: "The result of the resolution [of the Consortium to permit general competition for industrial loans] will be the competition of the real ability of the Powers which means ultimately the competition of financial power. This will lead Japan to a very difficult position."[8] The *North China Herald* was editorially more outspoken. It remarked that, "in the scramble for concession and loan agreements, which will certainly be attempted if not realized under the new freedom of finance, success will presumably be to the longest purse, which is also able to allow the longest credit; in such competition Japan is greatly at a disadvantage as compared with almost any other of the Five Powers."[9] These predictions were fully realized by the summer of 1914, for by that time, in spite of their "open door" and "equal opportunity" avowals, the European powers had divided China, south of the Great Wall, into a series of economic enclaves within which their respective nationals enjoyed what amounted to an exclusive monopoly of railway financing and construction.[10]

[5] MacMurray, *Treaties and Agreements with and concerning China,* Vol. I, pp. 841–49, Chinese currency reform and industrial loan agreement, April 15, 1911.

[6] *Infra,* p. 37.

[7] The decision referred to was embodied in a resolution accepted by the Consortium groups at Paris on September 26, 1913. *Japan Times,* weekly edition, October 4, 1913.

[8] *Ibid.*

[9] *North China Herald,* October 18, 1913, p. 163.

[10] The extent to which this economic "break-up" of China had progressed at the time of the outbreak of the war can be fully realized only as the result of close study of the various railway and mining concessions granted by the Chinese

In this pre-war scramble for railway concessions, Japanese interests fared very badly. Up to the opening of the war, Japanese interests had not succeeded in obtaining a single important railway concession south of the Great Wall. Japanese capitalists had participated in the financing of two short lines, but both of these lines had been completed and opened for traffic prior to the Revolution of 1911.[11]

The results of the situation described above were threefold. In the first place, Japanese capitalists were finding that China, with the exception of Manchuria, was rapidly being closed to them as a field

government, and especially by the new republican government, up to that time. Generally speaking the situation was somewhat as follows: France held a monopolistic position in regard to railway concessions in Kwantung, Kwangsi, Yunnan, and southern Szechwan. In the provinces bordering on the lower and middle Yangtze, Great Britain held a preferential railway position, and in the province of Honan, a Sino-British corporation had received a monopoly of all mining development for sixty years. The Hukuang Railway Agreements divided the construction of railways between Canton and Hankow, and from there westward into Szechwan, among British, American, French, and German interests. In northwestern China, Franco-Belgian interests held concessions which gave them preferential railway and considerable mining rights in Shensi and Shansi. In Chihli the powerful British and Chinese Corporation held a preferential right to railway construction and financing which offered a potential menace to Japan's pretensions to a special position in Eastern Inner Mongolia. In Shensi and around Jehol, the Standard Oil Company had received a 60-year monopoly of oil development, and in Fukien, the only province freely open to Japanese enterprise, it was rumored that the Bethlehem Steel Corporation was negotiating for a contract for harbor improvements. Furthermore, north of the Wall, Russia was planning a system of railways which would eventually encircle North China and Manchuria. This was to be accomplished by constructing a line from Kashgar to connect with the Franco-Belgian line at Lanchow in Kansu. This latter line was to stretch from Kansu to Haichow on the coast north of Shanghai. A second line was to be built from Omsk in Siberia to connect with the Peking-Kalgan line, and a third line from Manchouli southward via Dolon Nor to join with the Peking-Kalgan line at Kalgan. In addition to these serious threats from the north, Japan's position in South Manchuria was also threatened from the south, as the Chinese were seeking to persuade British interests to build a line from Hulutao, the Chinese port on the Gulf of Chihli to Chaoyang and thence to Chihfeng. Such a line would strengthen Peking's hold over Inner Mongolia to the detriment of Japan's ambitions in this direction.

See an article entitled "International Intrigues in Chinese Railways," *Far Eastern Review,* January 1914, for an excellent description of the web of railway concessions held by the concessionaires of the European powers; see also an article entitled "Control of Inner Mongolia," in the same journal, for March 1914, for an account and map showing the plans of China to build a series of lines in Eastern Mongolia in order to bring this area under her control.

[11] These railways were the Kiukiang-Nanchang Railway (80 miles), which was opened to traffic in December 1910, and the Chaochowfu-Swatow Railway (6 miles), completed in November 1906.

for railway and mining investments. Secondly, in part because of the relative unimportance of Japan's participation in railway construction and financing enterprises in China proper, the inferior political influence which the Japanese government possessed with the Chinese government as compared to that wielded by any of the leading Occidental powers threatened to decline even further. Finally, the access to the natural resources of China, which was vitally important to the continued growth of Japanese industry, threatened to be cut off by the monopolistic character of many of the mining and railway concessions which the Chinese government had granted to European and American interests.

Furthermore, there were many indications that Japan's favored position in South Manchuria was open to serious threats of economic penetration by rival, if not even hostile, American and European financial groups. The "Open Door" doctrine of the United States promised to raise difficulties in the future as it had in the past.[12] Such difficulties could be avoided only by securing from China specific treaty rights which would give Japan a paramount, if not an exclusive, position in the development of this great area.

From the Japanese viewpoint the outlook for the future was not reassuring either in China proper or in Manchuria unless strenuous measures were taken to overcome the situation which confronted Japan. The results of open financial competition with the powers in the rivalry for concessions had been unsatisfactory. It was decided, therefore, to use political measures to overcome Japan's inferior position in China rather than to rely further upon the precarious results of economic competition.[13]

The outbreak of the World War and the consequent absorption of the European powers in the conflict gave Japan the opportunity to replace the piecemeal methods, which under the circumstances of peace would have been more appropriate to the task, with a wholesale measure designed to place Japan immediately in a commanding position in China and South Manchuria. The Twenty-one Demands were designed to bring about this change. A favorable acceptance of the demands by the Chinese government would permanently safeguard Japan's paramount interests in South Manchuria against any attempt to undermine it by means of economic penetration on the part

[12] For example, the revival of the Chinchow-Aigun Railway project. See *infra*, p. 123.

[13] *Supra*, pp. 28–30.

of hostile interests; and in China, the handicap imposed by Japan's financial inability to compete with the other powers for concessions would be overcome by inheriting the influential position and valuable economic rights formerly enjoyed by Germany in Shantung. A preferential position would be secured in the development of Fukien, and through the construction of a series of Japanese-controlled railways, Japanese enterprise would dominate the region between the middle Yangtze Valley and the Fukien coast. Japan's contractual rights to immense quantities of iron from the Han-Yeh-ping smelters and mines in Central China would be further safeguarded. Finally, if China could be induced to accept a series of proposals designated as "requests" or "wishes" of the Japanese government, Chinese political and military affairs would be brought effectively under the control of Japan.

The path to the attainment of these desires was not entirely free of obstacles. The necessities of the war could be depended upon to eliminate any effective opposition on the part of the European powers. There remained, however, the opposition which the American government inevitably would show to a program which would seriously threaten the "open door" and "equal opportunity" policies of the United States. In the main the American government had been the chief advocate of free and equal competition for concessions in Manchuria, and, diplomatically at least, had refused to recognize that Japan possessed any favored position there in this respect.

Any resistance on the part of the Chinese people to this program seems not to have been taken into consideration by the Okuma cabinet prior to the presentation of the demands. The demands, however, were the cause for an outburst of protest on the part of the Chinese people which was so widespread and so generally felt that it truly can be said to mark the birth of nationalism in modern China. This aggressive move on the part of Japan greatly stimulated an already growing sense of patriotism among the Chinese people and made them vividly conscious of the indignities which China had been made to suffer at the hands of the Powers. The demands were met by a totally unexpected resistance and hostility on the part of the Chinese people which eventually did much to defeat the aims Japan had in mind. Faced by a military power which they could not resist, the Chinese people used the weapon of publicity to counter the Japanese move, while the Chinese officials to whom the negotiations were entrusted succeeded by clever diplomacy and procrastination in so modifying the demands that Japan came away with much more of the appearance than she did of the substance of her original program.

The most important of the questions, the solution of which was proposed by the Twenty-one Demands, was that of Japan's special or paramount position in South Manchuria.[14] The primary aim of Japan's foreign policy following the Russo-Japanese War had been to establish her unquestioned hegemony over this great area. By a series of agreements which Japan had concluded with her former enemy in 1907, 1910, and 1912, she had been successful in getting Russia to acknowledge her paramount position in South Manchuria and Eastern Inner Mongolia.[15] In 1907 Japan concluded an agreement with France whereby the two powers recognized the special interests of each other "in the regions of the Chinese Empire adjacent to the territories where they have the rights of sovereignty, protection or occupation . . . ."[16] Finally, the British government's interpretation of the Anglo-Japanese Alliance assured Japan that she need fear no interference from that quarter in her efforts to consolidate her position north of the Great Wall.[17]

In recent years, however, there had occurred several incidents

[14] The term "special position," as applied to Japan's relationship to South Manchuria, was quite differently interpreted by the American and the Japanese governments. This divergence in interpretation can be best illustrated through an inquiry posed by Minister Reinsch to the State Department on March 6, 1917. Mr. Reinsch inquired: "Is the Legation warranted in assuming that the 'special position' of Japan as thus recognized [in the Department telegram of January 27, 1917] must be understood as confined to those specific rights and privileges which have been obtained by the Japanese government from China and from Russia by way of international agreement; thus excluding an interpretation which upon the basis of these rights would claim for Japan a 'special position' implying general rights of preference and suzerainty in the regions affected?" (Reinsch to Lansing, March 6, 1917, *Foreign Relations, 1917,* pp. 182–83). On April 16, Secretary Lansing replied confirming Mr. Reinsch's assumption as set forth above (*ibid.,* Lansing to Reinsch, April 16, 1918 [*sic,* 1917], p. 187).

[15] See Ernest B. Price, *The Russo-Japanese Treaties of 1907–1916, concerning Manchuria and Mongolia,* pp. 107–20, for English translations, accompanied by facsimilies of the original French text, of these treaties.

[16] MacMurray, *op. cit.,* Vol. I, p. 640.

[17] The British government's refusal to lend its diplomatic support to the British interests involved in the Hsinmintun-Fakumen project of 1907–1908 had given concrete evidence of Great Britain's recognition of Japan's superior position in South Manchuria. See Paul Clyde, *International Rivalries in Manchuria, 1689–1922,* pp. 129–31, for a discussion of the British government's attitude in regard to this project. See also the conversations between Viscount Grey and Baron Kato in January 1913, wherein Grey assented to Japan's plan to extend the Kwantung Lease Agreement, *infra,* pp. 49 ff.

which revealed to Japan that the foregoing measures were not sufficient to secure her position in Manchuria from serious challenge,
especially from the United States. In 1909, the Chinese government
granted to American interests, with which were associated a British
construction firm, the Chinchow-Aigun Railway concession. This
railway was to traverse Manchuria from Chinchow, a point on the
Gulf of Chihli, to Aigun, on the Siberian border, and under any
other than Japanese control undoubtedly would have menaced the
economic position of the South Manchuria Railway. But, of even
more importance from the standpoint of Japan, such a line under
the control of American and British interests would have introduced
into Manchuria the complex of railway rivalries and diplomatic
intrigues which in China proper had left Japan in an inferior position.

The suspicions of the Japanese government as to the purely economic character of the Chinchow-Aigun project were aroused by the
fact that the same interests which were identified with this concession had been attempting to get the Japanese and Russian governments to sell the South Manchuria and Chinese Eastern Railways.
It looked as if the real motive of the concessionaires was to force
the sale of these two railways rather than actually to construct a
competing line.[18] Toward the end of 1909 the suspicions of the
Japanese government in this direction were further aroused by the
abrupt action of Mr. Knox, the American Secretary of State, who
suddenly brought forward a proposal for the neutralization and
international administration of all Manchurian railways.[19] Under
this plan, title to the railways would be vested in the Chinese government, but the administration of them would be entrusted to some sort
of international board during the period of the repayment of the loan

[18] Clyde makes the following statement (op. cit., p. 135) as to the aims of the
American group interested in the Chinchow-Aigun project: "A definite contract
was to be secured from the Chinese Government for the building of another railroad to Manchuria which might be used as a threat to force the sale of the
Japanese and Russian lines." In a footnote on the same page he quotes a letter
from Willard Straight to J. P. Morgan and Company and to Kuhn, Loeb and
Company which indicates that the limiting of Japanese activities in Manchuria was
one of the prime considerations of the American group.

[19] See the following for excellent accounts of the diplomacy of the Chinchow-
Aigun project and Secretary Knox's subsequent proposal for the neutralization and
international control of all Manchurian railways: Clyde, op. cit., chapter ix, "Railway Politics in Manchuria, 1907–1910; and C. Walter Young, Japan's Special Position in Manchuria, chapter v, "The Japanese Attitude toward Foreign Financed
Railways, 1909–1910."

furnished to the Chinese government by the participating powers for the purchase of the railways.[20] Both Russia and Japan, as was to be expected, were in no way attracted by the proposal of Mr. Knox, and on January 21, 1910, they declined to support the scheme for reasons so similarly expressed as to indicate previous consultation.[21] Subsequently, the Knox plan was dropped, but not before Japan and Russia were sufficiently alarmed to cause them to strengthen their Agreement of 1907, in which they had recognized each other's sphere of influence in Manchuria, by the secret treaty of July 4, 1910.[22] Although the Chinchow-Aigun project was temporarily abandoned, the United States government reserved the rights of its nationals in the project, which promised a repetition of the diplomatic unpleasantness that this concession had caused in 1909 if it should be revived in the future.[23]

Japan and Russia had no sooner warded off these threats to their special positions in Manchuria than a more subtle one arose. On April 15, 1911, an international consortium, composed of American, British, French, and German banking groups, signed an agreement with the Chinese government for a combined "currency reform

[20] The plan was first broached in a memorandum to the British government, dated November 6, 1909 (*Foreign Relations, 1910*, p. 234). On December 14, 1909, notes were dispatched to Tokyo, Peking, Paris, Berlin, and St. Petersburg setting forth the plan and asking for support of it (*Foreign Relations, 1910*, p. 236).

[21] *Ibid.*, pp. 248–52. See also *Entente Diplomacy and the World War*, by B. de Siebert, and George Schreiner, Documents 6, 8, and 11, for proof of the concerted action which Japan and Russia took to frustrate the Knox scheme.

[22] Price (*op. cit.*, p. 114; Article V, par. 2, of the Treaty of 1910) specifically states: "In the event that these special interests in North and South Manchuria respectively should come to be threatened, the two High Contracting Parties will agree upon the measures to be taken with a view to common action or to the support to be accorded for the safeguarding and defense of those interests."

[23] The reservation on the part of the United States of the rights of its nationals in the Chinchow-Aigun concession came up late in 1916 in connection with the contract concluded on December 27, 1915, between the Yokohama Specie Bank and the Chinese government for the building of the Ssupingkai-Chengchiatun Railway. In a note of October 13, 1916, addressed to the Chinese Foreign Office, Minister Reinsch again reserved the rights of Americans under the Chinchow-Aigun Agreement of October 6, 1909, and pointed out that the said railway concession granted to Japanese interests "if not actually in conflict with the prior grant to American interests, would at any rate prove such as to impair the value of the rights conferred upon the American Group . . . ." (*Foreign Relations, 1917*, pp. 168–69). It also led to a suggestion, reminiscent of the Knox proposals of 1909, on the part of Reinsch that the United States and Japan co-operate in railroad construction in South Manchuria (*ibid.*); see p. 123, for correspondence relative to this suggestion.

and Manchurian industrial development loan." Although out of the total amount of the loan, which was to be for £10,000,000, only £1,000,000 was to be spent on industrial development in Manchuria, very important revenues of the three Manchurian provinces were hypothecated to the service of the entire loan. In addition, the signatory banks were to be given a prior right on all future loans for the industrial development of Manchuria.[24] As a direct result of the terms of this loan agreement, Russia and Japan, in order to protect their interests in Manchuria, requested to be admitted to the Consortium. Their real desire, however, was to exclude Manchuria from any general monopoly of loans as was anticipated by the Consortium.[25] They were not, however, completely successful in this attempt and had to be satisfied with the right of the Russian and Japanese groups to withdraw from the Consortium if, in the face of the disapproval of either of them, the Consortium nevertheless advanced a loan to China. In such a case either of the two governments could notify the other that "the business proposed is contrary to the interests of Russia and Japan."[26] Reference has already been made to the fact that subsequently the Consortium groups decided to open industrial loans to China to the free competition of all banking groups and to the effect which the resulting competition for concessions had had upon Japan's position in China proper.[27]

The foregoing incidents led the Japanese government to the decision to come to some arrangement with China which would definitely safeguard Japan's paramount position in Manchuria against such attempts to undermine it.[28]

[24] MacMurray, *op. cit.,* Vol. I, pp. 841–49. The interest and principal of the loan was to be made a first charge on the tobacco and spirit taxes, the production and consumption taxes, and the salt surtax of Manchuria (Art. V). In case of default, all the services mentioned above were to be transferred to the administration of the Maritime Customs (Art. V, par. 4). The signatory banks were to be given a first preference on all future foreign borrowings for the purposes of the loan (Art. XVI).

[25] See C. Walter Young, *Japan's Special Position in Manchuria,* pp. 173–78, for a detailed account of Japan's and Russia's efforts to get the Consortium to exclude Manchuria from its field of activities.

[26] *Ibid.,* p. 178 and note. Presumably, in such a case as this, Russia and Japan would take action as provided in Art. V, par. 2, of the treaty of July 4, 1910. See *supra,* p. 36, note 22.

[27] *Supra,* p. 30.

[28] Japan had heretofore depended largely upon the so-called "parallel clause" in the Protocol accompanying the Peking Treaty of December 22, 1905, to curb China in granting railway concessions in South Manchuria. This clause reads as

Furthermore, Japan had no intention of relinquishing the Kwantung leased territory in 1923 when the old Russian lease would expire. This leasehold was the *point d'appui* of Japanese activities in Manchuria. It embraced the southern end of the Liaotung Peninsula and contained the port of Dairen, the terminus of the South Manchuria Railway and the headquarters of the Japanese military forces in Manchuria. The Russian leasehold had been transferred to Japan at the conclusion of the Russo-Japanese War, but no new lease agreement had been made with the Chinese government.

Japan wanted also to be assured continued control of the Kirin-Changchun Railway.[29] This railway was designed to become an important link in Japan's economic and strategic hold on Manchuria, as plans had been made to extend this line to some point on the Korean seacoast (at Yuki or Seishen) and from there to connect it with a Korean line running south to Seoul.[30] This system, when completed, would be of the utmost strategic and economic importance to Japan, as it would considerably reduce the distance between Japan and Changchun, and, in case of need, would enable Japan to throw troops into Central Manchuria much more rapidly than she could via

---

follows: "The Chinese Government engage for the purpose of protecting the interests of the South Manchuria Railway not to construct prior to the recovery by them of the said railway, any main line in the neighborhood of and parallel to that railway or any branch line which might be prejudicial to the interests of the above mentioned railway" (Manchuria, *Treaties and Agreements,* p. 83, quoted in Clyde, *op. cit.,* p. 129 n.).

[29] The Kirin-Changchun Railway was a Chinese government railway constructed with Japanese capital. The loan agreement was to expire in 1934. The Japanese government desired to extend the period of the loan (subsequently extended by the Agreement of October 12, 1917, to 1947) and to substitute Japanese management during the extended period of the loan for the existing Chinese administration. The Sino-Japanese agreements providing for the financing and construction of this line were as follows: Convention regarding the Hsinmintun-Mukden and Kirin-Changchun Railways, April 15, 1907 (MacMurray, *op. cit.,* Vol. I, p. 627); Supplementary Agreement for a Loan to the Hsinmintun-Mukden and Kirin-Changchun Railways, November 12, 1908 (*ibid.,* p. 767); Detailed Agreement for the Kirin-Changchun Railway Loan, August 18, 1909 (*ibid.,* p. 785).

[30] This plan was first definitely revealed in the Sino-Japanese Agreement of September 4, 1909, relating to the Chientao region, which, by Article 6, provided for an extension of the Kirin-Changchun Railway to the southern boundary of Yenchi (Chientao) and for the connection of the said extension with a Korean railway. MacMurray, *op. cit.,* Vol. I, p. 797.

The plan to extend the Kirin-Changchun line to the Korean coast was not realized until August 1933, when the last section was completed. The present (1936) connection is with the port of Yuki, but the construction of a line between Yuki and Rashin, the new port being constructed by the Japanese, will soon be completed. Connection is also made with the Korean railways via Seishin.

the Antung-Mukden and the South Manchuria lines.[31] The lease-hold and the railways formed the basis of Japan's control of South Manchuria. The Russo-Japanese War had convinced the Japanese people that the control of South Manchuria was necessary to the safety of the homeland. In Japanese opinion, South Manchuria had become the strategic frontier of the Empire.

In a somewhat less degree Japan wanted also to obtain from China a recognition of her special interests in what came to be called East-ern Inner Mongolia, the vast territory which stretched along China's northeastern border.[32]

The situation in this area was extremely complicated by reason of the conflicting interests, both strategic and economic, of the three Powers, Russia, China, and Japan. The territory had originally been a part of Mongolia, but by successive extensions of the northern boundary of Chihli much of it had gradually been incorporated in that province and was considered a part of China proper.[33] In Octo-ber 1913 the Chinese government, in order to check Russian advances into Inner Mongolia, voluntarily opened six of its most important towns to the trade and residence of foreigners.[34] It was rumored that in order to make its hold more secure the Chinese government was planning to build a series of railways which would radiate from Peking and traverse the entire area.[35] Furthermore it was said that

[31] It reduces the distance between Changchun (now Hsinching) and Osaka by 460 miles and the time of travel between Tokyo and Harbin by two days. See article by H. J. Timperly, "Japan in Manchukuo," *Foreign Affairs,* January 1934, for the latest developments of the plan mentioned above.

[32] This territory has recently become prominent in Far Eastern history under the names of Jehol, Chahar, and Suiyüan. Jehol is now part of the new state of Manchukuo. This territory had long been a field of colonization for the Chinese. They had gradually infiltrated into this area, pushing the nomadic Mongol tribes before them, until it had become largely Chinese in character. This infiltration was still going on and threatened eventually to absorb the entire area into China proper. In the Russo-Mongolian treaty of November 3, 1912, and the Sino-Russian agree-ment of November 5, 1913, provision was made to curb this Chinese colonization, as it was in harmony with the Russian policy "to treat Mongolia as a natural barrier against Chinese colonization movements in the direction of the Russian Dominions" (Prince Koudacheff, in conversation with Minister Reinsch, Reinsch to Lansing, October 31, 1916, *Foreign Relations, 1916,* p. 199).

[33] In 1914 the northern border of Chihli extended more than one hundred miles to the northwest of Mukden in Manchuria.

[34] The towns to be opened were Kalgan, Kweihuachêng, Dolon Nor, Chihfeng, Taonanfu, and Lungkow.

[35] See "The Control of Inner Mongolia," *Far Eastern Review,* March 1914, pp. 390 ff., and the map on p. 393, for a description of the projected railways re-ferred to above.

these railways were to be constructed and financed by the British interests which held an option on railway construction in Chihli.[36] So persistent were these rumors that on June 13, 1914, the Japanese Foreign Office issued an extremely frank statement as to its attitude toward such enterprises. The statement declared:

Reports have been circulated with persistency in the newspapers to the effect that British capitalists have obtained certain concessions regarding railways in South Manchuria and in Eastern and Inner Mongolia. Japan possesses in these regions special rights, and the Imperial Government of Japan had declared the fact to the Powers. In promoting or utilizing these rights, the Japanese Government has always been active to seize every possible opportunity, and the Powers, cognizant of these special rights, have shown respect for them. In view of the situation the Japanese Government firmly believes that no Power should assist its capitalists in obtaining concession for railways that have important bearing—economic and strategic—on the interests of Japan, without her previous consent. . . .[37]

Some sort of clear definition of Japan's relationship to Eastern Inner Mongolia seemed to be all the more imperative because of the virtual control which Russia had attained over Outer Mongolia after this nominal Chinese dependency had declared its independence of the Chinese Republic.[38] By the Urga Agreement of November 3, 1912, and the annexed Protocol, Russia obtained from the newly independent government of Outer Mongolia important privileges

[36] The right of the British interests to finance and construct railways in Chihli province was based on the Sino-British (British and Chinese Corporation) Agreement of October 10, 1898, Article 3, and on the Supplementary Agreement of April 29, 1902, Article 5 (MacMurray, *op. cit.*, Vol. I, pp. 173–79, and pp. 333–34). These two agreements gave the British and Chinese Corporation the first right to supply funds for railway construction in Chihli until 1934, the date of the expiration of the original agreement. In agreeing to the Scott-Mouravieff Agreement of April 28, 1899, the British government expressly reserved the rights acquired under the Agreement of October 10, 1898 (MacMurray, *op. cit.*, Vol. I, pp. 204–5, Sir C. Scott to Count Mouravieff).

[37] The *Japan Weekly Mail*, June 20, 1914, Supp., p. iv. In the negotiations leading to the new Consortium Agreement of October 15, 1920, one of the most important points at issue was the question of the extension of the proposed Jehol-Taonanfu Railway toward the north and that of a line to connect this projected railway with the seacoast on the Gulf of Chihli. Japan claimed the right to finance the construction of both extensions on the basis of the Sino-Japanese (Four Manchurian Railways) Agreement of September 18, 1918. She eventually receded from this position and acknowledged the right of the Consortium to participate in the financing of these projected railways. See C. Walter Young, *The International Relations of Manchuria*, pp. 160–69.

[38] The Mongols of Outer Mongolia declared their independence of China in December 1911. MacMurray, *op. cit.*, Vol. II, p. 992.

which later the Chinese government tacitly condoned in the Sino-Russian treaty of November 5, 1913. These privileges were elaborated by the Russo-Mongolian Agreement of September 30, 1914, by which Russia obtained the right to direct the construction of all railways in Outer Mongolia in the interests of her strategic and economic necessities.[39] Although Japan had arrived at an understanding with Russia in the secret treaty of June 25, 1912, as to their respective spheres of influence in Inner Mongolia, Japan had not as yet secured from China a recognition of her sphere of influence such as Russia had in the treaties mentioned above. Japan now proposed to remedy this defect.

Japan wanted also to remove the treaty restrictions in South Manchuria which confined her nationals to a few inland treaty ports and to a narrow strip of territory along the right of way of the South Manchuria Railway. She wanted the entire area opened to the commercial, industrial, and agricultural enterprises of her nationals. This last privilege was particularly important in view of the increasing numbers of her Korean subjects who were settling in South Manchuria as agricultural colonists.[40]

In China proper Japan was desirous of establishing a preferential position over other powers in the development of Fukien, whose close proximity to Formosa she felt gave her a claim to a favored position in this province. Japan's concern for her special interest in Fukien had been aroused just prior to the outbreak of the World War by rumors that the Bethlehem Steel Corporation had secured a contract from the Chinese government for the construction of a

---

[39] MacMurray, op. cit., Vol. II, p. 1178. Article 5 of the Russian Agreement provided that Russia would not interfere if Mongolia wished to construct a railway with its own means, but: "However, as regards the granting of railway concessions to anyone, the Mongolia Government shall, by virtue of the relations of close friendship with the neighbouring Great Russian Nation, previous to granting the concession enter into conference with the Imperial Russian Government, and consult with it as to whether the projected railroad is not injurious to Russia from an economic and strategic standpoint...."

[40] By the Chientao Agreement of September 4, 1909, between Japan and China, Koreans were permitted to settle as farmers in certain districts of Chientao, a portion of Manchuria adjacent to the Korean border, but they were subject to Chinese laws and jurisdiction. Upon the annexation of Korea by Japan in 1910, whereupon Koreans became Japanese subjects, this Agreement was continued in force in so far as it applied to the Chientao region. In the rest of Manchuria, however, Koreans, while enjoying full extraterritoriality, were restricted in residence and enterprise, as were the native Japanese. See MacMurray, op. cit., Vol. I, p. 796, for the Chientao Agreement of September 4, 1909.

naval dock, with gun emplacement, at Ma-Moi near Foochow.[41] This rumor revived the apprehension Japan had exhibited in 1900, when the Japanese government had been somewhat surprised by a request of the American government that it give its approval to the establishment of an American coaling station on the coast of Fukien. At that time the Japanese government declined to give its support to the proposal on the grounds that the Chinese government, in 1898, had tacitly recognized Fukien as a Japanese sphere of influence when it had promised not to alienate "to any other Power" territory in this province.[42]

Somewhat closely connected with Japan's desire to share in the development of South China by establishing a sphere of interest in Fukien was the plan Japanese interests had entertained for some years for the construction of a series of railways which would connect the growing industrial centers of Hankow, Hanyang, and Wuchang, on the Middle Yangtze, with the South China coast. These lines were to connect the cities named with Nanchang, the capital of Kiangsi, and thence were to branch, one line crossing Kiangsi and Chekiang to its terminus on the coast at Hangchow, and the other to traverse Kiangsi and Fukien, connecting at Chaochowfu with the short line to the port of Swatow. These lines would become the main arteries of traffic for these three populous provinces and would draw considerable traffic from the Middle Yangtze region to the South China coast. Japan had been pressing China for these concessions for some time, but, here again, the prior privileges obtained by other powers and the distinct preference shown by the Chinese government for European concessionaires stood in the way of Japanese interests obtaining them. Japanese interests had earlier succeeded in obtaining the concession for the Kiukiang-Nanchang line, but this line was only eighty miles long and by itself was not of much importance. As a link, however, to connect the three cities of Hankow, Wuchang, and Hanyang with the South China coast, it would become exceedingly valuable. Japanese ambitions in this direction received a severe setback in the spring and summer of 1914, by the

[41] MacMurray, op. cit., Vol. II, p. 1236. MacMurray says that the contract referred to was "apocryphal" and "fabricated out of false rumours" emanating from Chinese sources.

[42] Foreign Relations, 1915, pp. 113–15, note. This reference gives the correspondence between Secretary Hay and Minister Buck at Tokyo regarding the proposal for an American naval base on the coast of Fukien and the Japanese answer to this proposal.

conclusion, on March 31, 1914, of an agreement between the Chinese government and the British and Chinese Corporation for the construction of a line from Nanking to Pingsiang via Nanchang.[43] This agreement was followed on August 24, 1914, by the Chinese government entering into an engagement whereby British firms would be given preference for the projected line from Nanchang to Chaochowfu.[44] The rather pointed discrimination against the Japanese exhibited in this latter engagement of the Chinese government was all the more marked because this line would connect the only two railways in China proper in which Japanese interests had succeeded in obtaining the rights of construction and financing.[45]

Japanese quasi-governmental interests for many years had been involved in the largest and most important coal and iron properties in China. These properties were owned by the Han-Yeh-ping Company and were for the most part located in the Middle Yangtze Valley near the company's smelting works at Hanyang. Japanese concerns had purchased ores from the Tayeh iron mines since 1899, and from time to time had made contracts with the company whereby iron ore was to be supplied to Japan, principally to the Imperial Steel Foundry.[46] In 1908 the company, heretofore operated under the supervision of the Chinese government, was turned into a purely commercial concern by Imperial edict, which at the same time forbade the ownership of any of the shares by any other than Chinese subjects. Thus, Japanese capitalists were precluded from becoming shareholders. They, however, had been for some time seeking to gain a voice in the administration of the mines in order to protect their investments, since, following the Revolution of 1911, the financial condition of the company had fallen into a very bad state.[47] On

[43] Shanghai-Hangchow-Ningpo Railway Agreement of March 6, 1908, MacMurray, *op. cit.*, Vol. I, p. 707 ff. Nanking-Hunan Railway Agreement of March 31, 1914, *ibid.*, Vol. II, p. 1113 ff.

[44] This agreement is inferred from the Chinese official statement issued at the end of the negotiations. See *Sino-Japanese Negotiations of 1915*, Official Statement of the Chinese Government, Carnegie Endowment for International Peace, Pamphlet No. 45, pp. 66 ff.

[45] The Kiukiang-Nanchang Railway and the Chaochowfu-Swatow line.

[46] F. R. Tegengren, "The Iron Ores and Iron Industry of China," *The Geological Survey of China, Memoirs*, Ser. A, No. 2, pp. 366–80, gives an excellent historical account of the affairs of this company, one very sympathetic to the Chinese viewpoint.

[47] Tegengren ascribes the bad financial state of the company to three causes: (1) the damage caused during the Revolution; (2) the contracts under which the company had to deliver large amounts of iron ore and pig iron to Japan at un-

December 2, 1913, the company entered into an agreement with the Yokohama Specie Bank, acting on behalf of the Japanese Imperial Steel Foundry, whereby the Bank loaned the company 15,000,000 yen, the loan to be repaid over a period of forty years in up to 17,000,000 tons of iron ore and 8,000,000 tons of crude iron.[48] Because of the enormous amounts of the deliveries of iron and iron ore involved, this loan caused considerable adverse comment in China and increased the agitation, which had been going on for some time, to nationalize all the Han-Yeh-ping mines.[49] Pressure was brought to bear upon the government to declare the loan invalid.

In 1914, in connection with the decree nationalizing iron ores, promulgated by presidential mandate on November 22, 1914, the Chinese government took up the question of placing the company under government control. It was suggested that the government acquire possession of the Han-Yeh-ping mines, but no decision had been made at the time of the presentation of the Twenty-one Demands.[50] Despite the fact that from the Chinese viewpoint the deliveries under the contract were so enormous as seriously to hamper the development of the Chinese iron industry, Japan, in view of her extreme dependence upon foreign sources for her supply of iron ore, was not likely to acquiesce in any attempts to restrict the deliveries due to her under the agreement of 1913. Provision, therefore, was made in the demands for transforming the company into a Sino-Japanese concern.[51]

Finally, Japan, in view of the uncertain outcome of the war and in the light of her past experiences in dealing with the European powers at the council table, believed it highly desirable and necessary to come to some definite arrangement directly with China as to the

-----

profitable prices; (3) the Chinese custom which compelled the company to pay dividends to its shareholders regardless of the finances of the company. He states that 8 per cent was paid annually (Tegengren, *op. cit.*, p. 370).

[48] MacMurray, *op. cit.*, Vol. II, p. 1077 ff.

[49] On August 22, 1912, the shareholders had gone on record as favoring that the government take over the concern by purchase (*China Year Book for 1913*, p. 524).

[50] Tegengren, *op. cit.*, pp. 371–72.

[51] In commenting upon the deliveries contracted for under this loan, Tegengren states: "We arrive at the momentous conclusion that the fulfillment of the company's obligations under the 1913 loan agreement alone....would not only completely exhaust the Ta-Yeh reserves but still require large additional supplies of iron ore from elsewhere" (*ibid.*, p. 380).

disposition of the former German rights in Shantung as soon as possible and without waiting for the war to come to an end. Reference has already been made to the divergence in views with which the Chinese and the Japanese governments regarded the scope and aim of Japan's action against the German base at Kiaochow. Despite the Chinese thesis that once the German base had been captured and the possibility of Germany carrying on hostilities in the Far East had been eliminated Japan's task was done and all that remained for her to do was to garrison the former German leased territory until the end of the war, Japan was determined to take every measure she considered necessary to prevent Germany from regaining a foothold on the China coast and to secure for herself the economic rights which Germany had possessed in Shantung. The presence of the German fortified area had inevitably involved the Far East in the war. Germany refused to recognize China's attempts to escape responsibility through the declaration of a war zone and had stated in no uncertain terms that she would hold China responsible.[52] Therefore, there was every reason to suppose that if she were at all successful in the war, Germany would take advantage of the clause in the Kiaochow Lease Agreement which permitted her to claim another leasehold if she gave the Kiaochow one up before its expiration.[53] At no time in the interchange of views with Japan regarding the area of hostilities in Shantung did the Chinese government guarantee that Germany would not be permitted to return to the China coast.[54] In fact the closing sentences of the Chinese note of October 9 to Japan seemed to indicate that China rather expected Germany to resume possession of Kiaochow at the end of the war.[55]

However, it was not only the desire of preventing Germany's return to the Far East which now decided Japan to demand that China agree to the transfer of the former German rights to her at the end of the war. Japan wanted to secure certain of those rights for herself, and she wanted to guard against being maneuvered out of those rights at the peace conference which would take place at the

[52] See *supra*, pp. 21–22, for the answer of the German government to China's declaration of a war zone.

[53] Clause V, Section 1, Kiaochow Lease Agreement of March 6, 1898. MacMurray, *op. cit.*, Vol. I, p. 114.

[54] Because of her position as a neutral, China could hardly make such a declaration. But from Japan's point of view this only made the necessity of Japan taking action to preclude Germany's return all the more necessary.

[55] The sentences referred to are quoted *supra*, p. 25.

end of the war. Her humiliating experience following the Treaty of Shimonoseki in 1895, when by the action of Germany, France, and Russia she had been forced to relinquish the Liaotung Peninsula, and her almost equally unsuccessful experience at the Portsmouth Conference in 1905, where she felt that Russian diplomacy succeeded in evading the full consequences of military defeat, had taught Japan the wisdom of being as fully prepared as possible when confronting the European powers at the council table.

Furthermore, the government of Count Okuma was under pressure to show some compensation for the loss of life and expenditure which the eviction of Germany from Shantung had entailed. Japanese public opinion demanded some tangible compensations for the loss of over 2,000 Japanese lives and the expenditure of 50,000,000 yen, which the capture of Kiaochow had cost. The Okuma government was already under severe criticism for what many considered to be its premature promise to return Kiaochow to China, and some of the more radical journals were pressing for its retention.[56] The domestic political situation in Japan did not permit the government to commit Japan definitely to the return of Kiaochow to China without at the same time receiving some advantages for having eliminated Germany from her leasehold on the China coast. Therefore among the proposals advanced to China were ones asking that China give her consent to any arrangements Japan would make with Germany at the end of the war covering the disposition of the former German rights in Shantung.

In addition to the proposals advanced to meet the specific situation, the Okuma cabinet, partially in view of the vital importance of Japan's interests in China but primarily to placate the jingoistic desires of certain political factions, included in the demands a group of items which were termed "wishes" or "desires." These proposals were designated by Baron Kato, in his original instructions given to the Japanese Minister in Peking on December 3, 1914, as "wishes" of which "an adjustment at this time" was "highly desirable."[57] Baron Kato, in conversation with the American Ambassador, made the somewhat dubious distinction between the demands and the "wishes" by saying that "while it was Japan's wish to gain the latter and while

---

[56] For example, interpellation in Japanese Diet, December 8 and 9, 1914; see enclosures, *Foreign Relations, 1914, Supp.*, pp. 206–11; also Guthrie to Bryan, November 23, 1914, *ibid.*, p. 202.

[57] *Foreign Relations, 1915*, pp. 159–60.

she would continue to press them she did not expect to compel obedience by force."[58]

Despite the fact that out of the seven proposals which comprised these "requests" or "wishes" of the Japanese government, only one (Article 6, relative to Fukien) eventually formed a part of the Treaties and Agreements of May 25, 1915, the episode of the Twenty-one Demands has generally been more identified with these "wishes" than it has with the far more important demands of the first four groups which the Chinese government actually accepted. The reasons for this are apparent.

The general nature of these proposals and the ambiguity of the language in which they were expressed permitted the widest speculations as to Japan's purpose in including them with the more specific items. They led to the belief that Japan was actually seeking to set up a protectorate over China.[59] The Chinese quickly grasped the fact that the inclusion of this group of items was a grave diplomatic blunder on the part of the Japanese which could very effectively be used against them. In the first place, the equivocal meaning which could be read into them permitted the Chinese press to give them the most extreme interpretations. A press campaign was launched which concentrated chiefly upon these so-called "wishes." This campaign was carried on with such vigor that it led the ordinarily restrained *North China Herald* to remark in retrospect that "never a Chinese, rich or poor, high or low, stupid or intelligent, but knew that Manchuria was going as Formosa and Korea had gone, and that Mongolia and Shantung and Fukien were going too, and that henceforth no Chinese would be master of his own soul, if the Japanese demands were to prevail."[60] Furthermore, the Chinese officials seized the opportunity offered by the distinction the Japanese government was making between the items designated as "demands" and the

[58] Guthrie to Bryan, March 21, 1915, *ibid.*, pp. 113–15. Baron Kato's semi-official biography states that Kato did not want these items included in the demands and that he consented to their inclusion only after they had been reduced to "wishes." He believed that they would be quickly withdrawn and gave that as his reason for not informing the United States of their existence at the outset of the negotiations. See *Kato Biography*, Vol. II, pp. 200, 209.

[59] "The plan of Japan was not to make any annexations of her territory, but with the maintainance of the formal sovereignty of China, to place the Chinese State in a position of vassalage through exercising a control over important parts of its administration and over its industrial and natural resources, actual and prospective" (Reinsch to Bryan, February 10, 1915, *Foreign Relations, 1915*, p. 86).

[60] *North China Herald*, July 24, 1915.

proposals referred to as "wishes" to refuse to negotiate upon the latter, thus helping to prolong the negotiations and finally to force Japan to present an ultimatum in order to bring them to a close.[61]

The domestic political situation in Japan at the time of the presentation of the demands undoubtedly influenced the Okuma cabinet to include these more chauvinistic proposals among the demands. In January 1915 the Okuma government's supporters were outnumbered in the Diet by its opponents almost two to one. These opponents were savagely attacking the government upon every issue, particularly charging it with carrying on a weak and vacillating policy toward China. By early January, the opposition had become so recalcitrant that the Diet was dissolved. A general election was held on March 25, in the midst of the Sino-Japanese negotiations. The result was to give the Okuma government an overwhelming majority, thus assuring it that its China policy received the enthusiastic approval of the electorate. The Okuma government, now in a strong position, was able to take a less exigent attitude toward China, and after the election the pressure upon the Chinese government was markedly lessened.

In the Japanese ultimatum of May 7, 1915, which brought the negotiations to a close, these so-called "wishes" were withdrawn. They had served the double purpose of temporarily appeasing certain political elements in Japan and, at the same time, of making their withdrawal appear to be a generous concession to the Chinese, somewhat easing the force of the ultimatum.

---

[61] There exists a conflict of authorities as to whether the Japanese government in presenting the demands to China did or did not make a distinction between the "demands" and "wishes." Baron Kato informed Ambassador Guthrie on February 21, 1915, that "he was particularly anxious that you [Secretary of State] should understand that the reason for confining the statement sent you strictly to Japan's 'demands' was that the other items were 'requests' and were so designated when presented to China" (Guthrie to Bryan, February 21, 1915, *Foreign Relations, 1915,* p. 96).

On the other hand, Minister Reinsch reported on April 2: "Although the Japanese Government is understood to have explained that the demands suppressed in its first communication to the Powers were merely requests, I now learn that when that explanation was first reported in the newspapers the Secretary of the Japanese Legation called especially at the Foreign Office to state in the Minister's name that his Government recognized no such distinction and particularly would insist upon Group V of the demands equally with the others" (Reinsch to Bryan, April 2, 1915, *ibid.,* p. 118).

CHAPTER III

THE SINO-JAPANESE DISCUSSIONS OF THE TWENTY-ONE DEMANDS

The responsibility for the decision to present to China in January 1915 a list of demands the purpose of which was to bring to a favorable solution, from the standpoint of Japan, certain outstanding questions between the two countries rests without doubt upon Baron Kato. As early as January 1913 he had revealed to Sir (later Viscount) Edward Grey the necessity which Japan faced to extend the lease agreement for the Kwantung leasehold in Manchuria and for a similar extension of the agreements covering the South Manchuria and Antung-Mukden Railways.[1] The conversations with Sir Edward Grey were entirely informal and were not undertaken because of instructions from the Japanese government. They were initiated by Kato because he was about to leave his post as Ambassador to Great Britain in order to become Foreign Minister in the Katsura cabinet. His purpose was to acquaint Grey with the necessity Japan was under to seek sooner or later an understanding with China relative to the above-named concessions.

There were two conversations, the first on January 3, 1913, and the second some days later. In the first conversation Kato discussed the problem of the Kwantung leased territory. He pointed out to Grey not only that Japan's material welfare was involved in the Manchurian leasehold but also the emotional attitude of the Japanese people because of the two wars which had been fought there, and that, because of the historical basis of this feeling, the Japanese people were determined to keep the leased area permanently.[2] Kato said that in order to accomplish the continuance of Japanese control it would be necessary to seek some reason which would be easy for the Chinese to accept.[3]

Sir Edward Grey replied that he understood Kato's point relative to the historical events in Manchuria, and that the problem was one

[1] *Kato Biography,* Vol. II, pp. 132–36.
[2] *Ibid.* [3] *Ibid.*

to be settled between Japan and China, and also that there would be no necessity for other nations to interfere.[4]

On the tenth of the same month Kato raised the question of the extension of the agreements for the South Manchuria and the Antung-Mukden Railways. Grey, however, listened to Kato's discussion without expressing any idea one way or the other.[5]

Kato's general argument with Grey was that these problems had to be met sooner or later regardless of the cabinet which was in power in Japan, and that the settlement would be attempted at a favorable psychological opportunity. The fall of the Katsura cabinet before Kato could assume office, however, prevented any immediate move toward the realization of the foregoing plans.

Baron Kato came into office with the Okuma ministry in 1914. This gave him the opportunity to seek a chance to open negotiations with China. The outbreak of the war and Japan's capture of Kiaochow offered, from Kato's viewpoint, a fortuitous opportunity to settle both the question of Japan's leasehold and railway concessions in Manchuria and to overcome the inferior economic and political position of Japan in China. The European powers were absorbed in the war, but how long the war would last was difficult to foretell. Kato felt that Japan had to seize the opportunity for a general settlement with China while the opportunity was there.

Shortly after the war began, on August 26, 1914, Hioki, the Japanese Minister in Peking, proposed to Baron Kato that the time was now opportune to present to the Chinese government the demands Kato had in mind.[6] Kato, however, preferred to postpone the presentation for the moment. At the same time he ordered Hioki to prepare the way for the negotiations of the demands when they would be presented.[7]

Immediately following the fall of Tsingtao, which surrendered on November 10, Baron Kato outlined to the cabinet the proposals he wished to make to the Chinese government. On November 12 Hioki was recalled to Tokyo in order to receive instructions.[8]

The so-called Twenty-one Demands and the instructions accompanying them were given to Mr. Hioki by Baron Kato on December 3, 1914. The written instructions specified no particular date

[4] *Kato Biography,* Vol. II, pp. 136–37.   [5] *Ibid.,* pp. 137–40.

[6] Kato evidently had already informed Hioki of his intentions to present the demands to China.

[7] *Kato Biography,* Vol. II, p. 154.   [8] *Ibid.*

when the demands should be presented; this, presumably, depended upon further instructions and a favorable opportunity. The instructions opened by stating:

> In order to provide for the readjustment of the affairs consequent on the Japan-German war and for the purpose of ensuring a lasting peace in the Far East by strengthening the position of the Empire, the Imperial Government have resolved to approach the Chinese Government with a view to conclude treaties and agreements mainly along the lines laid down in the first four groups of the appended proposals....[9]

The distinction implied in this paragraph between the proposals of the first four groups and those in Group Five was definitely stated in a further paragraph as follows:

> As regards the proposals contained in the fifth Group, they are presented as the wishes of the Imperial Government. The matters which are dealt with under this category are entirely different in character from those which are included in the first four Groups. An adjustment, at this time, of these matters, some of which have been pending between the two countries, being nevertheless highly desirable for the advancement of the friendly relations between Japan and China as well as for safeguarding their common interests, you are also requested to exercise your best efforts to have our wishes carried out.[10]

The possibility of the Japanese government offering to restore Kiaochow, as a *quid pro quo* for the acceptance of her demands was somewhat guardedly mentioned as follows:

> If the Chinese Government will accept our proposals as above stated, the Imperial Government may, with due regard to the principle of China's territorial integrity and in the interest of the friendship of the two countries, well consider the question with a view to restoring the said territory to China, in the event of Japan's being given free hand in the disposition thereof as the result of the coming peace conference between Japan and Germany. As, however, it will be absolutely necessary, in restoring the said territory to China, to lay certain conditions such as the opening of the territory for foreign trade, establishment of a Japanese settlement, etc., you will ask for further instructions when you propose to declare to the Chinese Government the willingness of the Imperial Government to consider the question.[11]

The demands were arranged in five groups, the so-called "wishes" being brought together in the fifth group.

---

[9] *The Sino-Japanese Negotiations of 1915,* Japanese and Chinese Documents and Chinese Official Statement, Carnegie Endowment for International Peace, Division of International Law, Pamphlet 45, pp. 1–2 (hereafter cited as *Sino-Japanese Negotiations of 1915*). The official Japanese translation is used for Japanese documents and the official Chinese translation is used for Chinese documents.

[10] *Ibid.*, p. 2.   [11] *Ibid.*

Group One dealt with the German leasehold and economic rights in Shantung. The Chinese government was asked "to give full assent" to any arrangements Japan would arrive at with Germany as to the disposition of the German rights. Certain towns within the province were to be opened to the trade and residence of foreigners. Finally Japan asked that China agree not to cede or lease any territory within Shantung or along its coast "to any other Power." This latter phrase had been the one used by Great Britain, France, and Japan in 1898 when they were marking off their respective spheres of interest in South China. Presumably Japan intended it to have the same significance in this instance.

Group Two was concerned with South Manchuria and Eastern Inner Mongolia. The preamble to this group would have committed the Chinese government to a recognition of the "predominant position of Japan in South Manchuria and Eastern Inner Mongolia." Provision was made for the extension of Japanese control of the Kwantung leasehold and the South Manchuria Railway and its branches for a "further period of 99 years." The whole of these two great areas was to be opened to the trade and residence of Japanese subjects, and they were to be accorded the right to lease and own land there for farming, mining, and industrial purposes. Finally, the Chinese government was asked to agree that whenever it was proposed to give to foreign interests the right to construct or finance the construction of railways in South Manchuria and Eastern Inner Mongolia and the taxes of these two areas were to be made the security of a foreign loan, the consent of Japan would be obtained in advance. Japan was also to be consulted whenever the Chinese government desired to employ political, financial, or military advisers in these territories.

Under the provisions of Group Three the coal and iron properties and smelters of the Han-Yeh-ping Company were to be placed under Sino-Japanese control and the Company was to become a joint concern of the two nations. Furthermore, it was asked that the Chinese government engage that "no mines in the neighborhood of those owned by the Company were to be worked by anyone other than the said Company." The Company was not to be nationalized without Japan's consent.

The single article of Group Four was designed to notify the other powers that Fukien was a Japanese sphere of interest. This was to be done through the conventional diplomatic subterfuge of asking

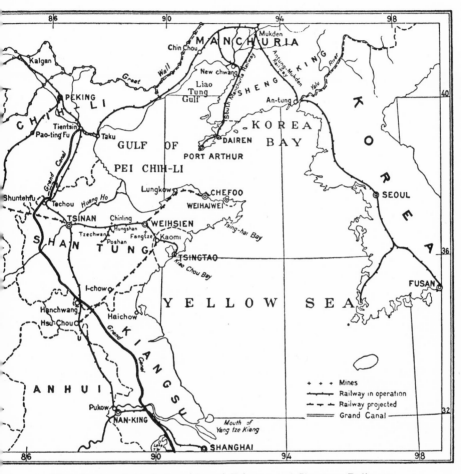

Map showing strategical position of Tsingtao and Shantung Railways

the Chinese government to promise that no portion of the coast of Fukien would be ceded or leased to "any other Power."

Group Five served as a catch-all for the items which could not be fitted into any other groups. These items comprised "wishes" preferred by the Japanese government in order "to safeguard the common interests of the two countries." The Chinese government was to engage influential Japanese as political, military, and financial advisers. Japanese temples, hospitals, and schools in the interior of China were to be given the right to own land. The police in localities in China "where such arrangements are necessary" were to be placed under joint Sino-Japanese management. Japanese capitalists were to be given the right to construct three important railways designed to connect the middle Yangtze region with the South China coast. Japan was to be consulted first whenever foreign capital would be needed for the development of railways in Fukien or whenever harbor improvements were to be made on the Fukien coast. Finally, it was asked that Japanese subjects be given the right to preach throughout China.[12]

The general background of these proposals and the ends the Japanese government hoped to attain in approaching China with them have already been described. They represented the specific means whereby these ends were to be translated into the legal realities of treaties and agreements.

When the demands were first presented to the Chinese government, Mr. Hioki, the Japanese Minister at Peking, to whom the negotiations were entrusted, enjoined secrecy upon Yuan Shih-k'ai and his Ministers.[13] The Chinese officials, however, recognized that wide publicity would be the most effective means with which to counter the Japanese move. Unofficial channels conveyed knowledge of the proposals to the American Minister, Mr. Paul Reinsch, whose attitude could be depended upon to be sympathetic. He was informed of the substance of the demands as early as January 21, just two days after they had been officially brought to the attention of the Chinese Foreign Office.[14] Garbled accounts of the various items and specula-

---

[12] For the complete text of the demands as originally presented, see Appendix, pp. 241–47.

[13] Reinsch to Bryan, January 23, 1915, *Foreign Relations, 1915,* p. 79.

[14] Paul S. Reinsch, "Secret Diplomacy and the Twenty-one Demands," *Asia,* November 1921; see also his *An American Diplomat in China,* p. 144. The active, although totally unofficial (and to the Department of State, somewhat embarrassing), part played by Mr. Reinsch in advising the Chinese throughout the

tions concerning their scope and character soon appeared in the Chinese and foreign press, so that, by the time the negotiations opened on February 2, any hope that the Japanese government had entertained of bringing them to a rapid and secret conclusion had to be given up.

The negotiations began on February 2 and continued without interruption until April 17, when the unwillingness of either side to make further concessions brought the discussions to a halt. In order to meet the situation, on April 26, the Japanese government brought forth what it termed "an amended project." This project, while keeping the basic intent of the original demands, accepted many of the modifications which the Chinese officials had insisted upon. Finally, as a *quid pro quo* for the unqualified acceptance of the new Japanese project, a definite promise was given to return the leased territory of Kiaochow to China "in the event of the said territory being left to the free disposal of Japan as the result of the peace conference upon the conclusion of the present war." The Chinese government, however, did not care to accept the conditions under which Kiaochow was to be returned, as it considered that Japan would still be in a position to dominate the affairs of Shantung by retention of a settlement at Tsingtao and through retaining control of the Tsingtao-Tsinan Railway. Therefore, on May 1, the Chinese government countered the amended Japanese proposals by a new project of its own. This project was termed the maximum which China could accept. The Japanese government found the Chinese final project unsatisfactory, and, faced by the choice of abandoning some of the important items in its demands or compelling acceptance by a threat of force, it chose the latter alternative. On May 7 an ultimatum was presented to the Chinese government which, under the circumstances, it felt compelled to accept. Shortly afterward related treaties and notes were signed embodying those demands to which the Chinese had acceded. Objectionable as the Japanese démarche must have been to the Chinese negotiators, nevertheless it is

negotiations can be best judged in his own words. He says of his activities: "While not taking responsibility of giving advice to the Chinese, I could give them an idea as to how the tactical situation, as it developed from week to week, impressed me. Dr. Wellington Koo all through this time acted as a liaison officer between the Minister for Foreign Affairs and myself: .... Some objection was hinted by the Japanese Legation to Dr. Koo's frequent visits to my office and house, but his coming and going continued, as was proper." See Reinsch, *An American Diplomat in China*, p. 144.

not true that the entire series of treaties and agreements of May 25, 1915, were forced upon China by the Japanese ultimatum. By April 17 some sort of compromise on most of the items had been reached between the Chinese and Japanese representatives. In view of the subsequent plea of the Chinese government, before the Paris Peace Conference, that the Sino-Japanese treaties of 1915 should be abrogated because they were imposed by *force majeure,* it is important to distinguish between the demands to which the Chinese government agreed prior to April 17 and those items which it was forced to accept under pressure of the Japanese ultimatum.

At the opening conference, on February 2, Mr. Hioki requested Lu Chêng-hsiang, the Chinese Minister in charge of the negotiations, to agree in principle to the full list of proposals, leaving the settlement of the details of each to subsequent negotiation. The Chinese representatives refused to do this, however, having been forewarned against this procedure by Mr. Reinsch, who had suggested that each item be debated separately.[15] At this meeting, the Chinese Minister "agreed in principle" to the transfer of Germany's rights in Shantung to Japan."[16] The Chinese assent, however, was accompanied by a series of counterdemands which the Japanese government considered nullified China's acceptance of its Shantung proposals. Before it would formally consent to the transfer of the German rights, the Chinese government asked that

The Japanese Government declare that, when the assent of the Chinese Government in regard to the interests above referred to has been given, Japan will restore Kiaochou to China, and they recognize the right of the Chinese Government to participate in the negotiations mentioned in the preceding clause between the Japanese and German Governments.

The Japanese Government agree that they will be entirely responsible in regard to indemnification for losses of all kinds occasioned by Japan's military operations in Kiaochou; and although the Customs, telegraphs and posts within the leased territory of Kiaochou will, pending the restoration of Kiaochou, be administered for the present as heretofore, the military railways and telegraphs which were constructed for the use of the Japanese troops will be immediately removed; and the Japanese forces remaining outside the leased territory of Kiaochou will first be withdrawn and those remaining within the said territory will be completely withdrawn at the time of the restoration of Kiaochou to China.[17]

[15] Reinsch, *Asia,* November 1921, *loc. cit.*

[16] *The Sino-Japanese Negotiations of 1915,* Chinese Official Statement of May 7, 1915, p. 66.

[17] *Ibid.,* Counter-Project of the Chinese Government of February 12, 1915, p. 8.

These counterproposals raised again the entire question of the scope of Japan's action in Shantung and emphasized the wide divergence in views with which the Chinese and Japanese governments regarded this question.[18] Yuan Shih-k'ai, anxious to overcome the "loss of face" caused by the presence of Japanese troops in Shantung outside the leased territory, desired the immediate restoration of the *status quo ante bellum* in this province. The Japanese government, on the other hand, was not willing to relinquish control of the Tsingtao-Tsinan Railway, which it considered to be German government property and inseparable from the leasehold, until the outcome of the war was finally decided. The Japanese government interpreted the request of the Chinese government that Japan formally commit itself to restore Kiaochow, in addition to the promise voluntarily made in her ultimatum to Germany, as a demand for the unconditional restoration of the leasehold at the end of the war.[19] The Chinese government, on the other hand, in its official statement issued shortly after the conclusion of the negotiations, explained that the Chinese requests "left the entire question of the conditions of the restoration to be determined by Japan . . . ."[20] In any event, the Chinese government refused throughout the subsequent months of negotiations to withdraw or modify these counterdemands. The Japanese government, in turn, refused to accept them. Thus the negotiations reached a deadlock which was broken only after the Japanese government resorted to the diplomatic extremity of an ultimatum.

On February 12 the Chinese government expressed its willingness to negotiate upon twelve of the Japanese proposals, provided certain modifications were accepted by Japan. The twelve items covered the demands relating to Shantung, South Manchuria, and the Han Yehping Company. The communication made no reference to Eastern Inner Mongolia nor to the "wishes" of Group Five, thereby indicating the unwillingness of the Chinese government to consider these items.

In framing their counterproject, the Chinese officials sought to avoid the full force of the original Japanese demands by imposing negative restrictions upon the Chinese government rather than by granting positive rights to Japan. For instance, with regard to Japan's plea for a preferential position in the financing and construc-

---

[18] *Supra,* pp. 25–26.
[19] *Sino-Japanese Negotiations of 1915,* Japan's Ultimatum to China, p. 33.
[20] *Ibid.,* Chinese Official Statement, p. 66.

tion of railways in South Manchuria, the Chinese government offered to pledge that it would not go outside its own resources in seeking capital for future railway enterprises.

The Chinese government fully agreed to the extension of the lease of the Kwantung area to a period of ninety-nine years.[21] It also agreed to extend the South Manchuria Railway Agreement for a similar period. These two items were undoubtedly the most important of the Japanese demands and constituted very great concessions upon the part of the Chinese government.

While the request for the extension of the Kwantung leasehold had been united with that of the South Manchuria Railway, the Chinese rights involved were very different in the two projects. Theoretically, at least, the Chinese government had the right to recover the control and administration of the leasehold in 1923, the date of the expiration of the Russian lease agreement. In the case of the South Manchuria Railway, however, the Chinese government had only the right to purchase the railway in 1939, and then only upon paying in full all the capital involved, the debts, and accrued interest contracted for the railway. Failing to avail itself of this option, which necessarily would have involved a tremendous financial operation, the railway was to pass to China in 1983 free of charge.[22]

The desire of the Japanese government to have the entire area of South Manchuria and Eastern Inner Mongolia opened to the residence, trade, industrial and agricultural enterprises of Japanese subjects was met by the Chinese proposal, which, while excluding Mongolia entirely, promised to open certain additional inland treaty ports in Manchuria in which Japanese and other foreign merchants could reside and trade and rent land required for commercial and industrial purposes. Merchants who took advantage of these privileges were to be subject to the same taxes and contributions imposed upon the

[21] The original Sino-Russian Convention of March 27, 1898, providing for the lease of the Liaotung Peninsula, stipulated that the terms of the leasehold "may be prolonged subsequently by mutual consent of both Governments." MacMurray, op. cit., Vol. I, p. 119, Article 3.

[22] The rights referred to above were derived from Article 8 of the Sino-Russian Convention of March 27, 1898, for the lease of the Liaotung Peninsula, whereby the provisions of the contract agreement of September 8, 1896, providing for the construction of the Chinese Eastern Railway, were to apply to the South Manchuria Railway. Sino-Russian Convention of March 27, 1898, MacMurray, op. cit., Vol. I, p. 119; and Article 12 of the Sino-Russian Contract for the Construction and Operation of the Chinese Eastern Railway, September 8, 1896, MacMurray, ibid., p. 74.

Chinese residents.[23] The Chinese contended that unlimited rights of residence, trade, and purchase of land for farming in South Manchuria were incompatible with the existence of extraterritoriality and that only in so far as foreigners were willing to give up such rights and place themselves under the jurisdiction of Chinese authorities should they be permitted to reside outside of the treaty ports.[24]

Article 4 of Group Two, asking that Japanese subjects be given the right to carry on mining operations in the above-named areas, the Chinese modified to cover merely the right to prospect for mines in South Manchuria with the privilege of mining one-half of the mines thus prospected. Advantage of this right, moreover, had to be taken within one year of the agreement going into date.

Japan had asked that the control of the Kirin-Changchun Railway should be extended for a term of ninety-nine years. This request was not immediately accepted, but subsequently, on March 23, the Chinese government agreed to a revision of the Kirin-Changchun Railway Agreement, and this revision was accomplished by the Agreement of October 12, 1917, whereby the railway was placed under the control of the South Manchuria Railway until 1947. The latter railway, in turn, advanced to the Kirin-Changchun Railway a loan of 6,500,000 yen.[25]

The demand of Group Three, by which Japan sought to turn the Han Yeh-ping Company into a joint Sino-Japanese concern, was avoided by the vague promise that if the "Company desires on a future occasion to come to agreement with Japanese capitalists for the joint management of its present business, the Chinese Government will give permission in so far as such step does not conflict with the laws of the country."[26]

The request that no position of the Chinese coast be ceded or leased "to any other Power" was met by stating that the alienation or nonalienation of Chinese territory was a question involving the sovereignty of China and therefore not a question upon which the Chinese government could properly negotiate.[27]

---

[23] *Sino-Japanese Negotiations of 1915,* Chinese Counter-Project of February 12, 1915, p. 9.

[24] *Ibid.,* Chinese Official Statement, pp. 72–73.

[25] C. Walter Young, *The International Relations of Manchuria,* p. 142.

[26] *Sino-Japanese Negotiations of 1915,* p. 10.

[27] Agreed to on March 9, in the form of a voluntary pronouncement by the Chinese government; *ibid.,* p. 68.

Finally, the Chinese government reiterated its willingness to agree to the transfer of the German economic rights in Shantung and the temporary transfer of the German leasehold to Japan, provided the Japanese government pledged itself to restore the leasehold to China after receiving it from Germany and provided that in the meantime the Japanese troops along the line of the Tsingtao-Tsinan Railway were withdrawn within the leasehold.

It will be seen from this description of the Chinese counter-proposals that the major demands of Japan were readily accepted by the Chinese government. Japan was assured practically permanent control of her leasehold in Manchuria and the South Manchuria Railway. Many new towns in Manchuria would be opened to trade and residence of foreigners. Japan would inherit the economic rights and preferred position in China which Germany had held in Shantung. However, the Chinese government refused to recognize Japan's demand for a similar position in Fukien. The attempt of Japan to seize control of the iron and coal resources of the Yangtze Valley was also side-stepped. Japanese nationals, the majority of whom would be Koreans, would remain excluded from carrying on farming operations in South Manchuria. Finally, the Chinese refused to acquiesce in Japan's desire to bring Inner Mongolia under her domination.

The vague language of the items of Group Five and their classification as "wishes" gave the Chinese the desired loophole to escape consideration of these demands. The Chinese were aware that practically every one of these items conflicted with the treaty engagements of China with the Powers and were contrary to their own and Japan's pledges to preserve China's administrative and territorial integrity. It was felt, therefore, that these proposals could be ignored because Japan would not care to force them upon China in the face of the criticism which such a procedure would be sure to arouse in Great Britain and the United States.

Following the presentation of the Chinese counterproject, the meetings between the Chinese and Japanese representatives were resumed on February 22 and continued until April 17, when the unwillingness of either side to make further concessions upon the bases of the original demands and the Chinese counterproposals brought about an impasse. Between these two dates twenty-one meetings were held and some progress was made toward reaching a compromise on most of the items. There remained, however, several points of serious disagreement. The Chinese government refused to withdraw or modify its reservations with regard to Shantung and Kiaochow. Agreement had not been reached as to the extra-territorial rights to be enjoyed by Japanese subjects who would reside in Manchuria outside the treaty ports. At first the Chinese government had wished to bring such foreign residents, who for the most part would be Korean farmers, under the full control of Chinese authorities. The Japanese government wanted to retain complete extraterritorial jurisdiction over them. The Chinese representatives made a series of concessions from their original position with regard to the Manchuria demands and by April 2 had yielded so far as to meet all the Japanese original requirements as to residence and juris-diction, with the exceptions that land could not be purchased and that Sino-Japanese cases involving land leases were to be tried solely by a Chinese judge.[28] The Chinese government refused also to yield to the request that Japanese consuls should have the right to partici-pate in the drawing up of agricultural tax and police regulations for South Manchuria upon the grounds that to yield on this issue would amount to a surrender of sovereignty.[29]

Throughout the negotiations the Chinese government refused to link the proposals relating to South Manchuria with those relating to Eastern Inner Mongolia. At first, any concessions in this area were flatly refused, but on April 17 the Chinese Minister for Foreign Affairs consented to open certain additional treaty ports in Mongolia and even went so far as to say that "he might find it possible to consider this demand to extend to Eastern Inner Mongolia the rights asked for in South Manchuria on condition that the Japanese should wholly abandon the demands under Group V."[30]

The question of Japanese participation in the control of the Han Yeh-ping Company also offered difficulties upon which the negotia-tors could arrive at no agreement. The Chinese were unwilling to go beyond their original promise not to place any obstacle in the way of Chinese and Japanese capitalists interested in the Company coming to some agreement as to joint control. This, for some years, the Japanese had attempted unsuccessfully to do. The Japanese govern-ment, therefore, continued to press the Chinese government to agree to turn the company into a joint Sino-Japanese concern.[31]

[28] Reinsch to Bryan, April 2, 3:00 P.M., *Foreign Relations, 1915*, p. 118.
[29] *Ibid.*, Reinsch to Bryan, April 17, 2:00 P.M., p. 126.   [30] *Ibid.*, same telegram.
[31] See *supra*, pp. 43–44, for a discussion of Japanese interests in this concern.

Finally, the Chinese government, realizing the strength of its position in regard to the "wishes" of Group Five, was unyielding in its resolution not to discuss this group. Mr. Hioki, during the negotiations, had pressed the Chinese Minister for Foreign Affairs to make certain statements relative to some of these items and had insisted that such statements should be incorporated in the minutes. Later, in its revised project of April 26, the Japanese government asked the Chinese government to approve these statements, but they did not appear in the final ultimatum of May 7.

An exception to the reluctance of the Chinese government to discuss the items of Group Five was made with regard to the demand concerning Fukien. The Chinese indicated that they were willing to give Japan an assurance in regard to this province in accordance with Japan's wishes, after the Japanese government had modified its original proposal in response to pressure brought by the United States government.[32] The original demand stated:

> In view of the relations between the Province of Fukien and Formosa and of the agreement respecting the non-alienation of that province, Japan [is] to be consulted first whenever foreign capital is needed in connection with the railways, mines and harbour works (including dockyards) in the Province of Fukien.[33]

This proposal was plainly intended to prevent the Bethlehem Steel Corporation from carrying out the contract it was supposed to have entered into with the Chinese government for the construction of a naval dockyard near Foochow. On March 20 the American Ambassador in Tokyo had "a full and frank interview" with Baron Kato, at which Kato discussed the Fukien demand. Ambassador Guthrie reported:

> He [Baron Kato] dwelt especially on Fukien saying that Japan was very sensitive about it because of its proximity to Formosa, and that she had been made uneasy some years ago by Secretary Hay's suggestion that the United States desired to improve a harbour there for a naval coaling station, and that this uneasiness had been recently revived by published reports that the Bethlehem Steel Company was negotiating with China a contract for that harbour's improvement. He said that the purpose of Japan's request on this point was to guarantee her against any action by any power which would give the latter a foothold in that province, as any attempt by any power to gain a foothold there would be regarded as unfriendly and inimical to Japan.[34]

[32] *Sino-Japanese Negotiations of 1915,* Chinese Official Statement, p. 69.

[33] Instructions given by Baron Kato to Mr. Hioki, December 3, 1914, *ibid.,* p. 7.

[34] Guthrie to Bryan, March 21, 1915, *Foreign Relations, 1915,* pp. 113–14.

Baron Kato then went on to suggest that the United States and Japan "should agree upon a frank and friendly statement concerning this province by which all possibility of future uneasiness might be eliminated."[35]

On March 26 Mr. Bryan instructed Ambassador Guthrie to inform the Japanese government that

....this Government will view without the slightest objection any arrangement which Japan may make with China looking toward the withholding of any concession to any foreign Power which contemplates the improvement of any harbor on the coast of Fukien or the establishment of a coaling station or naval base along said coast by any foreign power....[36]

The Japanese government subsequently modified its demands for a preferred position in Fukien to meet the foregoing proposal of Mr. Bryan; that is, China was asked to pledge not to grant any concession to any foreigners whatsoever for the purpose of undertaking harbor improvements on the Fukien coast. Baron Kato's biography reveals some interesting details with regard to the Fukien demand.[37] He seems to have believed that the United States was actually attempting to get some sort of foothold in South China. His plan was to prevent such a move by proposing a general renunciation of concessions for harbor improvements, coaling stations, and commercial activities in Fukien.[38] This course was followed, and Mr. Bryan fell in with Baron Kato's scheme. In other words, Baron Kato secured the renunciation by the American government of any concession which American interests might have secured for harbor improvements in this province, and at the same time Kato secured what amounted to a renunciation of any idea that the American government had, or was thought to have, of securing a coaling station on the Fukien coast. Mr. Bryan, as was expected, did not agree to any restrictions upon American commercial activities within the province.

The American government was for some time without an authoritative text of the complete list of the demands. The Chinese government, upon learning that the Japanese government had not communicated the full text of the demands to the American government, forwarded a complete list of the Japanese proposals, which, however, contained inaccuracies of such a nature as to be seriously misleading

[35] *Ibid.*

[36] Bryan to Guthrie, March 26, 1915, *ibid.,* pp. 116–17.

[37] *Kato Biography,* Vol. II, p. 193.   [38] *Ibid.*

in several instances.[39] On February 22 the Japanese Ambassador at Washington left with the Secretary of State a memorandum containing an outline of the items of Group Five, which had been omitted from the original communication.

With a full list of the Japanese proposals in his possession, Mr. Bryan, on March 13, sent a long memorandum to the Japanese Ambassador which, in effect, was a protest against certain of the demands.[40] Secretary Bryan emphasized especially the distinction the Japanese government was making between the "demands" of the first four groups and the "wishes" of the fifth group. Commenting upon this distinction, Mr. Bryan remarked that "the American Government understands from this distinction between the 'demands' and 'requests' that the latter are not to be pressed if the Chinese Government should decline to consider them."[41]

Mr. Bryan then took occasion to review extensively the treaties and agreements upon which the United States based its rights in China and upon which its policy toward China rested. In summing up these treaty rights he made a statement which later was to have a great deal of significance in the discussions leading to the Lansing-Ishii notes of November 2, 1917. Mr. Bryan concluded his summary by saying:

> While on principle and under the treaties of 1844, 1858, 1868, and 1903 with China the United States has ground upon which to base objections to the Japanese "demands" relative to Shantung, South Manchuria, and East Mongolia, nevertheless the United States frankly recognizes that territorial contiguity creates special relations between Japan and these districts.[42]

Whereas the recognition of the special relations to South Manchuria and Eastern Inner Mongolia created by geographical contiguity was not exactly what Japan wanted, yet to get any recognition at all of her special relations to these two areas from the power which had hitherto offered the greatest resistance to such recognition repre-

---

[39] *Foreign Relations, 1915*, pp. 93–95. Memorandum of the Chinese Minister to Bryan, undated. These inaccuracies were repeated in the Department's telegram to Guthrie, of February 19, 1915, *ibid.*, p. 93.

[40] *Ibid.*, Bryan to Japanese Ambassador, March 13, 1915, pp. 105–11.

[41] *Ibid.*, p. 105. Minister Reinsch reported and continued to report that Mr. Hioki had made no distinction between the "demands" and the "wishes," and that he continued to press for the acceptance of the latter equally with the former throughout the negotiations. See Reinsch to Bryan, February 20, 1915, *ibid.*, p. 95; February 23, 1915, *ibid.*, p. 97; and April 5, 1915, *ibid.*, p. 119.

[42] *Ibid.*, p. 108.

sented a distinct diplomatic gain and more than compensated for the objections that were made to certain of the demands.[43]

Specifically the United States government objected to the following demands: It objected to the arms purchase demand (Article 4) of Group Five and the Fukien demand (Article 6) of this group as being in violation of the Open Door. With regard to the nonalienation article of Group Four, together with Article 1 of Group Five requiring China to employ Japanese subjects as advisers, and Article 3 of the same group providing for joint policing in certain areas (South Manchuria), the United States government objected on the ground that these items were "clearly derogatory to the political independence and administrative entity" of China. Mr. Bryan concluded his note by warning the Japanese government as follows:

> The United States is convinced that an attempt to coerce China to submit to these proposals would result in engendering resentment on the part of the Chinese and opposition by other interested Powers, thereby creating a situation which the Government confidently believes the Imperial Government do not desire.[44]

Toward the end of March there was a noticeable lessening of the pressure upon the Chinese government, but, at the same time, the Japanese government began making preparations for a show of force designed to threaten the Chinese into submission. The American Minister reported the arrival of "twelve hundred new Japanese troops along [the] Shantung Railway and six thousand in Manchuria."[45] The explanation given by Mr. Hioki for this increase of troops was that they constituted the usual reliefs for those already there "although the latter will be retained during the discussions of the demands."[46] The Japanese Minister of War, General Oka, seems to have been responsible for these military preparations. They were not in keeping with Baron Kato's policy, which was to conclude the negotiations if possible without resorting to force. General Oka, toward the end of March, proposed to bring the negotiations to an

[43] In June 1917 the Japanese government asked that the United States government confirm the recognition given above by Mr. Bryan of Japan's special relations to South Manchuria and Eastern Inner Mongolia. This request led eventually to the Lansing-Ishii notes of November 2, 1917. See Memorandum of the Japanese Government to the Secretary of State, June 15, 1917, *Foreign Relations, 1917,* p. 259.

[44] *Foreign Relations, 1915,* p. 111.

[45] Reinsch to Bryan, March 22, 1915, *ibid.,* p. 115.

[46] Reinsch to Bryan, March 25, 1915, *ibid.,* p. 116.

end by military pressure and had received the consent of the Emperor to this procedure. Kato, however, interceded and succeeded in getting the order countermanded.[47]

The Japanese general election of March 25 resulted in a complete victory for the Okuma government and gave it sufficient majority in the Diet to be assured that it could carry out its Chinese policy in a more leisurely fashion. This change of situation may have had something to do with softening the character of the negotiations.

The United States note of March 13 offered such a mild protest to the Japanese demands that it can hardly account for the easing of the pressure upon China. A more probable explanation seems to be that Japanese public opinion, as reflected in the Japanese press, was becoming apprehensive because of the unexpected slowness of the negotiations and the bitterness with which the Chinese press and sections of the foreign press were meeting the demands. Chargé d'Affaires Wheeler, at Tokyo, reports on April 28 that "the local press has been very generally denouncing Baron Kato's methods of negotiation."[48] The Japanese government and the Japanese people seemed not to have envisaged the possibility of the discussions being long drawn out, and concern for the final outcome was being manifested. The *Japan Daily Mail* remarked: "At first, it was thought that by the time the press in Europe and America took up the question of Japan's demands on China, the new arrangements will have been practically settled, so as to leave no room for any anti-Japanese movement to affect the new relations established . . . . the press campaign against this country is found to be realizing no small degree of success."[49]

Concern was also being shown, particularly among the more conservative statesmen, over the criticisms which were being made in the British Parliament and press against certain of the demands. Count Okuma attempted to allay this criticism by saying that "the criticism and uneasiness in England and America are caused by misinformation."[50] Uneasiness had been shown in the British Parliament as to the possible effect of certain of the demands upon the British position in the Yangtze Valley. In answer to a pertinent question in the House of Commons as to whether or not certain of

[47] *Kato Biography,* Vol. II, p. 165.
[48] Wheeler to Bryan, April 28, 1915, *Foreign Relations, 1915,* p. 127.
[49] *Japan Daily Mail,* April 10, 1915.
[50] *North China Herald,* April 10, 1915.

the Japanese proposals menaced Great Britain's interests in the Yangtze Valley, Mr. Primrose, Undersecretary of State for Foreign Affairs, had put the "Government's" position quite plainly. He remarked:

On the general question I must say that His Majesty's Government have no objection to the expansion of Japanese interests in China provided that the expansion in no way inflicts injury upon British interests. That is the principle we here laid down for ourselves because we here admitted that we should not apply for any concessions in China which would affect the South Manchuria Railway. We naturally expect that Japan should show us reciprocity and not apply for any concessions which would affect British interests.[51]

In other words the British government was willing to see Japan expand her interests in Manchuria as long as she did not venture into the British preserve in the Yangtze region.

All these factors tended to make the Okuma government less peremptory toward China and to bring it to a consideration of modifying its original demands. In the measure that Japanese pressure upon China slackened, the resistance of the Chinese increased. By April 17 it was evident that further discussions on the bases of the original proposals and the Chinese counterproject of February 12 were useless. The Chinese government was unwilling to make further concessions upon the points of dispute, and the Japanese government had placed itself in a position in which it was difficult to abandon the proposals upon which agreement could not be found. The *Japan Daily Mail* of April 24 remarked: "Now that the terms of the proposals have come to be known, the public opinion here will not permit the Government to be satisfied without carrying the negotiations to a considerable success with reference to those terms."[52]

At this point Baron Kato again exercised a pacific influence upon the situation. On April 17 Hioki advised him to send an ultimatum to China in which would be stated the final date for ending the negotiations. Hioki gave as reasons for adopting this course that:

1. Further negotiations were useless.

2. The Chinese were taking a very resistant attitude, as they believed that Great Britain and the United States would interfere.

3. The anti-Japanese movement among the Chinese was being intensified.

[51] *Parliamentary Debates, Fifth Series, 1915,* Vol. 70, p. 1722, March 11, 1915.

[52] *Japan Daily Mail,* weekly edition, April 24, 1915.

4. Finally, the American and British communities in China were extreme in their criticism of Japan, thus creating a dangerous situation.[53]

Baron Kato declined this advice, however, and continued to seek a compromise. This compromise took the form of the Amended Japanese Project of April 26.[54] The Amended Project accepted many of the modifications which had been proposed by the Chinese government and took into consideration the objections raised by the memorandum of the United States government of March 13, 1915.[55]

In its amended project, the Japanese government accepted the Chinese government's counterproposals with regard to future railway construction in South Manchuria and for the proposed Chefoo-Weihsien branch of the Tsingtao-Tsinan Railway whereby the Chinese government reserved to itself the right to construct such railways, merely promising that, in case foreign funds were needed, Japanese capitalists would be given the first opportunity to supply them. This modification left the initiative for railway construction in these areas up to the Chinese government but gave Japan the preferred position if foreign funds would be needed. Thus Japan attained her desire to exclude South Manchuria from the international rivalry which characterized the competition for railway concessions in other parts of China. At the same time the Chinese government kept the control of future railway construction in its own hands.[56]

Likewise the Japanese government contented itself with receiving an assurance that Japanese capitalists would be given first preference in supplying funds in case China wished to raise a foreign loan based upon the security of the taxes of South Manchuria.

The demand that Japanese subjects be granted the right to purchase land in South Manchuria was again made, as was the demand that the Chinese police laws and regulations and taxes applying to Japanese subjects must be approved by the Japanese consuls. In civil and criminal cases the usual rights of extraterritoriality were to be observed; that is, the case would be tried by a judge of the nationality of the defendant, except that in civil suits concerning land between

---

[53] *Kato Biography,* Vol. II, p. 170.

[54] *The Sino-Japanese Negotiations of 1915,* pp. 10–19.

[55] *Supra,* pp. 64–65.

[56] This control did not embrace concessions for railway lines which the Chinese government had already granted or promised.

Japanese and Chinese the case was to be tried and decided jointly by the Japanese Consul and the Chinese official according to the laws and local usages of China.[57] These three items remained unmodified, therefore, although they were the ones in the Manchurian group to which the Chinese government had made the most objection.

In the Japanese amended project the proposals concerning Eastern Inner Mongolia were separated from those relating to South Manchuria and showed great modification from the original demands, which had asked that the same rights be extended to this area as were asked for South Manchuria. In place of the entire area being opened up to the residence, trade, etc., of Japanese subjects, only certain suitable places were to be opened to the trade and residence of foreigners.[58] Agricultural and industrial enterprises in which Japanese subjects were involved were to be carried out as joint Sino-Japanese undertakings. The new Japanese proposal relative to future railway construction merely asked that Japan be given preference in financing such construction if foreign capital was needed. However, the Japanese government retained its request for the right to veto foreign loans which would use the taxes of this area as security.

The so-called Yangtze Valley Railways request of Group Five, whereby Japan asked for the right to finance the construction of three important projected railways designed to connect the Middle Yangtze Valley with the coast, was changed to the request that Japan be given the right to finance the construction of these projected railways "in case it is clearly ascertained that there is no objection on the part of any other foreign Power, or that China refrain from granting it to any other Power before the Japanese Government come to an understanding with the other Power which is interested in these railway schemes."[59] In other words, the Japanese government wanted an opportunity to arrive at an understanding with the British government with regard to these concessions.

The other proposals of Group Five were not entirely abandoned by the Japanese government. Measures were taken to provide an opportunity to raise these proposals at some time in the future by asking that certain statements which had been made by Mr. Lu, the

[57] *The Sino-Japanese Negotiations of 1915*, p. 13.

[58] *Ibid.*, pp. 15–16.

[59] *Ibid.*, p. 17. See *supra*, pp. 42–43, for a discussion of the British rights concerned in those concessions and the interests of Japan in them.

Chinese Minister for Foreign Affairs, be placed upon record by the Chinese government. Specifically, it was asked that the following observations of Mr. Lu be recorded:

> Mr. Lu, the Minister of Foreign Affairs of China, stated as follows:
>
> *a*) The Chinese Government will, in case of necessity in future, employ Japanese advisers.
>
> *b*) Whenever the Japanese subjects desire to lease or purchase land for the purpose of building schools and hospitals in the interior of China, the Chinese Government will permit them to do so;
>
> *c*) Some day in future when a suitable opportunity arrives, the Chinese Government will send military officers to Japan in order to make arrangements directly with the military authorities of Japan either for the purchase of arms from Japan or for establishing an arsenal in China under joint Japanese and Chinese management.[60]

The request for the right of Japanese subjects to preach in China was postponed for future discussion, and the proposal for joint Sino-Japanese police administration in certain places (South Manchuria) was definitely withdrawn.

The second demand relating to the Han Yeh-ping Company was dropped. However, the Japanese government, in addition to asking that the Chinese government approve any agreement for joint Sino-Japanese administration of the concern which the capitalists of the two countries would come to, asked that the Chinese government engage not to confiscate the Company, nor, without the consent of the Japanese interests involved in the Company, to nationalize it, nor to permit it to contract any foreign loan other than Japanese.[61]

Finally, in return for the complete acceptance of the Japanese project of April 26, the Chinese government was offered the return of the leased territory of Kiaochow, provided that it was agreed:

> 1. To open the entire territory as a commercial port.
>
> 2. To permit a Japanese settlement to be established in the area designated by Japan.
>
> 3. To permit an international settlement to be established, if desired by the Powers.
>
> 4. Arrangements to be made between Japan and China, before the restoration of the territory to China, regarding the disposition of the German establishments and with respect to the other conditions and procedures.[62]

In answer to the Japanese Amended Project of April 26, the Chinese government, on May 1, presented what was termed China's

---

[60] *The Sino-Japanese Negotiations of 1915*, pp. 17–18.

[61] *Ibid.*, p. 16.   [62] *Ibid.*, pp. 18–19.

Final Amended Project.[63] The outstanding fact about the Chinese project of May 1 was the retention in their original form of the Chinese counterproposals relating to Shantung which had been brought forward at the first meeting on February 2. It will be recalled that they asked that China be permitted to take part in the negotiations between Germany and Japan relative to the disposal of German rights in Shantung; that Japan be completely responsible for all losses occasioned by Japan's military campaign against Kiaochow; and that the Japanese forces remaining outside the leased territory be immediately withdrawn, with complete withdrawal of all Japanese forces at the time of the restoration of the territory. These proposals were interpreted to mean that the Chinese government was asking that Kiaochow be unconditionally returned to China at the end of the war and that, in the meantime, the *status quo ante bellum* in Shantung be restored.[64] Therefore, in view of the conditions Japan had set forth in its project of April 26, under which it would restore Kiaochow to China, the Chinese reservations were not acceptable.

The Chinese Final Project did not accede to the Japanese request that the right to purchase land in South Manchuria be accorded to Japanese subjects. Nor would the Chinese government admit that the agricultural tax and police regulations to which Japanese subjects would be liable should be approved by the Japanese consuls. Also, the Chinese government wished to keep the trial of cases arising out of land disputes exclusively under the jurisdiction of its own authorities, although a concession was made that an officer could be sent by the Japanese consul to watch proceedings.[65]

The most important concession made by the Chinese project was the acceptance of three of the four demands relating to Eastern Inner Mongolia. Here again, the granting of positive rights to the Japanese government was avoided by the Chinese government retaining in its own control the responsibility for railway construction and by engaging not to pledge the taxes of this area for the security for foreign loans. In answer to the proposal that Sino-Japanese joint agricultural and industrial undertakings be permitted in the area, the Chinese government answered that such an agreement was un-

[63] *Ibid.*, pp. 23–31.
[64] *Supra*, pp. 56–57.
[65] *Sino-Japanese Negotiations of 1915*, p. 27.

necessary as "Eastern Inner Mongolia is not an enlightened region as yet."[66]

The Chinese government refused to confirm and place on record the statements made by Mr. Lu in regard to certain of the "wishes" of the fifth group. It was somewhat ironically observed that "in view of their palpably objectionable features the Chinese Government persuaded itself that these could not have been intended by Japan as any other than Japan's mere advice to China."[67]

The attempt to reach a compromise involved in the Japanese revised project of April 26 and the Chinese reply of May 1 was not successful. The new Japanese proposals, while they were considerably modified over the demands as originally presented, retained substantially unmodified those proposals to which the Chinese government had shown the greatest objections. The Chinese project of May 1, which the Chinese Minister for Foreign Affairs informed Mr. Hioki were the maximum demands to which China could agree, offered no further concessions on the mooted points of land ownership and the extraterritorial rights of Japanese subjects in South Manchuria.

At the same time, the inclusion of the Chinese reservations with regard to the Shantung proposals of Japan raised again the entire question of Japan's motives in Shantung and called into question the sincerity of her promise to restore Kiaochow to China. The Japanese ultimatum of May 7 characterized these reservations as "inadmissible demands" the acceptance of which would render any agreement which had been reached upon the other points "to be of no effect."[68]

The Japanese government now had to make the choice either of attempting to carry the negotiations further with little hope of prevailing upon the Chinese government to withdraw its Shantung counterproposals or of resorting to an ultimatum in order to bring the negotiations to a close. The latter course was decided upon, and an ultimatum was presented to the Chinese government on May 7. A satisfactory response was demanded by 6:00 P.M. of May 9, 1915, failing which the Japanese government stated that it would take such independent action as it deemed necessary.[69]

Upon receiving the ultimatum the Chinese officials were somewhat astonished to find that the demands as finally asked were less exigent than were the demands as incorporated in the Japanese

[66] *Sino-Japanese Negotiations of 1915*, p. 21.   [67] *Ibid.*, p. 22.
[68] *Ibid.*, pp. 32–34.   [69] *Ibid.*, p. 36.

project of April 26.[70] The whole of Group Five, except the Fukien demand in its modified form, was withdrawn from "the present negotiations and reserved for future discussion."[71] The right of Japanese subjects to "purchase land in South Manchuria could be changed, at the option of the Chinese Government, to 'temporary lease' or 'perpetual lease,' or simply to 'lease' on the clear understanding that it means a long-term lease with the privilege of its unconditional renewal."[72] Similarly, the Chinese government was given the option of changing the phrase "the Japanese Government will be consulted" in connection with questions of railway loans and loans to be secured by the taxes in Eastern Inner Mongolia to the phrase "Japanese capitalists shall be consulted . . . ." This change also could be extended to the similar articles relating to South Manchuria.[73]

These modifications seemed to have come about in part because of a genuine wish on the part of Baron Kato to avoid an open break with China and in part because of the attitude taken by Great Britain and the United States at this juncture, an attitude unfavorable to any attempt on the part of Japan to use actual force to induce the Chinese government to accept the demands.

Following the reply of the Chinese government of May 1 to the Japanese Amended Project of April 26, the Japanese cabinet met on May 3 to discuss the sending of an ultimatum to China. Premier Okuma and others believed that if the ultimatum were to be sent, Group Five should be included in the demands. Baron Kato, however, argued for a milder form because of the adverse opinion with which Japan's démarche had been received by the powers, and because the items in Group Five were "wishes" and not demands. He also argued that the items in Group Five were not the most important items: that the real problem which the demands were attempting to settle was that of Manchuria and Eastern Inner Mongolia.[74]

The attitude of the Genro had also undergone a marked change since the beginning of the negotiations. The Genro assented to the demands prior to their presentation, and later they urged that the demands be pushed through *in toto,* including Group Five. However, the unsatisfactory course of the negotiations and the adverse criticism which had met the demands in Great Britain and the United

[70] Reinsch to Lansing, May 17, 1915, *Foreign Relations, 1915,* pp. 148–50.
[71] *The Sino-Japanese Negotiations of 1915,* pp. 36–38.
[72] *Ibid.*   [73] *Ibid.*   [74] *Kato Biography,* Vol. II, p. 174.

States caused them to urge a compromise upon Kato.[75] According to his biography Kato was not adverse to withdrawing the "wishes" of Group Five in order to assure the acceptance of the ultimatum. He had opposed the inclusion of these items originally but had been forced to include them because of political pressure from various quarters. He had succeeded, however, in getting them included as "wishes" rather than as demands.[76]

Toward the close of the negotiations the British and the American governments indicated their apprehensions at the prospect of an open break between China and Japan and began to caution the Japanese government to avoid such an eventuality. On April 28, Great Britain expressed to Japan the hope that relations would not be broken off with China, as it would create a difficult situation.[77] Again, on May 4, Sir Edward Grey sent a message saying that if Group Five were to cause a break with China, public opinion in Great Britain would consider such a course a violation of the spirit of the Anglo-Japanese Alliance.[78] Finally, on May 6, Grey asked that if it were necessary for Japan to use force to bring the negotiations to a close, Great Britain might be consulted first. Kato replied that the situation was so delicate and the matter so pressing that there would not be time to consult with Great Britain.[79]

Secretary Bryan also had been following the situation with concern. Some time in April he informally offered the good offices of the United States to aid in the negotiations.[80] The Japanese government, however, declined this offer. On the eve of the ultimatum Bryan resorted to more definite measures. Communicating directly with Premier Okuma, he expressed the hope that Japan would settle its difficulties with China peaceably. At the same time Mr. Bryan attempted to get Great Britain, France, and Russia to join with the United States in making joint representations to Japan advising a peaceful settlement. All of these governments, however, declined to support Mr. Bryan's suggestion, and he therefore withdrew it.[81]

The Chinese government signified its acceptance of the ultimatum on May 9, thus bringing to an end over four months of continuous negotiations. Treaties and agreements embodying the substance of the demands as finally accepted were signed on May 25 and have since been collectively referred to as "The Treaties and Agreements of May 25, 1915."

[75] *Kato Biography*, Vol. II, p. 198.   [76] *Ibid.*, pp. 200 and 209.   [77] *Ibid.*, p. 190.
[78] *Ibid.*, p. 191.   [79] *Ibid.*   [80] *Ibid.*, p. 195.   [81] *Ibid.*, p. 196.

The United States government, without waiting for the final treaties and agreements embodying the results of the negotiations to be signed, took the unusual step of entering a formal caveat against any of the agreements which might infringe the treaty rights of the United States. On this date, the following identic note was presented to the Chinese and Japanese governments:

> In view of the circumstances of the negotiations....the Government of the United States has the honor to notify the Imperial Japanese Government that it cannot recognize any agreement or undertaking which has been entered into or which may be entered into between the Governments of Japan and China, impairing the treaty rights of the United States and its citizens in China, the political or territorial integrity of the Republic of China, or the international policy relative to China commonly known as the open door policy.[82]

As the Japanese government had been very careful either to modify or to abandon all the demands to which the United States' note of March 13 had made objection, the foregoing statement was directed at the "circumstances of the negotiations" rather than to the actual agreements.

The prolongation of the negotiations had been very much in favor of the Chinese government, with the consequence that, despite its apparent helplessness to resist any demands Japan cared to make, the final treaties and agreements represented very important modifications favorable to China over the demands as originally presented. The Okuma government may have reasoned that the uncertain duration of the war made it imperative that the Japanese government should seize the opportunity offered to come to a general settlement with China. This task would be almost impossible when the other powers were once again free to thwart Japan's efforts. Baron Kato hoped that the Chinese government would be led to accept the Japanese proposals quickly and in secret. When this hope was not realized, considerable time for negotiation was required. This gave the Chinese the opportunity to resist the demands with a press campaign which, under the circumstances, could not be expected to be too careful in distinguishing between what the Japanese government was actually asking and what its critics would like to have it appear was being asked. The position of the Okuma government was none too strong, and as the negotiations were prolonged month after month, the Opposition in the Diet began to taunt the

[82] Bryan to Guthrie, May 11, 1915, *Foreign Relations, 1915*, p. 146.

government with pursuing a policy toward China which would result in losing China's friendship without any compensating gain.

Finally, in placing the Okuma government in a position where it was necessary to send an ultimatum to bring the negotiations to a close, Chinese diplomacy scored a marked success. It enabled Yuan Shih-k'ai to escape the full responsibility for accepting the demands. What was much more important, it enabled the Chinese Delegation to the Paris Peace Conference to plead for the complete abrogation of all the 1915 treaties and agreements upon the grounds of *force majeure*.[83] While it was true that this plea was not heeded by the representatives of the Great Powers, it aroused tremendous popular sympathy, especially in America, for China's case, which, in turn, was one of the factors leading to the inclusion of the problem of China's relation to the powers in the agenda of the Washington Conference.

When balanced against the black eye which Japanese diplomacy received because of this episode, the gains to Japan were not sufficient compensation. Japan's most important gain was the extension of the leasehold and railway agreements in South Manchuria. These extensions, however, probably could have been secured by the ordinary means of diplomacy. Germany was eliminated from the Far East, but this elimination was decided by the outcome of the war rather than by the actual eviction of Germany from Shantung. Eastern Inner Mongolia was brought into the Japanese sphere of influence in South Manchuria. In Fukien and the Yangtze Valley, Japan did not accomplish her original objects, and, as subsequent events proved, Japan received very little of any value in Shantung. Against these gains must be placed the ill will which was created among the Chinese people against Japan.

The episode revealed the situation brought about in the Far East by the war. The European powers were completely absorbed in the conflict, and Japan was left with practically a free hand in her relations with China. The mutual jealousies and conflicting interests of the powers upon which China depended to mitigate the aggressive designs of any one of them was temporarily suspended. The United States was the only power which the Chinese government could hope to play off against Japan. In this crucial test it was fully demonstrated that the United States could not be depended upon to go

[83] *Infra*, pp. 204–5.

beyond a friendly protest, and that only in protection of her own treaty rights.

Back of the immediate demands was the struggle Japan was carrying on to make herself a Great Power. The paucity of her own natural resources and the weakness of her financial ability to compete with the other Great Powers in China dictated that she could overcome her economic handicaps only through political action. But any political action looking forward to secure a stronger hold over the natural resources of South Manchuria or the iron resources of the Han Yeh-ping Company, for instance, meant that Japan would thereby endanger the market for her manufactured goods in China by arousing the ill will of the Chinese people. In this particular instance the Okuma government seemed to have chosen to strengthen the position of Japan upon the Asiatic continent at the expense, temporarily at least, of endangering its good relations with the Chinese Republic.

CHAPTER IV

CHINA'S ENTRANCE INTO THE WORLD WAR

The conclusion of the Twenty-one Demands incident, which resulted in the Treaties and Agreements of May 25, 1915, between Japan and China, left Yuan Shih-k'ai outwardly unshaken in his role of dictator. By placing the Japanese government in a position whereby an ultimatum had to be sent in order to bring the negotiations to a close, Yuan was able to escape blame for accepting the demands, and the resentment of the Chinese people was focused entirely upon Japan. A boycott was launched against any buying or selling of Japanese goods and against all dealings with Japanese merchants, banks, etc. May 25 became a symbol of national humiliation. A national patriotic salvation fund was started by popular subscription for the purpose of raising a permanent fund with which to combat any further invasions of China's sovereignty.

By the end of the summer popular interest in the boycott and the salvation fund had somewhat died down. There remained, however, the intense resentment against Japan which had been aroused through the vigorous campaign carried on against the demands by the comparatively new and vociferous Chinese press. This resentment was widespread and marked the beginning among the Chinese people of a more general resentment against the indignities which China suffered as a consequence of her inferior position among the nations. The virtual birth of a feeling of nationalism in China, which arose in opposition to the aggressive action of Japan, was undoubtedly the most significant aftermath of the Twenty-one Demands.

More than two years were to elapse before China entered the war on the side of the Allies. In the interim, internal political conditions in China became exceedingly chaotic and were characterized by a series of factional struggles between several groups or cliques. These cliques, in their attempts to gain control of the Central Government, weighed every question, domestic or external, from the viewpoint of their own particular advantage. Consequently, when in March 1917 China broke off diplomatic relations with Germany at the invitation of the United States, the question of actively joining the Allied side became the focal point in the struggle being waged between the Kuomintang Parliament, dissolved in 1913 by Yuan Shih-k'ai but reconvoked following his death in June 1916, and a coterie of military chiefs or tuchuns who were attempting to gain absolute control of the Central Government.

In the meantime, the external crisis which China had experienced as a result of the Twenty-one Demands had hardly passed before an internal crisis arose which eventually led to the reopening of the civil war that had been temporarily subdued by Yuan Shih-k'ai in 1913 at the time of the Nanking Rebellion. This crisis was brought about by Yuan Shih-k'ai's attempt to bring to a realization his long-suspected desire to become the first emperor of a new dynasty.

It will be recalled that following the abortive Nanking Rebellion, which had marked the high tide of resistance of Sun Yat-sen and his followers to Yuan's assumption of dictatorial power, the Kuomintang party had been driven from active participation in politics and the parliament set up by the Provisional Constitution of 1912 had been dissolved.[1] The Provisional Constitution of 1912 had been thrown into the discard and had been replaced by the Amended Constitution of May 1, 1914, which provided for a highly centralized form of government with power concentrated in the hands of the executive. This document also provided for a procedure for drawing up a permanent constitution which insured Yuan a controlling voice in the form which the permanent government should take.

By midsummer of 1915 it had become quite generally evident that it was Yuan's design to set up a monarchy with himself as emperor.[2] This plan for a monarchy, which was to be patterned much after the despotic form that had characterized the former Manchu regime, at the outset made no provision for representative institutions. The movement, however, had no sooner been launched than it was seized upon first by one political faction and then by its rivals in order to promote their own selfish ends.

The men surrounding Yuan were divided into several factions or cliques, whose aims and composition at any given time were difficult to determine. However, because of the prominence of their leaders and the intense rivalry which existed between them, there were two groups who stood out more prominently and clearly than the

---

[1] *Supra,* pp. 3–4.

[2] MacMurray to Lansing, August 25, 1915, *Foreign Relations, 1915,* p. 46.

others. These two groups were the so-called Cantonese party and the Anhui party. They were described at the time as follows:

The terms Anhui and Cantonese parties as applied to the parties who are struggling to control finances, for that is what it amounts to, are misleading for the provincial origin of their respective adherents has little to do with their political colour; it merely happens that the principal leaders hail respectively from Anhui and Kuangtung.

It is difficult to define the policy of either party, but the Anhui party includes those with military influence who desire that a larger share of the revenues should be devoted to the purpose of the army. This party is believed to be inimical to the employment of foreigners, and is generally regarded as reactionary.

The Cantonese party is more farseeing and realizes the necessity of foreign assistance and might be termed progressive. Both parties, unfortunately, are credited with a common ambition, namely, scheming to achieve their personal ends regardless of the welfare of the State.[3]

During the negotiations between Japan and China relative to the Twenty-one Demands, these two factions somewhat abated their rivalry, but with the close of that incident the struggle between them broke out with renewed vigor. Toward the end of June 1915 the Anhui group attempted to get control of the government's sources of revenue and to rid themselves of their rivals by bringing about the dismissal from office of several important officials belonging to the Cantonese party.[4] Faced with the prospect of being overcome by the Anhui group, Liang Shih-yi and other leaders of the Cantonese party decided to undermine their opponents by coming out strongly in support of the monarchical movement, which heretofore had been fostered by the Anhui.[5] By and large, the Cantonese group attempted to give the monarchical movement a constitutional form with representative institutions, whereas the Anhui group wanted to concentrate all power in the hands of Yuan Shih-k'ai, who would govern with the support of certain powerful military and civil officials.

Preparations for the contemplated change in the form of government were pushed forward with great vigor during the summer of 1915, and no open signs of opposition were encountered. By early

[3] *North China Herald,* June 26, 1915. The Cantonese party here referred to is not to be confused with the Kuomintang, which had been exiled from politics in 1914.

[4] MacMurray to Lansing, September 24, 1915, *Foreign Relations, 1915,* p. 63.

[5] *Ibid.*

October Minister Reinsch reported that ". . . . most Legations now expect its successful consummation within a short time."[6] The attempts of the Cantonese party to give the movement a popular form was shown in the decision to hold a referendum on the question of the form of the state. Arrangements were made for representatives elected on a class basis to pass on this question on November 15. In the meantime Peking was deluged by a steady stream of memorials from the provinces urging the speedy restoration of the monarchy.

Suddenly, in the midst of all these signs which indicated a successful culmination of the monarchical project, there occurred an event which doomed the movement to failure, although it was not outwardly given up until the late spring of 1916. On October 27 the Japanese government notified the United States that it had invited the governments of Great Britain, France, and Russia to join with it in offering immediate advice to the Chinese government to defer the execution of the plan to restore the monarchy because of the dangers of internal disorders and the consequent threat to foreign interests which the Imperial Government believed would follow if the plan were carried out.[7] The United States was invited to extend similar advice to the Chinese government.

On the same day the British government informed Washington that "they had agreed with the Japanese Government that no time should be lost in tendering advice to the Chinese Government" and trusted that "the United States Government will appreciate the reason for proceeding at once with the communication without awaiting the reply of the United States."[8] On the following day, October 28, the Japanese chargé d'affaires in Peking, accompanied by the British and Russian Ministers, called on the Minister for Foreign Affairs and suggested the advisability of postponing the contemplated change in the form of the government.[9] On November 3 the French Minister tendered similar advice, and on November 12 the Italian government joined in these representations.

The United States government did not reply to the invitation

[6] Reinsch to Lansing, October 2, 1915, *ibid.,* p. 65.

[7] Memorandum of the Japanese Embassy to the Secretary of State, October 27, 1915, *ibid.,* p. 69.

[8] Memorandum of the British Embassy to the Secretary of State, October 27, 1915, *ibid.,* p. 70.

[9] Reinsch to Lansing, October 29, 1915, and Enclosure 1, *ibid.,* p. 73.

from Tokyo until November 4. On that date the State Department informed the Japanese government that it was of the opinion that "any change by the Chinese in the form of their government, however radical, is wholly a domestic question and that any sort of interference by the Government of the United States would be, therefore, an invasion of China's sovereignty and would be without justification unless convincing evidence, which is not now in the possession of the United States Government, should show that any foreign interests which is the privilege of the United States to safeguard would be imperilled."[10]

The Chinese government replied to these representations on November 2. It denied that there existed any signs of opposition to the movement, and it was of the opinion that if trouble did occur it would probably arise from the "small number of turbulent rebels who are seeking refuge in foreign countries and in other localities beyond Chinese jurisdiction."[11] This was plainly a hint at the activities carried on by the opponents of Yuan from the shelter of the International Settlement at Shanghai and to the hospitable asylum which Sun Yat-sen and his followers were then enjoying in Japan.

In spite of the unfavorable attitude of Japan, Great Britain, France, and Russia, the necessity of "saving face" on the part of the advocates of the monarchical movement caused them to proceed with their plans, but with a great deal more caution than had been shown heretofore and with increasing concessions in the direction of setting up a constitutional monarchy. Without the support of the powers named, however, the movement had little chance of success. The Central Government was almost completely dependent upon the monthly surpluses of the customs and salt revenues, and the transfer of these revenues could be held up whenever the Consortium banks or the Ministers of the Consortium Powers in Peking decided that conditions justified such a procedure. The Ministers of these powers displayed the pressure they could exert upon Chinese domestic affairs by withholding for several months during the summer of 1915 the transfer of £750,000 due to the Chinese government out of the £2,000,000 provided by the Quintuple Loan of 1911 for the reorganization of the Salt Gabelle. The transfer was held up because of

[10] Department of State to the Japanese Embassy, November 4, 1915, *Foreign Relations, 1915*, p. 76.

[11] Reply of the Chinese Government to the Chargé d'Affaires of Japan and the Ministers of Great Britain and Russia, *ibid.*, pp. 74–75.

the attempt of the Anhui party to interfere with the Salt Gabelle administration.[12] The money was not handed over until the Chinese government had assured Sir William Dane, the British chief of the Salt Gabelle, that this attempted interference would immediately cease.[13]

Following the representations of the Allied governments, Yuan and his supporters, in order to give the movement a popular complexion, carried through the referendum on the question of the change in government. The support of the change to a monarchy was so unanimous as to indicate that the plebiscite had been engineered from Peking, as was subsequently proved to be the case.[14] Early in December, the Council of State nominated Yuan as emperor, and he, after the customary thrice refusals, accepted the honor thus thrust upon him.

The seemingly defiant attitude of Yuan and his supporters in face of the united opposition of the Entente Powers in carrying their monarchical plans to the point of actually having the Council of State nominate Yuan as emperor had a deeper explanation than that of the necessity of "saving face." The fact was that the proposal to bring China into the war against Germany had arisen among the Allies, and along with it the possibility of extending recognition of the monarchy as a *quid pro quo* if Yuan would ally himself with the Entente Powers.

The proposal to get China (Yuan Shih-k'ai) to declare war against the Central Powers was under discussion by France and Russia during the late autumn of 1915. Under date of November 12, Isvolsky, the Russian Ambassador at Paris, reported a discussion with Cambon, the French Minister of Foreign Affairs, in which the latter expressed his entire agreement with the idea of bringing China into the war.[15] Cambon feared, however, that "des objections peuvent être formulées, non seulement du côté japonaise, mais aussi du côté anglais, mais il pense qu'il sera possible de les écarter."[16] On November 20 Isvolsky reported that appropriate instructions had

[12] *North China Herald,* September 11, 1915.   [13] *Ibid.*

[14] See the instructions sent by Yuan Shih-k'ai's government to the Provincial authorities instructing them how to vote, etc., quoted in B. L. P. Weale, *The Fight for the Republic in China,* pp. 221–35.

[15] R.S.F.S.R. *Un livre noir, diplomatie d'avant guerre et de guerre, d'après les documents des archives russes, 1910–1917,* Vol. III, Part 2, p. 37, Isvolsky to Sazanof, November 12, 1915.

[16] *Ibid.*

been sent to the French Ambassador at Tokyo looking forward to getting China into the war, i.e., by getting the consent of the Japanese government to this course.[17] Evidently Yuan Shih-k'ai had asked for recognition of his monarchical designs as a *quid pro quo* for a declaration of war against Germany by China, for in December Conty, the French Minister at Peking, informed Cambon that the question of a rupture between China and Germany could be decided only after the Entente Powers should recognize Yuan as emperor.[18]

These preliminary exchanges of views between the European Allies having taken place, the proposal was now placed before the Japanese government. On December 6, Viscount Ishii, the Japanese Foreign Minister, informed the Ambassadors of Great Britain, France, and Russia that Japan could not approve the proposal to get China to declare war against the Central Powers. The disapproval of Japan necessitated giving up the idea, or at least postponing it until it came up early in 1917 as a result of the American invitation to all neutrals to break off diplomatic relations with Germany.[19]

The failure of the efforts of France and Russia to get China into the war and the support which the Allied Governments gave to Japan's representations of October 28, advising the postponement of the monarchical movement, made the Consortium banks of these countries reluctant to extend the loan which Yuan Shih-k'ai was negotiating in order to defray the costs of the change to a monarchy.[20] These costs included the funds necessary to pay the army and to make a revision of the abdication agreement with the Manchu Imperial family which would be favorable enough to cause them to hand over the Imperial seals. In Chinese eyes these seals were the symbols of legitimate authority, and Yuan dared not assume the Imperial power without first securing possession of them. This loan, because it was connected with a reorganization of the government, came within the scope of the Six-Power Consortium Agreement of June 18, 1912; therefore German interests were entitled to participate

[17] Isvolsky to Sazanof, November 20, 1915, *Un livre noir* . . . ., Vol. III, Part 2, p. 43.

[18] *Idem*, December 22, 1915, *ibid.*, p. 68. The proposal may have originally come from Yuan Shih-k'ai.

[19] *The Japan Weekly Mail*, December 11, 1915. Beyond a simple statement that the proposal had been made by the Entente Ambassadors and that the Japanese government had not approved of the proposal, the Japanese government maintained a strict silence as to any details of the démarche.

[20] *North China Herald*, November 6, 1915.

in it. The Allied bankers used this fact as an excuse to refuse the loan on the grounds that they would not be principals to a loan to which the Germans were signatory.[21]

Toward the end of December, the dead calm which the monarchical movement had encountered up to this time was suddenly broken. Armed opposition to Yuan's plans broke out in the isolated provinces of Yünnan and Kweichow. By the following March the opposition movement had spread to the provinces of Kwangsi, Kwangtung, and Hunan. Government troops were unable to make headway against the rebellious provinces, and on March 23 a mandate was issued canceling the inauguration of the monarchy.[22]

The extent to which the movement was used by the political factions in their struggle for power is indicated by the fact that the cancellation of the monarchy was brought about in part by the Anhui party, the original promoters of the movement, who now sought by this method to discredit the Cantonese group, which had been active in pushing through the movement. Thus, in the words of the American Minister, the paradox was presented that "the so-called Anhui party, who are old fashioned and reactionary and who have little idea of constructive action and modern efficiency, should again come back into prominence in connection with the restoration of the Republic."[23]

Gradually Yuan was stripped of all his power and the government was placed in the hands of a cabinet headed by Tuan Chi-jui, who during the next few years was to become the most prominent man in the affairs of China. The rebellion against Yuan continued, however, and in April Kwangtung province declared its independence of the Peking government.[24] In May a regularly constituted Provisional Government which embraced the provinces of Yünnan, Kweichow, Kwangsi, and Kwangtung was organized at Canton.[25] In the midst of all these events, on June 6, 1916, Yuan Shih-k'ai, overcome by the failure of his plans, suddenly died.

The death of Yuan Shih-k'ai temporarily united the warring elements. Li Yuan-hung, the Vice-President, succeeded to the office of President and was accepted by those in control in Peking and by most of the provinces in rebellion in the South. In an attempt to conciliate all factions, the Parliament, dismissed by Yuan Shih-k'ai

[21] *Ibid.*, November 13, 1915.   [22] *Foreign Relations, 1916*, pp. 69–71.
[23] Reinsch to Lansing, April 4, 1916, *ibid.*, p. 68.
[24] *Ibid.*, p. 73.   [25] *Ibid.*, p. 78.

in 1914, was summoned to resume its sessions, and the discarded Provisional Constitution of 1912 was declared in force until a permanent constitution could be drawn up.

These external signs of harmony, however, were merely the prelude to intense political discord. Upon the reassembling of Parliament on August 1, 1916, a struggle immediately broke out between the Kuomintang majority in this body and the group of provincial military governors, known as the Pei Yang party, who dominated the cabinet and held control of a majority of the provincial governorships. The Kuomintang members in Parliament hoped, by exercising the full powers which were legally theirs under the Provisional Constitution of 1912, to subordinate the military chiefs to their control. The military chiefs, on their part, wished to despoil the Parliament of its powers and set up an oligarchy of their own choosing.[26] Parliament showed its opposition by refusing the appointment of Tsao Ju-lin as special envoy to Japan and by refusing its consent to a loan of $5,000,000 negotiated by the Minister of Finance with Japanese capitalists.[27] Angered by the obstructionist tactics of Parliament, many of the military governors of the provinces met in a conference on January 1, 1917, when they demanded that Premier Tuan Chi-jui put an end to the interference of the Parliament in administrative and diplomatic affairs and that it be reduced to a mere consultative body.[28]

Into the midst of this purely internal political struggle there was suddenly precipitated, early in February 1917, the question of severing diplomatic relations with Germany. This question arose out of the blanket invitation which President Wilson issued to all neutral powers to follow the example of the United States in severing relations with Germany because of the latter's resumption of unrestricted submarine warfare. Mr. Paul Reinsch, the American Minister in Peking, interpreted the instructions to convey President Wilson's message to the Chinese government to mean that he should urge Premier Tuan and his cabinet to follow the action of the United

---

[26] See dispatch of Minister Reinsch to the Secretary of State, December 13, 1916, for an account of the political situation in China, *Foreign Relations, 1916,* pp. 96–98.

[27] *Ibid.*

[28] France, Ministry of Foreign Affairs, *Bulletin périodique de la presse chinoise,* Bulletin No. 1, June 12, 1917, p. 2. These bulletins, issued from 1917 to 1923, give a running account of Chinese politics based on the Chinese press reports.

States. This he immediately began to do with great energy and enthusiasm.[29]

The decision of the American government to break off relations with Germany came about as the result of the joint note of January 31, 1917, of the Austrian and German governments advising the United States that the unrestricted submarine campaign which the Central Powers had agreed to modify in the spring of 1916 was to be immediately resumed. On February 3 the American government severed diplomatic relations with Germany. In the instructions sent to the American diplomatic representatives in the various neutral countries to notify the governments to which they were accredited of this decision the representatives were instructed to add that President Wilson "believes that it will make for the peace of the world if the other neutral powers can find it possible to take similar action to that taken by this Government."[30] These instructions were received by Mr. Reinsch on February 4, and he immediately embarked upon a campaign to persuade President Li Yuan-hung and Premier Tuan Chi-jui to adopt the course suggested by President Wilson. In his memoirs the American Minister justified this activity in the following words:

I felt justified in assuming that the invitation to the neutrals to join the United States was more than a pious wish and that there was some probability that the European neutrals would support our protest. As to China I had already informed the Government that we could reasonably expect support there. I therefore considered it to be the policy of the Government to assure a common demonstration on the part of all neutral powers, strong enough to bring Germany to a halt. So far as my action was concerned, I therefore saw the plain duty to prevail upon China to associate herself with the American action as proposed by my government.[31]

Mr. Reinsch's overtures were met at first by certain pertinent inquiries upon the part of Premier Tuan and his cabinet. They wanted to know if assurances could be given that Chinese arsenals and military forces would not come under foreign control; secondly, if assurances could be given that China would be admitted to full membership in the Peace Conference at the end of the war; and, thirdly, what would be the relations of the powers now entering the war to the London agreement not to make separate peace.[32]

---

[29] See Paul S. Reinsch, *An American Diplomat in China*, especially pp. 241–59.
[30] *Foreign Relations, 1917, Supp. 1*, p. 108.   [31] Reinsch, *op. cit.*, p. 241.
[32] Reinsch to Secretary of State, February 6, 1:00 P.M., 1917, *Foreign Relations, 1917, Supp. 1*, p. 401.

On February 6 these inquiries were replaced by more specific suggestions of the conditions which the Chinese cabinet considered necessary to impose before China could break with Germany. These conditions were that the Chinese government be assured that $10,000,000 would be loaned from American sources to improve the military establishment and that the United States government agree to fund its share of the Boxer indemnity in long-term bonds and to urge the same course upon the Allied Powers.[33]

On the following day, February 7, Mr. Reinsch reported to the State Department the substance of a conversation he had had with the Minister of Finance, in which the latter informed him that

....the Chinese officials are increasingly disposed to associate their Government with the action of the United States but are deterred by the fear that evident necessity for more adequate military organization might lead the Japanese Government to seek from the Allies mandate to supervise such organization; and that to avert the possibility of Japan's creating such a situation the Chinese Government considers it to be of the utmost importance to have some assurance that means will be provided to enable it to undertake the requisite measures.[34]

The situation seemed to Mr. Reinsch to require immediate action upon the assurances asked for by the Chinese cabinet which could not await formal instructions from the State Department. His own words best describe the dilemma in which he found himself. He says:

All through Wednesday [February 7] I struggled with this difficult problem. I had to act on my own responsibility, as I could not reach the Department of State by cable. If all the influences unfavorable to the action proposed were given time to assert themselves, the American proposal would be obstructed and probably defeated. The Chinese Government would act only on such assurances as I could feel justified in giving to them at this time; if I gave them none, no action would be taken. It seemed almost a matter of course, should China follow the lead of the American Government, that the latter would not allow China to suffer through lack of all possible support in aiding China to bear the responsibility she assumed, and in preventing action from any quarter which would impose on China new burdens because of her break with Germany. Unable to interpret my instructions otherwise than that a joint protest of the neutrals had actually been planned by the American Government, and feeling that the effect upon Germany of the American protest depended on the early concurrence of the important neutral powers, I considered prompt action essential. I was sure that all sorts of unfavorable and obstructive influences would presently get to work in Peking.

When discussion had reached its limit, on the afternoon of February 7th,

[33] Reinsch to Secretary of State, February 6, 11:00 P.M., 1917, *Foreign Relations, 1917, Supp. 1*, p. 401. [34] February 7, 1917, *ibid.*, p. 403.

I felt it necessary to draw up a note concerning the attitude of the American Government. The tenor of this note I communicated to the Premier and the Foreign Office, with the understanding that I should send the note if favourable action were decided upon by the Chinese Government.[35]

Mr. Reinsch's desire to persuade Tuan and his cabinet to associate China with the United States in breaking with Germany was so great that he was prevailed upon to deliver the note containing the desired assurances before rather than after the cabinet decided to take action against Germany.[36] Consequently, Mr. Reinsch, acting without authority from the State Department, handed the following note to the Minister for Foreign Affairs:

I have recommended to my Government, in the event of the Chinese Government's associating itself with the President's suggestion, the Government of the United States should take measures to put at its disposal funds immediately required for the purposes you have indicated, and should take steps with a view to such a funding of the Boxer indemnity as would for the time being make available for the [purposes?] of the Chinese Government at least the major portions [of] the current indemnity installments: and I have indicated to you my personal conviction that my Government would be found just and liberal in effecting this or other such arrangement to enable the Chinese Government to meet the responsibilities which it might assume upon the suggestion of the President. I should not be wholly frank with you, however, if I were to fail to point out that the exact nature of any assistance to be given or any measure to be taken must be determined through consultation of various administrative organs, in some cases including reference to Congress, in order to make effective such arrangements as might have been agreed to between the executive authorities of the two Governments; and I, therefore, could not in good faith make in behalf of my Government any definite commitments upon your suggestions at the present time.

I do, however, feel warranted in assuming the responsibility of assuring you in behalf of my Government that by the methods you have suggested, or otherwise, adequate means will be devolved to enable China to fulfill the responsibilities consequent upon associating itself with the action of the United States, without any impairment of her control of her military establishment and general administration.[37]

Premier Tuan and his colleagues came to a decision on February 9 to dispatch a note of protest to the German government. Mr. Reinsch reported that "in order to bring it [the action of the cabinet] about, I found it imperatively necessary to give the assurances referred to

---

[35] Reinsch, *op. cit.*, p. 247.

[36] Reinsch to Secretary of State, February 7, 1917, *Foreign Relations, 1917, Supp. 1*, p. 407.

[37] *Ibid.*, pp. 403–4.

in my cipher telegram of February 7, 6 P.M., which, however, I have pointed out apply to the consequences of action taken concurrently with the United States."³⁸ The result of this procedure upon the part of the American Minister was to make it appear as if he, on behalf of the American government, was offering the above-mentioned assurances as a *quid pro quo* to induce the Chinese government to follow the lead of the United States. Apparently Tuan and his colleagues chose to take this view, for, in addition to the formal answer to Mr. Reinsch's note, the Foreign Office sent him a confidential *note verbale* in which it was promised that

In case an act should be performed by the German Government which should be considered by the American Government a sufficient cause for a declaration of war between the United States and Germany, the Chinese Government should [at] least break its diplomatic relations with Germany.³⁹

The Chinese note of protest to the German government was quite mild in tone. It contented itself with protesting against the submarine blockade and the prohibition of neutral shipping in certain zones and complained about the loss of life among Chinese nationals which had already resulted from German submarine operations. The note concluded by stating:

In case contrary to its expectations its protest be ineffectual, the Government of the Chinese Republic will be constrained to its profound regret to sever the diplomatic relations at present existing between the two countries.⁴⁰

The American State Department, now in touch with Mr. Reinsch, began, too late, to caution him against "giving any promises or assurances."⁴¹ He was warned that "the unwillingness of any other important neutral to follow the American example ought to be considered very gravely by China, who should in prudence avoid isolated action."⁴² Finally, the State Department advised that "the Chinese Government, therefore, would do well to consult its representatives in Allied countries."⁴³ The reference to the avoidance of isolated action and the hint to consult with the Allied governments plainly indicated that the State Department believed that China should not act in this case unless her action was supported by them. As the Japa-

---

³⁸ Reinsch to Lansing, February 9, 1917, *Foreign Relations, 1917, Supp. 1,* pp. 407–8.   ³⁹ *Ibid.*   ⁴⁰ *Ibid.*
⁴¹ Lansing to Reinsch, February 10, 1917, 1:00 P.M., *ibid.,* p. 408.
⁴² Lansing to Reinsch, February 10, 1917, 4:00 P.M., *ibid.,* p. 408.
⁴³ *Ibid.*

nese government had shown itself heretofore opposed to China's entering the war, it must be presumed that the State Department had in mind the desirability of the Chinese government being assured of support in that quarter before it ranged itself against Germany.

Mr. Reinsch held the opposite view. He believed that the best protection for China against any attempts on the part of Japan to bring the Chinese military establishment under Japanese control was to be found in China's closely associating herself with the United States. In reply to the admonitions of the State Department, he urged that

the Chinese be not rebuffed in the action they have taken or be made to feel that by being alone in committing themselves to our leadership they have merely risked having their military resources placed under Japanese control instead of being assisted by the United States to fulfill the responsibilities undertaken at the President's invitation.

It is here understood that leadership assumed by the United States entitles the American Government to a decisive voice as to the form to be given any military assistance that may be rendered China, that it could legitimately and with propriety take the initiative in planning the nature of such assistance, and certainly that a proposal for single control by any other nation could not be effectuated over the head of the American Government....[44]

On February 17 the Department of State followed its two telegrams of the 10th, counseling Mr. Reinsch to observe greater caution in his promises to the Chinese government, by a longer telegram in which the Department informed him that President Wilson's invitation to neutral powers "did not contemplate the offer to any neutral power of special inducements to take action similar to that of the United States in regard to Germany," and adding that "Since, however, you have given the assurances . . . . the matter is being most carefully reconsidered and you will be made acquainted with the result as soon as a definite conclusion is reached."[45] Reinsch was further instructed to suggest to the Chinese government that "China should not, unless compelled by extraordinary circumstances, do more than break off diplomatic relations with Germany until the definite decision of this Government in the premises is communicated to it."[46]

The decision of the Department of State in this matter was communicated to Mr. Reinsch on February 26. He was informed that,

[44] Reinsch to Lansing, February 12, 1917, *ibid.*, pp. 408–9.
[45] Lansing to Reinsch, February 17, 1917, *ibid.*, p. 410.
[46] *Ibid.*

whereas the American government would like to see China have proper representation "in any conference of the present belligerents as the hostilities conducted by them within the boundaries of China entitle it to receive," the Department "is not disposed, in the event of hostilities between the United States and Germany, to urge China to declare war also on Germany. The course of events may make such a course advisable, but it is evident that the United States would not be able to give China the assistance proposed . . . . if serious opposition should be offered to such assistance. Attempt to override that opposition might precipitate the very aggression which China fears."[47]

It is clear from this correspondence that the impetuous action of Mr. Reinsch in pressing the Chinese government to follow the United States in breaking with Germany and the unofficial promises he had made in attempting to bring about that eventuality placed the American government in a somewhat embarrassing position. This embarrassment was not lessened by the fact that none of the European neutrals cared to accept President Wilson's invitation and that the South American neutrals had shown an almost equal reluctance to take any positive action against Germany. The important element in the situation, however, was the evident fact that the American government did not wish to take the lead in influencing China to adopt a course of action which would not be supported by the Allied governments, and particularly one which would not have the support of Japan. Although Secretary Lansing shared the belief of Mr. Reinsch that the military establishment of China was in danger of falling under the control of Japan, he differed with Mr. Reinsch in the methods by which he believed this domination could be averted. Mr. Reinsch believed that, if China were to associate herself with the United States against Germany "without yet entirely associating herself with the Allies, China would be in a position to command their good will; any interference with China's sovereign rights would be rendered more difficult because of the situation thus created."[48] Mr. Lansing, on the other hand, believed that for the American government to attempt to protect China from this danger by assuming to induce China to enter the war and to render military assistance and advice to China, as was proposed by Mr. Reinsch, would bring

[47] Lansing to Reinsch, February 26, 1917, *Foreign Relations, 1917, Supp.* 1, p. 411.
[48] Reinsch to Lansing, February 14, 1917, *ibid.,* p. 415.

about Allied interference with China's military establishment which the Chinese government wished to avoid.[49]

The difficulties of the situation were not lessened by the fact that in persuading the Chinese government to dispatch its note of protest to Germany on February 9 Mr. Reinsch acted in such a manner as to give the impression that he was stealing a march upon the Allied Ministers in Peking.[50] Baron Hayashi, the Japanese Minister, was absent in Japan while Mr. Reinsch was busily consulting with the Chinese officials, and the other Allied Ministers were disregarded in favor of a group of non-official Americans and Britishers whose aid Mr. Reinsch enlisted to influence the Chinese to take action against Germany.[51]

Following the refusal of the State Department to confirm the unofficial assurances given to the Chinese government by Mr. Reinsch in his note of February 8, the American government attempted to restrain rather than to urge the Chinese government to enter the war.[52] The question of China's participation in the war was now taken up by the Allied Ministers in Peking, but apparently not until they had been first approached by Premier Tuan Chi-jui with a proposal looking forward to the adoption of such a course.

Without waiting for the decision of the American government as to whether or not it was prepared to confirm the unofficial assurances given by Mr. Reinsch, Premier Tuan Chi-jui approached first the British, French, and Russian Ministers, and, on the following day, the Ministers of Japan, Belgium, and Italy. In these interviews, which took place on February 13 and 14, respectively, Mr. Lu Chêng-hsiang, the Acting Minister for Foreign Affairs, informed the Allied Ministers that "the Chinese Government could not undertake the responsibility of taking any further steps in the direction of war without having the assurances of the powers that they would allow China certain financial benefits, particularly the postponement of the Boxer indemnity installments during the remainder of the war, and an increase of the customs duties to which China is entitled by treaty."[53] He also asked that the agreement (in the Boxer Protocol of 1901) for the exclusion of Chinese troops from Tientsin should

[49] Lansing to Reinsch, February 26, 1917, *ibid.*, p. 411.

[50] Reinsch, *op. cit.*, p. 244.   [51] *Ibid.*, p. 250.

[52] See Lansing to Reinsch, March 13, 1917, *Foreign Relations, 1917, Supp. 1*, p. 419; and *idem*, June 4, 1917, *Foreign Relations, 1917*, p. 48.

[53] Reinsch to Lansing, April 13, 1917, *ibid., Supp. 1*, pp. 441–42.

be canceled. On the same day that Mr. Lu conveyed the proposals of the Chinese cabinet to the Allied Ministers, he also had an interview with Mr. Reinsch. At this interview he informed Mr. Reinsch that "the Chinese Government was being strongly urged by Japan to commit itself to a war policy; that there was considerable opposition to such a policy in the interior of China; that particularly among the Mohammedans of western China the danger of an uprising appeared imminent." He (Mr. Lu) then asked "what financial assistance China could expect from the United States in order to enable her to face this danger." Apparently, however, he did not inform Mr. Reinsch of the overtures which had just been made to the Allied Ministers beyond saying that "he considered China, before committing herself to the war, should endeavor to obtain some assurances from the Allies as would guarantee her financial independence."[54] The State Department learned of these overtures through the French Ambassador in Washington and thereupon called Mr. Reinsch's attention to the fact that the Allies were being approached by the Chinese government. Mr. Reinsch was warned that "this indicates that the Foreign Office has not told you the whole situation."[55]

It seems quite clear that Tuan and his cabinet did not hesitate to take full advantage of the opportunity for bargaining which had arisen. On the one hand, they attempted to induce the American government to grant certain concessions to China by stressing the possibilities of China being driven into an alliance with Japan if these concessions were not forthcoming. On the other hand, without waiting for the decision of the American government as to whether or not it was going to confirm officially the assurances that the American Minister had made, they approached the Allied governments with a view to getting them to grant important desiderata as a *quid pro quo* in return for associating China with the Allies in the war against Germany. When it became apparent that the American government was not going to confirm the assurances given by Mr. Reinsch and that instead of wishing China to take action against Germany it was more concerned with counseling caution in this direction, Premier Tuan, Fêng Kuo-chang, the Vice-President, and other high officials in the government turned toward the Allies and more particularly toward Japan.[56]

[54] Reinsch to Lansing, April 13, 1917, *Foreign Relations, 1917, Supp. 1*, pp. 441–42. [55] Lansing to Reinsch, March 2, 1917, *ibid.*, p. 412.
[56] Reinsch to Lansing, March 9, 1917, *ibid.*, p. 428–30.

The failure of the French and Russian démarche toward the end of 1915 to induce the Japanese government to support the move to get China into the war revealed the differences of opinion existing among the Allied Powers as to the desirability of such an eventuality.[57] At that time the Japanese government had shown itself definitely opposed to China's joining the Allies against Germany, and until the Japanese government changed its attitude in this respect there seemed to be little chance of China's being drawn into the hostilities. However, the activities of the American Minister in connection with President Wilson's invitation of February 4, 1917, to neutral powers brought the question to the fore from a quarter over which Japan had no control. The question having thus been raised and the initial step taken by the Chinese government in dispatching its note of February 9 to the German government, it became necessary for the Japanese government to reconsider its previous attitude of opposition to China's entrance into the war, particularly in view of the possibility of China entering the war under the sponsorship of the American government.

The question of Japan's attitude toward China's entrance into the war became involved with another important question upon which the Japanese government had begun negotiations some time previously. This was the problem of getting the Allied governments committed to support the claims which Japan proposed to present at the peace conference at the end of the war. On January 27, four days before the German government announced its intention of resuming unrestricted submarine warfare and one week before the American government broke off diplomatic relations with Germany,[58] the Japanese government entered into negotiations with the British government, asking the latter for assurances of support to the claims of Japan for the transfer to her of the former German rights in Shantung and the German islands in the Pacific north of the equator.[59] The British government gave the desired assurances

[57] *Supra,* pp. 83–84.

[58] The time element is important here because at the Paris Peace Conference in 1919 Lloyd George defended the action of the British government in entering into this secret agreement on the ground that Japan required the above-named assurances of support before she would dispatch a destroyer flotilla to the Mediterranean in order to combat the submarine menace. See *infra,* p. 217. Remarks of Lloyd George at a meeting of the Council of Four, April 22, 1919.

[59] MacMurray, *op. cit.,* Vol. II, pp. 1167–68. Understanding between Great Britain and Japan relative to the ultimate disposal of German rights. Mr. Lansing

on February 16 and in return asked that Japan support its claims for the German islands in the Pacific south of the equator.[60]

In the meantime the extreme activity of the American Minister at Peking in pressing the Chinese government to break off diplomatic relations with Germany introduced the possibility of China entering the war under the leadership of the American government, which could be counted on to oppose the Japanese claims to the former German rights in Shantung.[61] Therefore, in order further to strengthen its position, the Japanese government on February 19 approached the French and Russian governments seeking from them assurances of support similar to those which it had received from Great Britain.[62] This gave these governments an opportunity to press the Japanese government to change its previous attitude of opposition to China's entrance into the war.

The publication by the Soviet government in the autumn of 1917 of certain documents in the archives of the former Russian government revealed that the foregoing question had already been the subject of conversations between M. Krupensky, the Russian Ambassador at Tokyo, and Viscount Motono, the Japanese Foreign Minister. On February 8, 1917, M. Krupensky reported to his home government the substance of a conversation he had had with Viscount Motono on this subject. He wrote:

I never omit an opportunity for representing to the Minister for Foreign Affairs the desirability, in the interests of Japan herself, of China's intervention in the war, and only last week I had a conversation with him on the subject. Today I again pointed out to him that the present moment was particularly favourable, in view of the position taken up by the United States and the proposal made by them to the neutral powers to follow their example, and more particularly, in view of the recent speeches of the American Minister at Peking. Viscount Motono replied that he would be the first to welcome a rupture between China and Germany, and would not hesitate to take steps in this direction at Peking if he were sure that the Chinese Government would

is responsible for the statement that Viscount Ishii and Lord Grey had reached an understanding in 1915 that the equator should be the dividing line between the Pacific islands to be acquired by Great Britain and Japan. (*United States Senate Document 7605*, 1919, pp. 216–17, Hearings on the Peace Treaty.)

[60] MacMurray, *loc. cit.*

[61] The American government had already indicated its opposition to any claims Japan would make to the former rights possessed by Germany in the province of Shantung. See *infra*, p. 122.

[62] MacMurray, *op. cit.*, Vol. II, p. 1169, Memorandum of the Japanese Minister of Foreign Affairs to the French Ambassador and (*mutatis mutandis*) to the Russian Ambassador at Tokyo, February 19, 1917.

go in that direction. So far, however, he had no such assurance, and he feared lest unsuccessful representations at Peking might do harm to the Allies. He promised me to sound the attitude of Peking without delay, and, in case of some hope of success, to propose to the Cabinet to take a decision in the desired direction.

On the other hand, the Minister pointed out the necessity for him, in view of the attitude of Japanese public opinion on the subject, as well as with a view to safeguard Japan's position at the future Peace Conference, if China should be admitted to it, of securing the support of the Allied powers to the desires of Japan in respect of Shantung and the Pacific Islands. These desires are for the succession to all the rights and privileges hitherto possessed by Germany in the Shantung province and for the acquisition of the Islands north of the equator which are now occupied by the Japanese. Motono plainly told me that the Japanese Government would like to receive at once the promise of the Imperial [Russian] Government to support the above desires of Japan. In order to give a push to the highly important question of a break between China and Germany I regard it as very desirable that the Japanese should be given the promise they ask—this the more so as, so far as can be seen here, the relations between Great Britain and Japan have of late been such as to justify a surmise that the Japanese aspirations would not meet with any objections on the part of the London Cabinet.[63]

The Russian Ambassador in Tokyo wrote very briefly on February 20, committing his government to the support of the Japanese claims.[64] The French reply was made on March 1, and the promise of support was made quite explicitly on the understanding that "Japan give its support to obtain from China the breaking of its diplomatic relations with Germany, and that it gives this act desirable significance."[65] The latter phrase was stated to mean:

First, the German diplomatic agents and consuls should be handed their passports.

Second, the obligation of all under German jurisdiction to leave Chinese territory.

Third, the internment of German ships in Chinese ports and the ultimate requisition of these ships in order to place them at the disposition of the Allies.

Fourth, requisition of German commercial houses established in China, forfeiting the rights of Germany in the concessions she possesses in certain ports of China.[66]

[63] Published in the *Manchester Guardian* of February 7, 8, and 22, 1918. Quoted from F. Seymour Cocks, *The Secret Treaties and Understandings,* Appendix C, pp. 84–85.

[64] *New York Times,* April 22, 1919. Quoted in MacMurray, *op. cit.,* p. 1168. A telegram published by the Bolsheviks in 1917 indicates that up to March 1, 1917, the Russian government had not given Japan the desired assurances (Cocks, *Secret Treaties,* Appendix C, p. 85).

[65] MacMurray, *op. cit.,* Vol. II, p. 1169.   [66] *Ibid.*

Viscount Motono, upon receipt of this, replied by promising on behalf of the Japanese government to help persuade the Chinese government to break off relations with Germany.[67]

The decision to break off diplomatic relations with Germany was arrived at by Premier Tuan Chi-jui and his associates on March 3 but was not formally carried out until March 14.[68] On February 24 the French ship "Athos" was sunk in the Mediterranean by a German submarine. There were over 900 Chinese coolies aboard bound for work behind the lines in France, of whom 543 were drowned.[69] This fact, coupled with the formal reply of the German government on March 10 to the Chinese note of protest of February 9 that it was unable to restrict the operations of the submarine campaign to meet the Chinese protest, gave the Chinese government the basis in international law for its break with Germany.

The decision to adopt this course gave rise to an open quarrel between Premier Tuan Chi-jui and President Li Yuan-hung. This quarrel had been brewing for some time and was to be one of the important factors in causing the question of a declaration of war upon Germany to become a decisive issue in the political struggle between the Northern military tuchuns and the Kuomintang majority in Parliament.

The quarrel between President Li and Premier Tuan arose because Li was still convinced that the best course to follow was for China to remain neutral. Tuan was anxious to break off relations with Germany and to do so without consulting Parliament. President Li refused to sign a telegram which was to announce the break of diplomatic relations to the provincial authorities and gave as his reason that Parliament had not been consulted. Further, Li refused to consent to Tuan's desire "of informing the Japanese Government of the steps to be taken before the policy had been passed on by Parliament."[70]

The differences of opinion between President Li and Premier Tuan led the latter to resign on March 4 and to leave Peking for Tientsin. He returned to Peking, however, on March 7, after being assured that the President would approve the break with Germany and that he would no longer intervene in the transmission of dis-

---

[67] MacMurray, op. cit., Vol. II, p. 1169.

[68] Reinsch to Lansing, March 9, 1917, Foreign Relations, 1917, Supp. 1, p. 427.

[69] N. Ariga, La Chine et la Grand Guerre Européenne, p. 145.

[70] Reinsch to Lansing, March 9, 1917, Foreign Relations, 1917, Supp. 1, p. 428.

patches to the Chinese diplomatic agents abroad or to the provincial authorities.[71]

The extent to which the professed rupture with Germany was being used purely as an adjunct to the political maneuverings of the various factions in Peking and the little sympathy it had among the Chinese generally is revealed in the following extract from the *Bulletin périodique.* Commenting on the manner in which the Chinese received the news of the contemplated break, the editors of this publication remark:

> The publication of the note to Germany [of February 9] produced everywhere in China a profound impression and was very diversely received: notably it provoked consternation in Chinese commercial circles. Numerous meetings were organized at Shanghai by the Guilds and by the Chinese General Chamber of Commerce with the consequence that telegrams were sent to the government and to the two Chambers [of Parliament] protesting against the eventuality of a rupture to which the true sentiment of the nation was not favorable. "If China abandons her neutrality," concludes one of these telegrams, "she will be ruined for a long time, no matter which side is victorious."[72]

Tuan led Parliament to believe that he had already received assurances from the powers which made it safe for China to sever relations with Germany and to look toward taking further appropriate action.[73] Consequently, on March 11, the lower house of Parliament, after a long debate, finally adopted a vote of confidence in the government by a vote of 331 to 87, and on March 14 diplomatic relations with Germany were formally broken off.[74]

Immediately following the break with Germany, the Minister for Foreign Affairs formally presented to the Entente Powers and the neutrals a list of desiderata which "the Chinese Government proposed . . . . as due to China from nations desirous to strengthen her position and not as conditions for entering the war."[75] These desiderata were a more detailed statement of the concessions which Premier Tuan, on February 13 and 14, had brought to the attention of the Allied Ministers as being prerequisite to taking further action against Germany. They were:

[71] *Bulletin périodique de la presse chinoise,* No. 1, p. 5.

[72] *Ibid.,* p. 3; my translation from the French.

[73] Reinsch to Lansing, April 13, 1917, *Foreign Relations, 1917, Supp. 1,* p. 442.

[74] Ariga, *La Chine et la Grande Guerre Européenne . . . . ,* p. 144.

[75] Reinsch to Lansing, March 18, 1917, *Foreign Relations, 1917, Supp. 1,* pp. 420–21.

1. Suspension of the Boxer installments for ten years.
2. The immediate imposition of a surtax of 50 per cent on the present import duty; thereupon a revision of the tariff so as to produce an effective 7.5 per cent duty; and finally after abolition of likin, [the introduction of] the customs régime of the MacKay treaty.
3. Cancellation of the provisions of the 1901 protocol relating to Legation guards and to the exclusion of Chinese troops from Tientsin.[76]

The Chinese government, as represented by Tuan and his cabinet, still cherished the hope that the American government could be caused to give favorable consideration to these desiderata by bringing up the bogey of China being forced into a military alliance with Japan. In discussing these items with Mr. Reinsch, the Minister for Foreign Affairs declared that "should the American Government now abandon interest in China, the Chinese Government would be driven into the arms of Japan. . . . ."[77] Secretary Lansing was evidently impressed by this argument, as he promised to support the efforts of the Chinese government to get these concessions provided the Entente Powers also agreed and under the condition that "China will agree that Chinese military forces and equipment, arsenals, and munition factories are not to be placed under control of any foreign power."[78]

At the time that the Chinese government advanced these desires the Ministers of the Allied Powers inquired "as to the effect which the Chinese Government was ready to give the action taken, with respect to the treatment of German residents, disposal of German vessels, the rights of the German Bank, and the treatment of German employees in the Chinese public service."[79] The Chinese government replied on March 23, indicating that it had taken no further measures than to place police control over the German vessels in Chinese ports and that it had dismissed German employees in the operating department of the railways.[80] These measures were deemed insufficient by the Allied Ministers who wanted all German employees of the Chinese government dismissed, the Deutsche Asiatische Bank closed, and all German ships sequestered by the Chinese government to be placed at the service of the Allies.[81]

The reluctance of the Chinese government to take any other measures than these against the German residents in China gave an indi-

---

[76] Reinsch to Lansing, March 18, 1917, *Foreign Relations, 1917, Supp. 1,* pp. 420–21.   [77] *Ibid.*   [78] Lansing to Reinsch, March 26, 1917, *ibid.,* p. 423.
[79] Reinsch to Lansing, March 28, 1917, *ibid.,* p. 436.
[80] *Ibid.*   [81] *Ibid.*

cation of the uncertainty which pervaded government circles as to what attitude should be adopted now that the break of relations had occurred. The break had been brought about by Premier Tuan and the Northern military clique largely with a view to strengthening their political position, and more particularly with a view "to getting the upper hand over Parliament and the President."[82]

Opposition, however, to an actual declaration of war against Germany was beginning to appear, particularly in the South. The American Consul General at Canton reported:

> The news of the action of the Central Government in breaking off relations with Germany is not being received with enthusiasm by the natives of the southern provinces. . . . . Many influential southern men and institutions have expressed themselves strongly and fearlessly against any rupture of relations with Germany. On the other hand, I have been unable to find a single official, public institution, or newspaper advocating such a course.[83]

Sun Yat-sen, the leader of the Kuomintang, sent a telegram to Lloyd George protesting against the attempts of the Allies to drag China into the war.[84] In Shanghai, the Chinese General Chamber of Commerce organized a movement against a declaration of war and encouraged the provincial Chambers of Commerce to do likewise.[85]

The opposition which had arisen to the course upon which Premier Tuan had embarked reflected the attitude of the Chinese people toward the war. Although not indifferent to the World War, the Chinese people had shown no disposition to ally themselves actively with one side or the other. They were, however, distinctly pro-German in their sympathies and remained relatively so up to the signing of the armistice.[86]

This sympathy for Germany was in part ascribable to the policy of cultivating the friendship of the Chinese people which the German government had pursued after the Germans had once established themselves at Kiaochow. In part it was due to the fact that German business methods in China had brought the German business man into much closer contact with the Chinese than did the methods pursued by the British and French merchants. The Germans ventured into the interior and established direct contact with their Chinese

---

[82] Reinsch to Lansing, March 1, 1917, *ibid.,* pp. 424–25.

[83] Consul General at Canton to Minister Reinsch, March 16, 1917, *ibid.,* pp. 438–39.

[84] *North China Herald,* March 10, 1917.

[85] *Bulletin périodique de la presse chinoise,* No. 1, p. 3.   [86] *Ibid.,* pp. 2–3.

clients instead of remaining in the ports and working through a Chinese comprador, as was the usual foreign custom. In great contrast to the exclusiveness of the British and French clubs, the German clubs were thrown open to Chinese guests. The Chinese people were also convinced of the military superiority of the Germans and firmly believed that Germany would emerge victorious in the war.

The general popularity of the Germans and the Chinese belief in the ultimate victory of Germany was sedulously cultivated by Von Hintze, the German Minister in Peking. Von Hintze had at his command the monthly payments of the German share of the Boxer indemnity, which was paid regularly by the Chinese government into the German Bank in Peking. These payments, totaling over one million marks monthly, were used by Von Hintze to carry on extensive propaganda in favor of Germany.

Furthermore, the unexpected delay of the American government in following its severance of diplomatic relations with Germany by a declaration of war and the outbreak of the Russian revolution made the course upon which Tuan Chi-jui had embarked much less attractive than it had seemed early in February.

The most important factor, however, which caused Tuan and the cabinet to hesitate to take further action was that the Allied governments had not taken any favorable action upon the desiderata which had been advanced as the necessary conditions for committing China to a positive stand against Germany. Tuan Chi-jui and his supporters among the military governors of the Northern provinces were thus deprived of the financial benefits which were expected from the increased revenue in customs which a change of the tariff rates would have brought about. In addition, the expected financial assistance in the form of a loan from the Consortium banking groups had not materialized. Nor had financial assistance in any large amount from Japanese sources been forthcoming, although negotiations for a large loan were pending.

The failure of the Allied governments to grant to the Chinese government the concessions which it had asked were due in part to the fact that these governments were unable to agree upon a common basis of action.[87] This was explicable because of the obvious fact that the concessions asked by the Chinese government would bear unequally upon the various governments if they were granted. The Japanese government opposed the increase of the customs tariff to

---

[87] Reinsch to Lansing, May 10, 1917, *Foreign Relations, 1917, Supp. 1*, p. 447.

an effective five per cent on these grounds, and the Russian Minister informed Mr. Reinsch that "it would seem unjust to ask Russia to postpone all her Boxer indemnity because . . . . Russia would be giving up much more than the other powers."[88]

Furthermore, the Allied Ministers were not satisfied with the mildness of the measures which the Chinese government had taken against the German residents in China. These measures did not go further than to require all Germans in China to register with the local authorities and to secure permission if they wished to move from one locality to another.[89] In all other matters they were left entirely free to pursue their professions and business. These mild regulations were particularly criticized by the British and French merchants in China, who had hoped to see the Germans strictly circumscribed in their actions if not actually interned.

Difficulties had also arisen in connection with the extraterritorial status of the German residents. Upon the break of diplomatic relations with Germany, the German Minister and the German Consuls in China had been requested to leave Chinese territory. German interests had been entrusted to the Dutch Minister and consular officials in China. The Chinese government tentatively held that the severance of relations with Germany abrogated all treaties and agreements between China and Germany and that, therefore, German residents in China lost their rights of extraterritorial jurisdiction. The Dutch Minister, on the other hand, held that the severance of relations did not affect the legal rights of the German residents and that under the régime of extraterritoriality consular jurisdiction over such residents temporarily passed to the Dutch Consuls in China.

The Chinese government, while not admitting the contention of the Dutch Minister, nevertheless permitted the Dutch Consuls to assume this jurisdiction "out of courtesy."[90] This situation gave rise to a great deal of dissatisfaction among the British and French residents, particularly in Shanghai, where the Dutch Consul was accused of defeating the interests of the Allies by the way in which he exercised jurisdiction over German residents.[91] There also occurred difficulties in Shanghai in connection with the registration of German residents. The authorities of the International Settlement claimed

---

[88] *Ibid.*   [89] Ariga, *La Chine et la Grande Guerre Européenne* . . . ., pp. 203–4.
[90] *Ibid.*, pp. 244–45.
[91] Notably in the Seubert case. See editorials in the *North China Herald,* April 21, 1917, showing Allied opinion relative to the action of the Dutch Consul in this case.

the right to register German residents within the Settlement as against both the Dutch Consul and the Chinese government.[92]

The Allied communities in the Treaty ports were also disturbed by the independence which the Chinese authorities had shown when they took over the jurisdiction of the German concessions at Tientsin and Hankow without consulting the Allied representatives. This action gave rise to the problem of police jurisdiction in these concessions over the numerous German residents who lived in them. Certain of the Allied Ministers wished to see these former German concessions placed under the administration of one or more of the Allied Powers, but the Chinese insisted upon retaining the administration in their own hands.[93]

The effect of these difficulties, which had arisen as a result of China's break in relations with Germany, was that, whereas the Entente Ministers and the British and French merchants wished to see the Chinese government take stricter measures against the German residents in China, they at the same time did not relish seeing the Chinese authorities take independent action to control the German residents which threatened to make a break in the system of extra-territoriality and other unilateral privileges enjoyed by the Treaty Powers. The Chinese government was faced with the reverse of this situation. The desire to abolish the extraterritorial rights of Germans in China and to do away with the German concessions at Tientsin and Hankow inclined them to declare war upon Germany, in which case there would be no question of the right of the Chinese government under international law to take these measures. On the other hand, the attempts of the Settlement authorities at Shanghai to assume jurisdiction over German nationals and the high-handed act of the French authorities at Shanghai in forcibly closing the German School of Medicine in the French Concession caused Chinese public opinion to become increasingly unfavorable to the Allied cause.[94]

These considerations, however, had little actual influence on the question of declaring war upon Germany. This question became the point of issue in the political duel which had developed between Tuan

[92] This was an important point, as the majority of the German merchants in China resided in the International Settlement and the Settlement authorities were attempting to bring them under their control rather than leave them to the control of the Chinese authorities.

[93] Reinsch to Lansing, March 28, 1917, *Foreign Relations, 1917, Supp. 1,* p. 434.

[94] *Bulletin périodique de la presse chinoise,* No. 2, August 18, 1917, p. 1.

Chi-jui and his military supporters and the Kuomintang-dominated Parliament.[95] The quarrel between these two groups was frankly as to which should control the Central Government. The situation was complicated by the personal antagonism which existed between President Li Yuan-hung and the Premier, Tuan Chi-jui. Tuan had attempted to reduce the President to a figurehead and to draw the control of affairs into his own hands. President Li was determined to retain the prerogatives which he believed belonged to his office. Therefore, when the question of entering the war arose and Tuan attempted to force the issue over President Li's objections, Li allied himself with the Kuomintang majority in Parliament, who were striving to bring about the downfall of Tuan and to bring the Peking government under their control. It was a continuation of the same struggle which had gone on in 1912 and 1913 between the Parliament, dominated by the "Young China" elements who had brought about the revolution, and Yuan Shih-k'ai, who represented the autocratic traditions of the old regime. As in the case of Yuan Shih-k'ai in 1912 and 1913, Tuan was faced with the necessity of getting funds from any source available in order to overcome the chronic poverty of the government. He was desirous of allying China with the Allied Powers in order to secure loans and other financial concessions. Parliament, on its part, was fearful that to consent to a declaration of war would place in Tuan's hands the means by which he could reduce this body to impotence.[96] Tuan was supported in his war policy by three important groups. The first group consisted of the provincial military governors of the Northern provinces, generally known as the Pei Yang party. The second group consisted of the so-called Communications clique, headed by Tsao Ju-lin. This group leaned decidedly toward a policy of working in close co-operation with Japan and became prominently identified with the Sino-Japanese loans of 1917 and 1918. The third group was known as the Chin Pu Tang and was led by Liang Ch'i-ch'ao. It was a conservative group and tended to oppose the radical Kuomintang.[97]

In order to strengthen his policy and to overcome the opposition of Parliament, Tuan Chi-jui convoked at Peking, on April 25, a meeting of the provincial military governors. Nine governors were present, and the military governors of the other provinces and

[95] Reinsch to Lansing, June 6, 1917, *Foreign Relations, 1917*, pp. 54–55.
[96] Reinsch to Lansing, May 10, 1917, *Foreign Relations, 1917, Supp. 1*, p. 448.
[97] *Ibid.*

territories were represented by delegates.[98] These military governors or tuchuns during their stay in Peking were feted by the American and Allied Ministers with the object of influencing them favorably toward a declaration of war. On April 27 they were invited to the British Legation, where they were shown a great war film, "The Battle of the Somme," and in the evening they were entertained at the American Legation by Mr. Reinsch, where they were addressed upon the "War Aims of America." On April 28 the military governors passed a resolution supporting a declaration of war upon Germany.[99] They thereafter remained in the capital and attempted to press Parliament to consent to a declaration of war.

Closely connected with the question of declaring war was the question of modifying the draft constitution which Parliament had prepared. This draft constitution was modeled after the Provisional Constitution of 1912 and envisaged a form of government in which the executive would be subordinated to the legislature. The military governors wanted this draft amended so as to make the executive independent of the legislature.[100]

The action of Premier Tuan in calling the convention of military governors increased the antagonism and fears of Parliament and also determined President Li not to support a declaration of war except coming as a mandate from Parliament.

The question of declaring war was brought before the lower House of Parliament on May 10. On the previous day the Allied Ministers called in a body upon the Minister for Foreign Affairs and expressed to him their concern for the Allied cause because of the weak measures which the Chinese government had taken to restrict the activities of German nationals in China. He was warned that the Allied governments feared they would be constrained to devise methods to meet the situation.[101]

When the lower House met to discuss the question of a declaration of war the Parliament building was surrounded by a hired mob, which attempted by duress to force the members to vote for the declaration. In the face of this situation the Parliament refused to discuss the question and were held prisoners by the mob until after

[98] Reinsch, *An American Diplomat in China*, p. 261.

[99] *Ibid.*

[100] *Foreign Relations, 1917*, p. 68. Enclosure includes petition of the tuchuns relative to the provisions in the draft constitution to which they objected.

[101] *North China Herald*, May 19, 1917.

midnight. The result of this tour de force was that Parliament became determined to force Tuan to resign. All the cabinet ministers resigned except Tuan Chi-jui and the Minister of Education. Thereupon, Parliament refused to treat with Tuan, as it did not consider that he and the Minister of Education constituted a cabinet. The military supporters of Tuan, on their part, demanded the dissolution of Parliament.[102]

On May 23 President Li attempted to combat the pressure of the military tuchuns to dissolve Parliament by suddenly dismissing from office Premier Tuan and by bringing under his control all the military forces of the capital. This coup d'état gave the military governors the opportunity, for which they had been seeking, to declare openly against President Li. The military governors of Honan, Shantung, Manchuria, and Anhui declared their intention to sever relations with the Central Government unless Parliament was dissolved.[103] In order to avoid a military movement upon the part of the governors against Peking, President Li called in General Chang Hsün to mediate with them. Before proceeding to Peking, Chang Hsün, who was a reactionary general of the old regime, insisted that Parliament should be dissolved.[104] Faced by the prospects of a military movement against Peking on the part of the military governors, who had set up a provisional government at Tientsin, President Li yielded and dissolved Parliament on June 11.

Upon his arrival in Peking, General Chang Hsün, instead of attempting to mediate between President Li and the military governors, judged the time ripe to set up a restoration of the Manchu regime by placing upon the throne the young Emperor Hsüan Tung, who, in accordance with the arrangements made at the time of the abdication in 1912, was living in the Imperial palace in Peking. This plan was suddenly carried out on the night of June 30, and the young emperor was set upon the throne.[105] The insufficient preparations made by Chang Hsün to carry through such a coup became immediately apparent. The tuchuns assembled at Tientsin began to move upon Peking under the command of Tuan Chi-jui. Peking was subjected to bombardment during July 11 and 12. Chang Hsün fled

---

[102] *Foreign Relations, 1917*, pp. 67–68, Mandate Dissolving Parliament, June 12, 1917.

[103] Reinsch to Lansing, May 30, 1917, *ibid.*, p. 47.

[104] Reinsch to Lansing, July 3, 1917, *ibid.*, p. 84.

[105] See Reinsch to Lansing, August 9, 1917, *Foreign Relations, 1917*, pp. 90–96, for a detailed description of this coup d'état.

to the Dutch Legation, and on July 14 General Tuan entered the city.

The restoration movement thus was over as suddenly as it had appeared. Its effects, however, were far-reaching. Most of the Kuomintang members of the dissolved Parliament fled to Shanghai or Canton, and President Li resigned. Thus the way was left open for a complete ascendancy to power of the military and pro-Japanese groups who supported Tuan Chi-jui. Fêng Kuo-chang, the Vice-President, assumed the office of Acting President, and Tuan Chi-jui reformed his cabinet, excluding representatives of the Southern provinces from participation in the government. These provinces, thereupon, set up an independent government at Canton and prepared to move against the Peking government.

On August 3 the cabinet decided to declare war upon Germany, and on August 14 this decision was carried out by presidential mandate countersigned by the Premier. Mr. Reinsch was informed that "the adoption of this policy is prompted by a desire to strengthen China internationally, as well as particularly [protect?] the present Government against internal opposition which would probably, after the declaration of war, be treated as treasonable negligence."[106]

The real reasons for the declaration of war, however, were stated more succinctly and to the point in the *Bulletin périodique*. This official publication of the French Foreign Office remarked:

Le nouveau Gouvernement comprend en effet; parfaitement que pour affermir son autorité et calmer l'agitation du Sud, sa tâche la plus urgente est de prendre parti pour l'Entente et d'obtenir par ce moyen les réssources financières et le prestige indispensables.[107]

When earlier in the year it had become apparent that the question of declaring war upon Germany was being subordinated to the exigencies of domestic politics, the Allied Ministers in Peking had adopted an attitude of watchful waiting pending the outcome of the internal political struggle described above. With regard to the desiderata which the Chinese government had advanced as necessary to be granted before further action against Germany could be taken, the Allied governments had adopted the position that "China should not attempt to get definite assurances but should take action friendly to the powers who would then reciprocate in the same spirit."[108]

[106] Reinsch to Lansing, August 3, 1917, *Foreign Relations, 1917*, p. 89.
[107] *Bulletin périodique de la presse chinoise*, No. 3, p. 6.
[108] Reinsch to Lansing, May 10, 1917, *Foreign Relations, 1917, Supp. 1*, pp. 447–48.

The American government on its part had showed apprehension over the possibility of the war issue giving rise to a renewed outbreak of civil war. When this possibility became imminent upon the dismissal of Tuan Chi-jui by President Li with the threat of the military governors gathered at Tientsin to restore him to power by force, the American government, in a note of June 4, communicated to the Chinese government its apprehensions on this score and added:

The entry of China into war with Germany, or the continuance of the *status quo* of her relations with that Government, are matters of secondary consideration. The principal necessity for China is to resume and continue her political entity and to proceed along the road of national development on which she had made such marked progress.[109]

Under the same date, June 4, the American government dispatched notes to the governments of Great Britain, France, and Japan proposing that they make identic representations to the Chinese government in this sense. The American Minister was instructed to communicate the contents of the American note to the Chinese government without awaiting the replies to this invitation. This he did on June 5.

The replies of Great Britain, France, and Japan, while expressing concern over the disturbed internal situation, took issue with the American government with respect to China's entrance into the war as being a matter of secondary consideration. The British Foreign Office, replying under date of June 15, stated:

. . . . His Majesty's Government thus consider China's entry into the war to be primarily to her own interest, and moreover, as far as they themselves are concerned, they feel it would be inconsistent with all the steps which they have taken to bring China in, if they were suddenly to qualify the importance which they have hitherto attached to that eventuality.[110]

The note of the French government, delivered to the American Ambassador, Sharp, on June 17, stated:

It did not, in fact, appear happy . . . . to say to the Chinese Government that we consider the entry of China into the war against Germany as of entirely secondary importance . . . .[111]

The reply of the Japanese government, delivered through the Japanese Ambassador in Washington on June 15, while not specifi-

[109] Lansing to Reinsch, June 4, 1917, *Foreign Relations, 1917*, pp. 48–49.

[110] Great Britain: Foreign Office to Page, June 14, 1917, *ibid.*, p. 74–75.

[111] France: Minister for Foreign Affairs to Sharp, June 14, 1917, *ibid.*, pp. 75–76.

cally commenting on the relative importance of China's entrance into the war, definitely opposed making any identic representations in the sense proposed by the United States government. It was considered by the Japanese government that the moment was inopportune for making such representations; that the lives and properties of foreigners remained essentially unmolested; and that to make such representations would be interfering in the domestic affairs of China.[112]

The action of the American government was not well received by the Japanese press or by the Japanese government.[113] The Japanese government used the incident to ask that the American government confirm the recognition of Japan's special and close relations, political as well as economic, with China given by Mr. Bryan in his note of March 13, 1915.[114] This request of the Japanese government led eventually to the Lansing-Ishii notes of November 2, 1917.[115]

All during the struggle of Tuan Chi-jui and his supporters among the military governors with the Kuomintang majority in Parliament over the question of declaring war upon Germany, the Chinese government was suffering from its usual lack of funds and was turning in every direction in its attempts to secure foreign loans. In fact one of the most compelling motives which urged Tuan to push through a declaration of war over the opposition of Parliament was to enhance the possibilities of obtaining a large loan either from the American government or from the Allied banking groups in the Consortium. A third possibility was that of obtaining loans from Japanese sources, other than those bound by the Consortium Agreement of June 18, 1912, which, in any case, would expire on June 18, 1917. All three of these sources were being approached; but Parliament opposed the consummation of any loans, as a part of its attempts to get rid of Tuan and because it feared that the proceeds would be

---

[112] Japanese Ambassador to Lansing, June 15, 1917, *Foreign Relations, 1917,* pp. 71–72. It is of interest to note that in this instance the two governments completely reversed the positions they had taken under somewhat similar circumstances in the autumn of 1915. At that time the American government had declined to participate in making representations to Yuan Shih-k'ai advising him to abandon his plans to make himself emperor, giving reasons almost identical with those of Japan at the later time, as the basis for its refusal. *Supra,* pp. 81–82.

[113] Wheeler to Lansing, June 9, 1917, *Foreign Relations, 1917,* p. 58.

[114] *Supra,* p. 64.

[115] See *infra,* pp. 129 ff., for a more detailed treatment of the bearing this incident had upon the Lansing-Ishii notes.

used to force the Kuomintang from political life. Its fears in this direction gave it another reason for opposing the declaration of war. However, it was not only the internal political conflict which stood in the way of the Chinese government securing the funds which it was seeking and which it needed if any kind of order were to be brought out of the troubled internal situation. The question of rendering adequate financial assistance to China, which had been raised by the Chinese government as a necessary requisite to China's participation in the war, became immediately lost in the morass of international rivalries and conflicting policies which seem inevitably to meet any attempts of the Powers to deal collectively with China.

The war demands of the European Allied governments eliminated any possibility of securing funds from them, and, therefore, Japan and the United States were left as the only sources from which loans could be secured. The American government for some time had shown itself desirous of assisting the Chinese government in its financial difficulties.[116]

Shortly after the American government entered the war the State Department virtually committed the American government to extend to the Chinese government some sort of financial assistance under circumstances which led the Chinese government to believe that such assistance would be forthcoming if it declared war upon Germany. This assistance was to be extended under legislation passed on April 24, 1917, providing for loans to nations at war with Germany. Prior to its passage the State Department informed the Chinese Minister in Washington that "if China should be among those then [when the bill was passed] engaged in war with our enemies she might have some reason to expect such financial assistance."[117] It was subsequently decided, however, that China entered the war after the law was passed, and therefore she was not eligible to loans under its provisions.

In view of the difficulties encountered by the American government to extend financial assistance to China through the channels described above, the situation resolved itself into the American government either extending a direct loan to the Chinese government or proposing that the Consortium be reorganized upon a new basis with American participation. The situation was somewhat delicate,

---

[116] See *infra*, p. 124, for the efforts of the American government to encourage American bankers to loan money to China.

[117] Lansing to Reinsch, April 23, 1917, *Foreign Relations, 1917, Supp. 1*, p. 432.

as the Chinese government had already approached the Consortium groups with proposals for a loan of £10,000,000 to £20,000,000.

The alternative to either of the courses indicated was to acquiesce in having Japanese banks, either within the Consortium or independently, extend loans to China under conditions which would give Japanese interests a paramount influence in the financial affairs of the Chinese government.

The idea of extending a direct loan to China, which was "intended as a substitute for the Consortium loan now under consideration in Peking," was given up.[118] In its place the American government decided to propose the formation of a new international financial Consortium which would have for its purpose the maintenance of a balance of power in rendering financial assistance to China. The American government was strongly urged to take this course by the British government, which evinced great concern over the possibility of Japanese interests attaining a predominant position in Chinese financial affairs if American interests did not participate in the loans for which the Chinese government was asking.[119]

The negotiations connected with the formation of a new Consortium were long and tortuous and involved so many delicate questions, particularly in regard to conflicts of Japanese and American policy, that the final agreement was not signed until October 1920, thus coming too late to have any constructive effect upon China's participation in the war.

In the meantime the failure of the American and the Entente governments to extend any financial relief to China forced the Chinese government to turn to Japanese sources, with the result that during the latter part of 1917 and in 1918 there were consummated a series of Japanese loans, which became generally known as the Nishihara loans. At the same time the secret Sino-Japanese Military Agreement of March 25, 1918, and the Naval Agreement of May 19, 1918, were signed. These agreements were designed to draw the Chinese military and naval establishments under Japanese control, at least during the period of the war.[120] This was the danger which Mr. Reinsch, the American Minister, had foreseen and which he believed could have been avoided if the American government had

---

[118] Lansing to Reinsch, September 20, 1917, *Foreign Relations, 1917*, p. 142.

[119] British Embassy to Lansing, October 3, 1917, *ibid.*, pp. 144–45.

[120] The Sino-Japanese Military Agreement of March 25, 1918, text, *Foreign Relations, 1918*, pp. 224–25.

seen fit to divert to China a few millions of the billions it loaned the Allied governments.[121]

In recognition of its declaration of war upon Germany, the Allied Ministers gave to the Chinese government the following vague assurances:

> My Government is pleased to take this opportunity to give to the Chinese Government the assurance of its solidarity, of its friendship, of its support. It will do all that depends upon it in order that China may have the benefit in her international relations of the situation and the regards due from a great country.[122]

The American Minister was authorized to join in giving these meaningless assurances to the Chinese government.

The immediate effect of China's entrance into the war was to place Tuan Chi-jui and the military governors of the Northern provinces in complete control of the Central Government. Backed by Japanese financial support, they were able to maintain themselves in power until the end of fighting in Europe. The dismissal of Parliament and the declaration of war, however, caused the provinces south of the Yangtze Valley to set up an independent government at Canton and to rebel openly against the Northern tuchuns. The civil war which ensued absorbed the energies of the Peking government to such an extent that China's participation in the war remained merely nominal. The question of China's entrance into the war, which temporarily had held the center of the stage, became in retrospect merely an incident in the domestic struggle being waged between the conservative forces left over from the old regime and the "Young China" elements which had come to the fore with the Revolution of 1911.

---

[121] Letter of resignation of Minister Reinsch, June 7, 1919, Reinsch, *An American Diplomat in China*, pp. 364–67.

[122] Reinsch to Lansing, August 12, 1917, *Foreign Relations, 1917, Supp. 1*, p. 455.

CHAPTER V

JAPANESE-AMERICAN RIVALRY IN CHINA AND THE LANSING-ISHII NOTES

The absorption of the European powers in the World War caused a suspension of their normal economic activities in China. Work already begun on the numerous railway concessions granted by the Chinese government to European concessionaires in 1913 and 1914 was stopped, and many other concessions remained dormant in the contract stage.[1] The flow of funds from foreign loans upon which the new republican government largely depended ceased with the outbreak of the war, causing the government to become almost solely dependent upon the monthly surpluses of the Salt Gabelle and the customs and upon the proceeds from several internal loans. In the diplomatic field, the Entente Powers withdrew into the background, leaving the leadership in affairs concerning their common interests largely in the hands of Japan.

Japan, as may be inferred from her actions, saw in the temporary withdrawal of the European powers from the Chinese scene the opportunity to establish her hegemony in South Manchuria upon a firm basis and to assume the position of leadership among the Powers in Chinese affairs to which she felt that her geographic proximity and her political and economic interests in China entitled her.[2]

The American government, meanwhile, continued to pursue its traditional policy of the Open Door, which by its nature implies the preservation of a balance of power in China. It was logical, therefore, that the policy of the United States should come into sharp conflict with the aims of Japan. In fact, the diplomacy of the Far East in the war years largely resolved itself into a prolonged diplomatic duel between Japan and the United States in which each government attempted to check and countercheck the efforts of the other in order to secure the lead in Chinese affairs. For the most part, the Entente

[1] See *supra*, p. 30, n. 10, for a general description of the railway and mining concessions granted to foreign interests by the republican government.

[2] See *supra*, pp. 28–32, for a discussion of the relative position of Japan in China as compared to that of the European Powers.

114

Powers remained in the background, emerging now and then in response to some critical situation but quickly returning to the shadow of Japan's lead.

The recession of the European Powers into the background caused the conflicting policies of the United States and Japan to be thrown more sharply into prominence than they would have been under ordinary circumstances. The conflict was accentuated by the fact that in the measure that Japan took steps to strengthen her position in Manchuria and China the American government increased its efforts to protect the treaty rights of its nationals and to preserve a condition of free economic competition. This course often tended to make it appear as if the American government were championing the cause of China rather than taking measures to protect its own treaty rights.[3] The impression was greatly strengthened by the sympathetic attitude of the American Minister at Peking for the Chinese side of the many Sino-Japanese problems which arose. At times Mr. Reinsch's sympathies led him into actions and to take views which were decidedly anti-Japanese. As the war progressed, he became increasingly *persona non grata* to the Japanese government and people.[4]

The Twenty-one Demands and the Treaties and Notes of May 25, 1915, marked the decisive step by which Japan obtained from China, although not as completely as she had hoped, treaty recognition of her paramount position in South Manchuria and of her right to inherit certain of the former German rights in Shantung. However, Japan did not obtain through this démarche the commanding influence in Chinese affairs for which she had hoped. This was, in part, due to the objections of the American government to certain of the Japanese demands which caused them to be either subsequently modified or abandoned.[5] The American government also pressed the distinction which Baron Kato had made between the "demands" of the first four groups and the "wishes" of the fifth group in such a way as to discourage the Japanese government from forcing these latter proposals upon the Chinese government.[6] Since among these "wishes" were the proposals designed to give Japan a leading influence over the Chinese government, when they were given up, other means had to be found to attain this objective. Furthermore, the Wilson administra-

---

[3] E.g., as in the case of the Twenty-one Demands.

[4] *Infra*, p. 130.

[5] *Supra*, pp. 64–65.   [6] *Supra*, p. 65.

tion adopted the position that it would not recognize that the 1915 treaties and agreements modified any American rights in China or that they affected the pledges of the Treaty Powers to support the Open Door and the administrative and territorial integrity of China.[7]

As the war progressed, the financial position of both Japan and the United States underwent a rapid transformation. Prior to the war both countries had been debtor nations, with the consequent necessity of devoting a considerable portion of their revenue to the payments of interest and principal upon their loan obligations.[8] The continuation of the war reversed this situation and placed both countries in a position where they had funds to loan to other countries.[9] The Allies had no funds to spare for loans to China. Japan and America, therefore, soon became the only countries from which the Chinese government could hope to obtain the funds of which it was in continual need. This situation gave rise to another source of conflict between the United States and Japan as each was fearful that the other would use the financial needs of the Chinese government as a means to further its influence at Peking.

The Wilson administration, soon after the outbreak of the war, began encouraging private American interests to make loans to China and in 1916 invited the American group in the International Consortium to become active again.[10] Later, when the Chinese government was about to enter the war, the American government considered making a direct loan to China.[11] The concern of the American government for the unfortunate financial situation of the Chinese government, shown by the efforts cited, was, in part, to be explained by the increasing importance of private American enterprise in China; but in addition there was the desire to prevent Japan from assuming

---

[7] *Supra*, p. 75.

[8] *Supra*, p. 29, n. 1.

[9] Arthur Morgan Young, *Japan under Taisho Tenno, 1912–1926*, p. 95. "In July [1916] it was announced that payments for the supply of war materials to Russia were over eighty million yen in arrears; but when in September the Russian Government placed seventy millions in treasury bills on the Japanese market, not only were they immediately subscribed, but there were bitter complaints because the money was not used for buying more stores, but for paying off liabilities already incurred. Ten million yen's worth of British treasury bills had already been taken up, and it was with no small satisfaction that Japanese found their country in a position to lend money to first-class Powers instead of being, as had been the case hitherto, a very poor relation."

[10] *Infra*, p. 125.

[11] *Supra*, p. 112.

the ascendancy over the Chinese government by becoming its chief source of revenue.[12]

The Japanese government, on its part, viewed with apprehension the considerable increase of American commercial activity in China. As the war progressed, American interests received concessions to build a great network of railways, and American banks began to make loans to the Chinese government. These activities, fostered and encouraged by the American government, seemed to herald a definite bid for hegemony in China on the part of the United States.

Finally, the activities of Mr. Reinsch in attempting to persuade the Chinese government to enter the war under the sponsorship of the United States were generally regarded by the Japanese as an attempt of the American government to substitute its leadership in Chinese affairs for that of Japan.[13]

The entry of the United States into the war in April 1917 did much to change the situation. The American government became completely absorbed in the task of defeating Germany. In accomplishing this task Japan became an important factor, while China became of very secondary interest. The result of this change was that the Japanese government, which heretofore had been vigorously challenged at every step in its program of securing a dominant position on the continent of Asia by the American government, was soon able to secure from Secretary Lansing and President Wilson a public recognition of the special interests of Japan in China. The resulting difference of opinion over just what the phrase "special interests" meant did not alter the fact that the Lansing-Ishii notes of November 2, 1917, were universally interpreted, other than by the American government, as being tantamount to a recognition of Japan's paramount interests in China.

It will be the aim of the following pages to describe the events which led to such an unexpected dénouement of the conflicting policies of Japan and the United States in China.

The years 1914 to 1917 were marked by an increase in American interests and activities in China. This was due in part to the en-

---

[12] See Lansing to Reinsch, September 20, 1917, *Foreign Relations, 1917*, p. 142. In order to prevent Japan from becoming the sole lender to China in the Consortium Loan which was being negotiated during 1917 and 1918, the American government offered to carry temporarily the British and French shares of the proposed loan. See Lansing to Sharp, November 22, 1917, *ibid.*, pp. 156–57.

[13] *Supra*, pp. 86–93.

couragement which the Wilson administration gave to American financial and business interests to push American enterprise and, in a part, it was a logical result of the practical suspension of the economic activities of the European interests which prior to the war had been active in advancing funds to the Chinese government and in railway enterprise.

Despite the fact that one of Mr. Wilson's first official acts upon assuming the presidency in 1913 was to disapprove American participation in the £25,000,000 Reorganization Loan which was then being negotiated between the Six-Power Consortium and the Chinese government, he did not intend thereby that American financial and industrial interests should be discouraged from taking part in the economic development of China. Mr. Reinsch, appointed as Minister to China by the incoming Wilson administration, informs us that:

> From my conversation with President Wilson before departing for my post I had formed the conclusion that the President realized that as America had withdrawn from cooperative effort to assist in the development of China, it was incumbent upon her to do her share independently and to give specific moral and financial assistance . . . .[14]

Upon assuming his post at Peking Mr. Reinsch entered with great enthusiasm into the task of encouraging and helping American enterprise. He believed that if Western skill could be induced to build a few trunk railway lines the local democratic institutions of the Chinese people could be linked into one great democracy.[15]

Shortly after Mr. Reinsch arrived in China, toward the end of 1913, two important contracts were signed between the Chinese government and American interests, and there was much talk of another one which did not materialize. Of the two contracts which were signed the first was with the Standard Oil Company, relative to the exploration of certain oil fields in North China, and the second was an important agreement with the American Red Cross concerning the Huai River Conservancy project.[16]

The contract, of which there were many rumors during the spring of 1914 but which was never carried to a final conclusion, was reported to be for the construction of a naval dockyard in Fukien province. The Bethlehem Steel Corporation was to undertake the

---

[14] Reinsch, *An American Diplomat in China*, p. 63.

[15] *Ibid.*, pp. 60–61.

[16] MacMurray, *Treaties and Agreements with and concerning China*, Vol. II, pp. 1109 and 1310 n.

work as a part of a $20,000,000 contract it had secured from the Chinese government in 1910 for the construction of merchant vessels, which in time of necessity could be transformed into war vessels.[17]

The rumors in regard to this concession had some basis in fact, as the Bethlehem Steel Corporation and the Chinese government had tentatively considered such a project.[18] The Japanese press became excited over the possibility of American interests invading the province of Fukien, where, because of its proximity to Formosa and because of the nonalienation promise which the Chinese government had given to Japan on April 26, 1898, it was considered that Japan possessed a preferred position. Reference has already been made to the concern with which the Japanese government regarded this project and how this concern led the Japanese government to include among the Twenty-one Demands an item providing for Japan to be first consulted whenever railways, mines, or harbor improvements were to be undertaken in Fukien with the aid of foreign capital.[19]

The Standard Oil contract gave the Company the right to explore oil fields in Shensi and around Jehol and the exclusive right to exploit these oil fields for a period of sixty years. The Japanese were particularly annoyed by this concession, as Japanese interests had been previously approached by the Chinese government with a proposal covering the same area, and negotiations had not yet been broken off with the Japanese interests when the Standard Oil Company agreement was concluded.[20] The Japanese press felt also that because of the proximity of the Jehol area to South Manchuria and because the Chinese government had already granted to Japanese interests the right to construct a railway which would traverse the oil fields, to grant to any other than Japanese interests the right of exploiting the oil fields around Jehol was a decided affront and an invasion of Japan's sphere of influence.[21]

Upon Mr. Reinsch's arrival in China in November 1913, one of his first tasks was to take up the Huai River Conservancy project. This scheme had arisen in connection with the American Red Cross relief work during the famine of 1911.[22] The project was designed to prevent the recurrence of such famines by draining and systematically irrigating the Huai River basin. This river, which runs from

---

[17] *Ibid.*, Vol. II, p. 1236, n. 2.   [18] Reinsch, *op. cit.*, p. 82.
[19] *Supra*, p. 62.   [20] *Japan Weekly Mail*, February 28, 1914.   [21] *Ibid.*
[22] MacMurray, *op. cit.*, Vol. II, p. 1310 n. See *Foreign Relations*, 1914, p. 97, for a description of this project.

west to east midway between the Yellow River on the north and the Yangtze on the south, has no adequate outlet to the sea and consequently periodically overflows its banks. A part of the scheme was to dredge and improve the Grand Canal, which had become silted up. The Chinese government was particularly anxious to make this an exclusive Sino-American enterprise, hoping thus to keep it free of political entanglements. It offered, in January 1914, to give the American Red Cross the exclusive right to undertake the necessary work. The American Red Cross, however, could not accept direct control of the work and therefore, after establishing conditions of construction, turned the contract over to the American International Corporation.

The project was eventually divided into two parts, that having to do with the drainage of the Huai River region and that having to do with the improvement of the portion of the Grand Canal in the provinces of Shantung and Kiangsu. Contracts covering the Grand Canal project were signed by the representatives of the American International Corporation and the provincial authorities of Shantung and Kiangsu in April and May of 1916.[23] The Corporation retained its option on the Huai River scheme with the intent of taking it up later.

Under the Kiaochow Lease Agreement of March 6, 1898, Germany had the right to be first consulted when public improvements were to be made in Shantung. In order to safeguard itself against any future claims Germany might make on the basis of this right, the Chinese government offered German capitalists participation in the loan for the Shantung portion of the Grand Canal Improvement loan, which offer, as was expected, was not taken up.[24]

The Japanese government now came forward in protest against the contract having to do with the Shantung portion of the Grand Canal Improvement scheme on the ground that the former German rights had passed to it as a result of its ejection of Germany from this province. On September 15, 1916, the Japanese government presented a memorandum to the Chinese government calling attention to the right enjoyed by Germany under Article 3 of the Kiaochow Lease Agreement of March 6, 1898, to have the first opportunity to undertake any public work or to supply the funds and

---

[23] MacMurray, *op. cit.*, Vol. II, p. 1287.
[24] Reinsch to Lansing, May 15, 1916, *Foreign Relations, 1916*, pp. 110–19.

materials for any such projects in which foreign labor, capital, or materials were required.[25] The memorandum then called attention to the circumstances that "Two years ago Japan engaged in war . . . . with Germany and expelled Germany from all influence in the Province of Shantung. The consequence was that all the rights and privileges which Germany had obtained in Shantung by treaty or otherwise reverted to Japan." The memorandum further stated that by Article 1 of the Shantung treaty of May 25, 1915, the Chinese government acknowledged that these former German rights now "appertained to Japan."[26]

The purpose of Japan in presenting this memorandum seems to have been to cause the Chinese government to recognize that Japan had taken over the position of Germany in Shantung rather than to attempt to secure participation in the Grand Canal project. This view was confirmed in a conversation between Mr. Debuchi, the First Secretary of the Japanese Legation in Peking, and Mr. W. F. Carey, the representative of the American International Corporation. Mr. Debuchi informed Mr. Carey that

. . . . we must not take their inquiries on the Grand Canal, for instance, as meaning anything more than they were anxious that China should recognize the fact that Japan had by might taken over the position of Germany in the Province of Shantung. He said that he realized quite fully that legally as yet Japan did not have the rights of Germany in Shantung; but that, inasmuch as they had put the Germans out of this province, and inasmuch as by the twenty-one demands made on China in 1915 (wherein one of these demands stipulated that should Germany and Japan come to an agreement whereby Germany relinquished her position in Shantung to Japan, that transaction should be recognized and binding upon the Chinese Government), therefore, while this procedure as yet had not actually taken place, nevertheless it was procedure that would at the close of the war take place; and that Japan was only anxious that China recognize the fact that Japan was actually now in Germany's position in this province.[27]

The American government, however, was not willing to admit Japan's claim of having succeeded to Germany's position in Shantung, thereby foreshadowing the reluctance to recognize Japan's claims in this province which President Wilson showed at Paris in 1919.

[25] Memorandum from the Japanese Legation to the Chinese Government, September 15, 1916, *ibid.*, pp. 126–27.

[26] *Ibid.*

[27] Quoted in Reinsch to Lansing, November 15, 1916, *ibid.*, pp. 127–28.

In an interview with the Japanese Ambassador, on January 25, 1917, Mr. Lansing, the American Secretary of State, stated that the American government did not recognize that Japan possessed any special interests in Shantung, nor had it ever recognized the claims of Germany to any special interests there.[28]

The upshot of the Japanese protest was that the American International Corporation, because it feared that otherwise it would not be able to dispose of the necessary bond issue, invited Japanese interests to participate in the Grand Canal Improvement project and in the Huai River Conservancy scheme.[29] This course caused a great deal of criticism on the part of the Chinese people who believed that the Americans were guilty of a breach of faith in permitting Japanese participation in an enterprise which had promised to be free of political entanglements.[30]

At the same time that negotiations were going on with regard to the Grand Canal Improvement project, the firm of Siems-Carey and Company, acting as agents for the American International Corporation, had been negotiating with the Chinese government for concessions to finance and construct an extensive series of railways in various parts of China. On May 17, 1916, there was signed a preliminary agreement whereby the Siems-Carey Company was given the right to construct railways totaling over 1,100 miles, with the option to construct 1,500 miles more upon completion of the first group.[31] The Russian, French, and British governments promptly protested against one or more of the projected railways on the grounds that they infringed rights already granted to their nationals.[32]

The Japanese government brought forward no protest with regard to the Siems-Carey concessions, as none of the projected railways specifically conflicted with rights previously granted to Japan. On the other hand, the conclusion of a contract between the Chinese and Japanese governments, on December 27, 1915, for the construc-

[28] Memorandum of a conversation between the Japanese Ambassador and Mr. Lansing, January 25, 1917, *Foreign Relations, 1917*, p. 117.

[29] American International Corporation to Its Representative at Peking, February 5, 1917, *ibid.*, p. 210; also *ibid.*, pp. 207–15.

[30] Reinsch, *op. cit.*, pp. 217–19.

[31] MacMurray, *op. cit.*, Vol. II, p. 1313.

[32] Reinsch to Lansing, October 19, 1916, *Foreign Relations, 1916*, p. 190; Conty (French Minister) to Reinsch, March 30, 1917, *Foreign Relations, 1917*, pp. 185–86; Spring Rice to Lansing, September 8, 1917, *ibid.*, pp. 195–96.

tion of the Ssupingkai-Chengchiatun Railway in South Manchuria caused Minister Reinsch to raise the question of the rights of American nationals reserved under the Chinchow-Aigun Railway Agreement of October 6, 1909.[33]

Mr. Reinsch, on his own initiative, decided to use this question as a method of combating the Japanese claim to participation in the Grand Canal project.[34] Accordingly, he addressed a note to the Japanese Minister in Peking suggesting the possibility of American and Japanese interests co-operating in railway construction in South Manchuria.[35] The Japanese Minister, thereupon, replied to Mr. Reinsch, assuring him that he shared the views of Mr. Reinsch with regard to the co-operation of Japanese and American capitalists in developing the natural resources of China; but he sidestepped Mr. Reinsch's proposal by saying that "as regards the practical side of the question in applying the said principle of co-operation to railway enterprises in South Manchuria and Eastern Inner Mongolia, it is more desirable that I shall be allowed to reply at a later date."[36] There the matter was temporarily dropped.

Mention has already been made of the decision of the American banking group in the Six-Power Consortium to withdraw from active participation in loans to China. This decision came as a direct result of the Wilson administration's refusal to give its official sanction and backing to the £25,000,000 Reorganization Loan of 1913.[37] This loan was completed on April 26, 1913, by the British, French, Russian, German, and Japanese banking groups. The advent of the war, however, quickly eliminated any possibility of the European groups from actively participating in any additional loans to China. This left the Japanese and American groups as the only sources from which the Chinese government could seek loans for political or governmental reorganization purposes. The Consortium Agreement of June 18, 1912, obligated the Chinese government for a period of five years to seek loans for these purposes only from the Consortium, and at the same time it restrained the banking groups in the Consortium from making loans to the Chinese govern-

---

[33] *Supra,* p. 35.

[34] Reinsch to Lansing, January 3, 1917, *Foreign Relations, 1917,* pp. 161–63.

[35] Reinsch to Hayashi (Japanese Minister), January 3, 1917, *ibid.,* p. 169.

[36] Hayashi to Reinsch, January 20, 1917, *ibid.,* p. 172.

[37] For a review of the American group's connection with the Consortium, see The American Group to Lansing, July 26, 1916, *Foreign Relations, 1916,* pp. 134–38.

ment for these purposes independently of the Consortium.[38] The Consortium Agreement, therefore, designed originally to place a monopoly of political loans to China in the hands of a few powerful banking houses, now, because of the war situation, practically prevented any such loans being made. Germany was at war with all the other Consortium Powers, and therefore they could not deal with the German group in the Consortium.[39] The American group was inactive and, in any case, was finding very profitable uses for its money in making war loans to the Allies or to American war industries. Japan, therefore, was left as the only member of the Consortium which could advance funds to China.

At first the European powers seemed to have acquiesced in permitting Japan to take the lead in loaning money to China, although such a course inevitably meant that Japan would attain a position of commanding influence with the Peking government. By the autumn of 1917, however, Great Britain and France expressed concern over the possibility of Japan securing a monopoly of loans to China and urged the United States to re-enter the Consortium in order to check Japan.[40] The American government at first attempted to meet the threat of Japanese ascendancy by inducing American banks outside of the Consortium to make loans to the Chinese government and also for a time considered making a direct intergovernmental loan to the Chinese government.[41] Later it proposed the organization of a new Four-Power Consortium to replace the old Six-Power group. This proposal, however, was preceded by much maneuvering on both sides.

The first two years of the war passed without any outward signs of the approaching conflict between Japan and the United States over the question of financial control in China. American banks had discussed for some time the possibility of making loans to the Chinese government, but the internal conditions in China had not been conducive to such transactions. Finally, on April 7, 1916, the American firm of Lee, Higginson, and Company concluded an agreement with the Chinese government whereby a loan of $3,000,000

[38] MacMurray, op. cit., Vol. II, p. 1007.

[39] The Allied Banking groups in the Consortium had refused in 1916 to be principals in a loan to which the Germans were signatory; supra, pp. 84–85.

[40] British Embassy to Lansing, October 3, 1917, Foreign Relations, 1917, pp. 144–45; Jusserand to Lansing, November 19, 1917, ibid., pp. 154–55.

[41] Lansing to Reinsch, September 20, 1917, ibid., p. 142.

was extended for a term of three years.[42] This loan was followed on November 16, 1916, by another American loan. This second loan was made by the Continental and Commercial Trust and Savings Bank of Chicago and was for the sum of $5,000,000. At the same time the Chicago bank received an option on further loans to the Chinese government up to $25,000,000.[43]

In addition to these evidences of growing American interest in the finances of the Chinese government, the American State Department in July 1916 invited the original American group in the Consortium to become active again and to extend to the Chinese government a loan of from $4,000,000 to $5,000,000. The American group, however, did not respond with any enthusiasm to the State Department's proposal. In the first place they were still bound by the Consortium Agreement of June 18, 1912, and therefore could make only independent loans for purposes outside of those embraced by the Consortium Agreement. Secondly, the reply of the bankers, because of their unfortunate experience in 1913 with the Wilson administration, plainly intimated their reluctance to take up again the Chinese business.[44]

Shortly after the agreement was signed with the Continental Bank of Chicago the Chinese government received a note from the Allied members of the Consortium protesting against this loan as being in violation of their rights under the Reorganization Loan Agreement of April 26, 1913.[45] The reply of the Chinese government, however, indicated that it was not inclined to take this protest seriously. The Chinese government considered that the inability of the Consortium to meet its financial demands released it from the agreement.[46]

The Consortium banks were thereupon faced with the possibility of competition from American banks, which, under the circumstances of the war, they could not hope to meet. In order to avoid this contingency the Consortium banks decided to invite the American group to participate in a Supplementary Reorganization Loan of

---

[42] MacMurray, *op. cit.*, Vol. II, p. 1279.   [43] *Ibid.*, p. 1337.

[44] American Group to Lansing, July 26, 1916, *Foreign Relations, 1916*, pp. 134–38.

[45] Consortium Representatives to the Minister of Finance, December 6, 1916, *ibid.*, p. 147.

[46] Memorandum concerning the reply of the Minister of Finance to the Consortium Representatives, December 1, 1916, *ibid.*, p. 147.

from £10,000,000 to £20,000,000 which the Chinese government was requesting. The proposal to invite the American group to become active and to participate in this loan was advanced by the representative of the Japanese group at a conference in London held on January 30, 1917.[47] If it be presumed that Japanese interests were attempting at this juncture to obtain control over the finances of China, it is difficult to explain the action of the Japanese group in proposing to invite the American group to enter the new Consortium. It seems likely that the Japanese government, in order to avoid American banks outside of the Consortium extending large loans to China, decided that it would be better to have such loans made through the American group in the Consortium than to have to face the competition of independent American banks. Some such action was necessary as the Consortium Agreement would expire in June 1917, and thereafter loans for political purposes would be thrown open to the competition of powerful American banks heretofore restricted by or excluded from making such loans by the Consortium Agreement.[48]

Before any action could be taken on the proposal for the American group to become active again in the Consortium, the American government broke off diplomatic relations with Germany and invited China and all other neutrals to follow suit. The activities of Mr. Reinsch and the response of the Chinese government to President Wilson's invitation have already been described in some detail.[49]

The reaction of the Japanese government to the activities of Mr. Reinsch in attempting to persuade the Chinese government to enter the war under the aegis of America can only be surmised. In view of the obvious fact that if China were to enter the war, Japan and Japanese interests would be seriously affected one way or the other, the Japanese government could hardly view favorably the efforts of Mr. Reinsch to persuade China to take this course without enlisting Japan's co-operation. In any event it must have added to the

[47] Morgan, Greenfall and Co., to J. P. Morgan and Co., March 2, 1917, *Foreign Relations, 1917*, p. 128.

[48] In June 1918 Mr. Lansing suggested to President Wilson that the United States assist in forming a new Consortium. President Wilson approved and negotiations looking to this end were initiated. The negotiations proved to be long and tortuous and did not result in an agreement until October 1920. See Carnegie Endowment for International Peace, *The Consortium*.

[49] *Supra*, pp. 86–93.

apprehensions which the Japanese government had already evinced over the evidences of increasing American activity in China.

The Japanese government had already indicated a certain concern over American activities in China when, on January 25, 1917, Aimaro Sato, the Japanese Ambassador, called on Mr. Lansing to inquire about the subject of co-operation between Japanese and Americans in loans and industrial enterprises in China. His inquiry was obviously designed to find out more about the proposal made by Mr. Reinsch to the Japanese Minister in Peking relative to co-operation in railway building in Manchuria. To quote from the State Department's memorandum of the conversation:

> The Ambassador inquired about the proposal to cooperate in railway building in Manchuria.
>
> The Secretary replied that the Ambassador must be aware that the American Government recognized that Japan had special interests in Manchuria. Although no declaration to that effect had been made by the United States yet this Government had repeatedly shown a practical recognition of the fact and did not desire to do anything there to interfere with Japan's interests.
>
> "But," asked the Ambassador, "was not the proposal made by the American Minister in Peking?" The Secretary said he did not know of it. "Was it not done then in accordance with instructions from the Department of State?" asked the Ambassador. The Secretary said that he did not recollect any such instruction.[50]

This conversation served two useful purposes for the Japanese government. It revealed that Mr. Reinsch's proposal was simply his own idea and was not, therefore, a move on the part of the American government to revive American interest in railway construction in Manchuria, which had been permitted to lapse following the unfavorable response of Japan and Russia to the Knox proposals of 1910.[51] Secondly, Mr. Lansing suggested, inadvertently, a means by which the Japanese government could hope to check the growing American influence in China.

Mr. Lansing's admission that "the American Government recognized that Japan had special interests in Manchuria" and that "although no declaration to that effect had been made by the United States yet this Government had repeatedly shown a practical recognition of the fact," suggested the possibility of obtaining a formal

---

[50] Memorandum of a conversation between the Japanese Ambassador and Mr. Lansing, January 25, 1917, *Foreign Relations, 1917*, pp. 117–18.

[51] *Supra*, p. 36.

and open declaration from the American government of that which Mr. Lansing had said was recognized in practice.

A few days after this interview, Viscount Motono, the Japanese Minister for Foreign Affairs, made the subject of Japanese-American co-operation in China the occasion for an address to the Diet. Although Viscount Motono spoke warmly of Japanese and American co-operation in China, his speech was in a sense a warning to China to cease the policy of playing off America against Japan. He concluded on the theme to which all Japanese Foreign Ministers revert whenever speaking about Japan's policy in China, by saying:

> The other point to which the Government must call your attention is the special position occupied by Japan in certain portions of China. I am speaking especially of South Manchuria and East Inner Mongolia. Our special situation in these parts has been acquired at the cost of immense sacrifice and immeasurable efforts on our part and on the strength of this circumstance our rights and interests in these parts have been consecrated by treaties and arrangements. It is therefore the most elementary duty of the Imperial Government toward the nation to safeguard these rights and interests. In the same way it is necessary that China should comprehend that it is not only a matter of compliance with international duty that China should respect these rights and interests of Japan, but it would be nothing more than the realization of the good understanding between the two countries . . . .[52]

Viscount Motono, in conversation with the American Ambassador, elaborated on the theme of Japanese-American co-operation in China. Mr. Guthrie reported that "He [Motono] expressed the opinion that such cooperation would strengthen the friendly relations between Japan and the United States, allay suspicion in China and aid in her development. All this was predicated on the understanding that Japan claims special rights in Manchuria and Eastern Inner Mongolia which she does not waive."[53] Motono's speech paved the way for the Lansing-Ishii negotiations which took place some months later. Meanwhile, the difficulties between the United States and Japan with regard to China increased rather than diminished.

The final agreement of the Continental and Commercial Trust and Savings Bank loan was not concluded until late in the spring of 1917, difficulties having been raised by French interests which claimed priority over the security which had been assigned to the loan.[54]

[52] *Foreign Relations, 1917*, pp. 119–21.
[53] Guthrie to Lansing, January 27, 1917, *ibid.*, p. 118.
[54] Reinsch to Lansing, November 29, 1916, *ibid.*, pp. 143–45.

This loan was only one of several factors in the complex situation which had arisen because of the financial needs of the Chinese government. The underlying factor was the diplomatic maneuvering which the United States and Japan were carrying on to prevent each other from attaining a position of control over Chinese finances. In addition Mr. Lansing and Mr. Reinsch were convinced that Japan was attempting to use the Chinese government's offer to enter the war as a means of obtaining control of China's military establishment.[55]

All these factors tended to create an atmosphere of suspicion between the United States and Japan. Japanese public opinion began to believe that the American government was carrying on a policy in China the deliberate intention of which was to give the American government a leading position in Chinese affairs to the detriment of Japan's interest.[56]

This growing suspicion among Japanese official circles and as expressed in the press was greatly enhanced by the action of the American government, which, at a crucial point in the internal political struggle that was going on in China over the question of declaring war upon Germany, suddenly announced to the Chinese government that in its opinion the entrance of China into the war was of quite secondary importance as compared to the settlement of her internal difficulties.[57] As we have seen, the American government invited the governments of Great Britain, France, and Japan to follow its lead and to make similar representations to the Chinese government, and delivered its note to China without waiting for the replies of the Entente Powers.

The Japanese press became aroused over this move on the part of the American government, which was considered an unwarranted interference in China's domestic affairs and a deliberate affront to Japan, exhibiting a disregard of Japan's special and close relations to China. Chargé d'Affaires Wheeler, at Tokyo, reported on June 9: "The Press today shows general irritation at the communication made by Reinsch to China, which is viewed as interference in the

---

[55] *Supra,* p. 92.

[56] For instance, Dr. Toyokichi Iyenaga, Chief of the East and West News Bureau in the United States, stated in the *New York Times* of June 15, 1917: "The activities of the Americans in China have created the fear in Japan that America was seeking to control the foreign policy of China."

[57] Lansing to Reinsch, June 4, 1917, *Foreign Relations, 1917,* pp. 48–49; see *supra,* p. 109.

latter's internal politics and a further indication of objectionable activity of the Legation at Peking."[58] Wheeler also pointed out that the Japanese Foreign Office assumed that the American proposal contemplated joint as well as identic representations.[59]

In the next few days it became clear that the Japanese government had come to the conclusion that this latest American démarche, in conjunction with the several other factors described above, had brought about a situation which required more than a mere note of protest. On June 12 Wheeler reported: "There are indications that pressure is being brought to bear upon the Foreign Office to utilize the incident to press the United States for an assurance which will virtually admit Japan's special and paramount position relative [to] China."[60]

The position of the Terauchi cabinet, which was in power in Japan at this juncture, was not an easy one. Upon assuming office the Terauchi cabinet had announced a renunciation of the aggressive policy of its predecessors toward China and had also announced its determination not to interfere in Chinese domestic affairs. Count Motono, the Foreign Minister in the cabinet, was the particular advocate of this policy and was striving to overcome the bad impression resulting from the Twenty-one Demands affair. The increasing, and from the Japanese viewpoint, objectionable, activity of Mr. Reinsch in the affairs of China made an adherence to this policy difficult. To what extent the State Department of the United States and President Wilson, of whom Mr. Reinsch was a close friend, were aware of the degree to which Mr. Reinsch had become *persona non grata* to the Japanese people and government can only be surmised. Apprehension on this score may have led Mr. Wheeler to report from Tokyo in some detail the state of Japanese opinion in this regard. He reported:

The belief that the activities of the Legation at Peking were being exerted against Japanese interests and influence in China has been growing here during the past three years. The first open expression which came to my notice was in the autumn of 1914 in connection with the allegation, printed in Tokyo, that Chinese officials were invoking American influence for the restoration of Kiau-chau, when a Tokyo newspaper made reference to the "deliberate ill-will" of the American colony in Peking and the "anti-Japanese propaganda of a certain Embassy Secretary." This distrust of

[58] Wheeler to Lansing, June 9, 1917, *Foreign Relations, 1917*, p. 58.
[59] *Ibid.*
[60] Wheeler to Lansing, June 12, 1917, *ibid.*, pp. 61–62.

our friendliness at Peking, then sufficiently vague, has since kept pace with Japan's growing nervousness where China is concerned. Since the question arose of the latter's entrance into the World War, the suspicion of American political activity in Peking has arisen. . . . . The Foreign Office, meanwhile, has held, under increasing pressure, to its policy of ostensible noninterference. In this programme it could be sure of its ground, however, only so long as Japan's position in China (as she conceives this to be) was not seemingly jeopardized. And there is no doubt that the Foreign Office has begun to regard the American activity in Peking which popular Japanese opinion finds objectionable, as a menace to that position. . . . .[61]

The prediction of Mr. Wheeler that the Japanese government would utilize this incident to press for a recognition of its special and paramount position in China proved correct.

On June 15 the Japanese government replied through its Ambassador at Washington to the American government's invitation to join with it in making representations to the Chinese government in the sense of the American note of June 4.[62] After indicating that his government declined the invitation of the American government, the Japanese Ambassador read a memorandum to the Secretary of State in which was set forth a positive statement of Japan's general relationship to China. This memorandum marked the opening move in the Japanese government's plan to obtain from the American government a formal and public recognition of Japan's paramount interests in China. The memorandum stated:

That Japan has special and close relations, political as well as economic, with China, is well and has long been understood by the American Government. In a note dated March 13, 1915, addressed to Viscount Chinda, my predecessor, by Mr. Bryan, the then Secretary of State, he recognized this state of affairs and declared that the activity of Americans in China had never been political. Reposing confidence in this statement, the Japanese Government has attached no importance to the recent rumor repeatedly finding its way to the press despatches from China to the effect that the American Minister at Peking was more or less involved in the present political crisis in China. Again, with regard to the recent important representations made by the American Government to the Chinese Government relative to the political situation in China without previously consulting Japan, the Japanese Government does not entertain the slightest doubt as to the fair and unselfish motives of the United States Government. However, it is constrained, much to its regret, to recognize as a fact that, since the Japanese public is specially sensitive toward Chinese problems, this action of the American Government, in conjunction with the rumor aforementioned, has

[61] Wheeler to Lansing, June 14, 1917, *ibid.*, pp. 68–71.
[62] *Supra,* pp. 109–10.

generated in the minds of a certain part of the people a feeling of uneasiness. In such circumstances, the Japanese Government believes that if
the United States Government sees its way by some appropriate means to
confirming the statement made by Mr. Bryan and clearly reasserting its
friendly attitude toward Japan in respect of Chinese problems, it would leave
a good impression on the minds of the Japanese public and would certainly
contribute in no small measure to the friendly relations between our two
nations, and accordingly it now communicates its conviction most frankly to
the American Government and desires to be informed of the latter's
opinion.[63]

Two days previous to this communication the Japanese government appointed Viscount Ishii Ambassador Extraordinary and
Plenipotentiary and ordered him to proceed to the United States.
Ostensibly the object of the Ishii mission was similar to that of
the war missions which most of the Allied countries sent to America soon after the United States entered the war. In general their
purpose was to discuss America's participation in the war, to arrange for supplies and loans, discuss embargoes, etc. The Ishii
mission, however, had for its most important purpose the discussion of Japan's relationship to China.

By the time the Ishii mission arrived in America the American
government had plunged into the task of defeating Germany, and
every other consideration was made secondary to this. Viscount
Ishii believed that the absorption of the American government in
the war would jeopardize the success of his mission, as he thought
that it would not permit time for the consideration of the Chinese
question. He found on the contrary that the tremendous concentration of the American government upon winning the war made
his task much easier than it would have been if the United States
had still been neutral.[64] It not only shifted the interest of the American government from China and focused it almost completely upon
the European battlefields but it also gave the Japanese government
some valuable trading points. Japanese warships were desperately
needed for convoy service in the Indian Ocean and the Mediterranean Sea, and the allocation of more Japanese merchant vessels
to Allied services was highly desirable.[65]

[63] Japanese Ambassador to Lansing, June 15, 1917, *Foreign Relations, 1917*,
p. 259.

[64] Viscount Kikujiro Ishii, *Diplomatic Commentaries* (trans. W. R. Langdon),
p. 112; hereafter cited as Ishii, *Memoirs*.

[65] At the time of the entrance of the United States into the war, the number
of Japanese merchant vessels devoted or chartered to Allied uses was compara-

From the moment that the Ishii mission landed in San Francisco it was the object of marked and cordial attention. Viscount Ishii was not altogether prepared for the enthusiastic reception which he and his colleagues received, but he quickly took advantage of it to make many speeches in which the friendly relations between Japan and the United States were emphasized and Germany was pointed out as the villain in the piece who had been largely responsible for any discord which had arisen between the two nations.[66]

Upon the arrival of the mission in Washington, Ishii first approached President Wilson with regard to the China problem. He found Wilson friendly and willing to discuss the subject. Mr. Wilson said that the United States wanted only the Open Door and equal opportunity but that the sphere of interest of the Powers violated these two principles. Wilson then directed Ishii to Secretary of State Lansing for further discussion.[67]

Following the foregoing conversation with President Wilson, Viscount Ishii cabled his government proposing that the United States and Japan enter into a general renunciation of spheres of interest in China. Ishii's idea was that if the American government would agree to this proposal then Japan could advance its claim for a general recognition of the special position she occupied in relation to China in the same way that the United States by virtue of the Monroe Doctrine enjoyed a special position in relation to Mexico and all Central and South America.[68] The Japanese

tively small. The major portion of the Japanese merchant fleet was engaged in the commerce of the Pacific and Far East, which it had taken over almost exclusively following the withdrawal of Allied vessels from these waters. Great Britain and the United States were anxious that Japan devote a larger portion of her merchant vessels to uses directly connected with the war. The Japanese government was unwilling to transfer any important portion of the tonnage devoted to the Pacific and Asiatic trade to European service. It was willing, however, that Japanese shipyards should build ships for the Allies in proportion to the steel and iron which the American government would permit to be exported to Japan, the American government having declared an embargo on the exportation of iron and steel except for purposes directly connected with the prosecution of the war. Negotiations between Japan and the United States relative to this latter question were being carried on at the time of the Ishii mission's visit but were voluntarily ended by Japan because she believed that the demands of the American government for the diversion of Japanese shipping to Europe and the Atlantic were such as to be incompatible with the national interests of Japan. *Foreign Relations, 1917, Supp. 2,* Vol. I, pp. 713–20.

[66] For the texts of many of these speeches, see Carnegie Endowment for International Peace, *The Imperial Japanese Mission to the United States, 1917.*

[67] Ishii, *Memoirs,* pp. 112–13.   [68] *Ibid.,* pp. 113–15.

government, however, delayed its reply to the proposal of Ishii until after the Lansing-Ishii notes had been signed.

In the first conversation between Secretary Lansing and Viscount Ishii the latter remarked that German propaganda was attempting to divide Japan and the United States by playing up the immigration and Chinese questions.[69]

Mr. Lansing replied in the same vein and added that German propaganda was saying that the Allies believed that Japan was using the war as an opportunity to strengthen her position in China and that her actions were making the Open Door and equal opportunity and China's territorial integrity meaningless. He therefore proposed a joint declaration of the Open Door.[70]

Viscount Ishii replied that such a declaration would not be sufficient, and that it had already been done in the Root-Takahira notes and also in the Anglo-Japanese Alliance and in the French and Russian agreements. A re-declaration would be meaningless and would throw doubts upon Japan's good intentions in these previous agreements. It would look as if the United States doubted the good faith of Japan. Viscount Ishii believed that a new item must be added to make the re-declaration meaningful.[71]

Viscount Ishii then brought up the idea of a declaration in regard to the special interests of Japan arising from the territorial contiguity of Japan to China. He said that such a declaration was unnecessary in the same way that a similar declaration in regard to the Monroe Doctrine was unnecessary but that such a declaration would overcome German propaganda, would remove the doubts held by the Japanese people, and would clarify the Far Eastern question.[72]

This conversation took place before Viscount Ishii's visit to New York. He used his visit there to make several speeches explaining Japan's policies in China. The main tenor of his arguments was that Japan desired to see the Open Door extended to all China and that there should be no special interests in China. The renunciation of all spheres of interest would lead logically to a Monroe Doctrine for the Far East which would have the same motive as the American Monroe Doctrine, that is, the preservation of the peace of the Far East by keeping the Far East free from the extension of the political influence of the Occidental powers to that region.[73]

69 Ishii, *Memoirs*, p. 115.   70 *Ibid.*, p. 116.   71 *Ibid.*, p. 116–17.   72 *Ibid.*, p. 117.
73 See *The Imperial Japanese Mission to the United States, 1917*, pp. 59–111.

Viscount Ishii's purpose in making these speeches in New York after he had once revealed the object of his mission to Secretary Lansing was not merely to create friendly feeling among the New Yorkers toward Japan; his aim was to influence President Wilson and Mr. Lansing favorably to the object of his mission. He says in his memoirs:

In the United States, where state policies are determined by the drift of public opinion, it is frequently necessary for a foreign envoy, at the same time as he is carrying on discussions with the authorities at Washington, to win the understanding of the people, so that the authorities, influenced by the wishes of the people, might more readily come around to his way of thinking. The place best adapted to cultivate the good understanding of the American public is, of course, New York. Accordingly, the author, unfettered by the hesitancy of the government and the timidity of certain elements in the Foreign Office, freely explained Japan's policy toward China.[74]

Ishii found the New York audiences most receptive. The general feeling seemed to be that Japan was now an ally in the great crusade against Germany and therefore everything she wanted in the Far East was all right.[75]

Upon Ishii's return to Washington his conversations with Secretary Lansing were resumed. At the second meeting Mr. Lansing inquired what words should be used to express Japan's special interests in China. Ishii said that he thought the word "paramount" would express exactly the interests of Japan in China.[76] Mr. Lansing replied that this word had a strong meaning and if the United States agreed to the use of this word then any nation accepting its use would have to acquiesce in anything Japan did in China. The United States could not recognize such a meaning.

Viscount Ishii then referred to the use of the word "paramount" by Secretaries Seward and Frelinghuysen in relation to the interests of the United States in Mexico. Lansing, however, remained adamant, and finally the phrase "special interests" was accepted as a substitute and the attached phrase "and influence" was omitted.[77]

After the word "paramount" had been given up, the negotiations progressed easily.

In the final draft of the notes there appeared two paragraphs reaffirming the policy of the Open Door in China and the maintenance

[74] Ishii, *Memoirs*, p. 118.   [75] *Ibid.*, p. 119.
[76] *Ibid.*   [77] *Ibid.*, pp. 119, 120.

of China's territorial integrity. In the State Department's press release given out at the time the notes were made public the re-affirmation of these two policies was emphasized as one of the principal results of the negotiations.[78] Rather than being the reason for Mr. Lansing to enter into the agreement, however, this portion of the notes seemed to have been inserted as an afterthought at the last moment by Dr. E. T. Williams, who was then in charge of the Division of Far Eastern Affairs in the State Department and who was charged with the composition of the notes.[79]

Viscount Ishii ascribed the successful outcome of his mission to the friendly attitude exhibited by President Wilson. He believed that because of the pro-Chinese leanings of Mr. Lansing the negotiations would have failed if they had been left to him alone.[80]

The part of the exchange of notes which was important and which marked a new step in Japanese-American relations toward China was the declaration that:

> The Governments of the United States and Japan recognize that territorial propinquity creates special relations between countries, and consequently the Government of the United States recognizes that Japan has special interests in China, particularly in the part to which her possessions are contiguous.[81]

A careful reading of this statement indicates that Mr. Lansing meant merely to repeat in more general terms the statement made by Mr. Bryan in his note of March 13, 1915, relative to the Twenty-one Demands. In that instance Mr. Bryan specifically mentioned South Manchuria, East Mongolia, and Shantung, and declared that "United States frankly recognizes that territorial contiguity creates

---

[78] Text of statement to the press is given in Lansing to Morris, November 5, 1917, *Foreign Relations, 1917*, pp. 266–67.

[79] According to Dr. Williams' statement he was directed by Mr. Lansing to draw up the notes embracing the words which had been decided upon. Dr. Williams states: "When I returned to my office, it occurred to me that there ought to be paragraphs re-affirming the Open Door and the preservation of Chinese territorial integrity." E. T. Williams, "Japan's Interest in Manchuria," *University of California Chronicle*, January 1932.

In 1919, Mr. Lansing, however, in his testimony before the Senate Foreign Relations Committee on the Versailles Treaty, stated: "One of the very reasons why that Lansing-Ishii agreement was entered into was on account of the 21 demands and the attitude that Japan was taking toward China, in order to secure from Japan a re-declaration of the open-door policy . . . ." *United States Senate Document 7605*, p. 148, Testimony of Secretary Lansing, August 6, 1919.

[80] Ishii, *Memoirs*, pp. 122–23.

[81] Text of the Lansing-Ishii Notes in *Foreign Relations, 1917*, p. 264.

special relations between Japan and these districts."[82] Mr. Lansing, some months previous to the visit of the Ishii mission, had gone to some length to indicate to the Japanese government that he was unwilling to go beyond recognizing that Japan's special relations to China arose out of the geographical proximity of the two countries. He specifically denied at the same time that it had been his intention, upon the occasion of receiving the Japanese government's memorandum of June 15, 1917, "to convey the impression that this Government recognized that Japan possessed in China a paramount interest."[83]

Despite these prior communications between the two governments and despite the subsequent explanations of Mr. Lansing, the term "special interests" inevitably gave rise to two different interpretations, and as one cannot expect any nation to interpret such terms in a way as to disparage its own interests, the Japanese people interpreted this term to indicate that Japan had a right to speak first and to be consulted on any important question arising with regard to China's foreign relations. In view of the circumstances under which the Lansing-Ishii notes originated, it would seem that there was some justification for the Japanese interpretation. At least, we can say that Mr. Lansing was guilty of unwise diplomacy in permitting himself to be drawn into making a declaration couched in such ambiguous terms. The United States gained nothing from the notes, and Japan was moved a little closer to the attainment of the "paramount" position in China which was her evident goal.

In the official statement given to the press by the State Department, the reason given for the exchange of notes was to dispel the feeling of suspicion as to the motives of the two powers in the Far East. Germany was made the *deus ex machina* who had come between Japan and the United States. It was charged that "the attitude of constraint and doubt thus created was fostered and encouraged by the campaign of falsehood which for a long time had been adroitly and secretly carried on by the Germans . . . ."[84] The State Department, optimistic as to the effects the notes would have in overcoming the machinations of Germany, was led to say that "in a few days the propaganda of years has been undone, and both

[82] Bryan to Reinsch, March 13, 1915, *Foreign Relations, 1915*, p. 108.

[83] Lansing to the Japanese Ambassador, July 6, 1917, *Foreign Relations, 1917*, pp. 260–62.

[84] Text in Lansing to Morris, November 5, 1917, *ibid.*, pp. 266–67.

nations are now able to see how near they came to being led into the trap which had been skillfully set for them."[85]

The statement to the press brought out, also, the fact that the Ishii mission had had the additional purpose of discussing the "military, naval and economic activities to be employed" in the war against Germany. It was said that these discussions included a "complete and satisfactory understanding upon the matter of naval co-operation in the Pacific for the purpose of obtaining the common object."[86] As every vestige of German naval armament had long been swept from the Pacific, it was difficult to see just what such an agreement could be about. The American and Japanese governments did arrange a few days prior to the signing of the Lansing-Ishii notes to withdraw the U.S.S. "Saratoga" from patrol duty around the Hawaiian Islands and to replace it with a Japanese cruiser of equal fighting value and speed.[87]

Secretary Lansing's real motives in entering into this agreement were stated much more candidly in his explanations to the Chinese Minister in Washington than they had been in the State Department's official release to the press. He informed the Chinese Minister that

. . . . our friendship for China [is] unchanged but the financing of the present war prevented large independent investments in China and made inadvisable attempts to secure such investments by financial competition with Japan; China could not longer, because of those conditions, continue to play the United States against Japan in the matter of such investments; that we were still anxious to manifest our friendship by aiding China financially; which, however, was possible only by some arrangement for co-operation with Japan thereby preventing Japan's sole appropriation of the Chinese investment field; I assumed China preferred us to join with Japan rather than to leave China to that country alone.[88]

The Chinese government, a few days after the publication of the texts of the notes, issued a caveat in which it guarded itself against any interpretation of the Lansing-Ishii notes which would give to either party greater rights in China than those already provided for by treaties. The Chinese note stated:

. . . . the rights enjoyed by the friendly nations derived from the treaties have been consistently respected, and so even with the special relations

[85] Lansing to Morris, November 5, 1917, *Foreign Relations, 1917*, pp. 266–67.

[86] *Ibid.*

[87] Ishii to Lansing, October 30, 1917, *Foreign Relations, 1917, Supp.* 2, Vol. I, pp. 697–98.

[88] Lansing to Morris, November 22, 1917, *Foreign Relations, 1917*, p. 273.

between countries created by the fact of territorial contiguity, it is only in so far as they have already been provided for in her existing treaties.[89]

The notes were quite generally interpreted in Japan and China as marking the acknowledgment by the United States of the leading position of Japan in the relations of the Powers with China. Mr. Reinsch, in commenting on the attitude of the Chinese toward the United States, reported late in April 1918 that:

. . . . the exchange of notes between the Secretary of State and Viscount Ishii was quite generally interpreted as indicating a withdrawal of the American Government, in favor of Japan, from any desire to exercise any influence in Chinese affairs.[90]

Ambassador Morris reported from Tokyo:

. . . . I have observed two tendencies in the comments of those Japanese with whom I have had the privilege of talking . . . . one is to interpret very broadly the definition of "special interests," and if possible to disconnect it from any geographical considerations. The second is to express a rather exaggerated delight at what is termed in official Government circles "Viscount Ishii's great diplomatic victory."[91]

The conclusion of the Lansing-Ishii agreement was an unfortunate episode in American diplomacy. The ambiguity of the language used benefited no one. If the American government acquiesced in the Japanese interpretation that the agreement constituted an acknowledgment of Japan's paramount interests in China, the traditional belief of the Chinese in the good faith of America in her dealings with them would be seriously jeopardized. On the other hand, if the American government did not acquiesce in this interpretation, Japanese-American relations would become more strained rather than bettered. The agreement became a dead letter at the time of the Washington Conference, although it was not actually abrogated until April 14, 1923. No one seems to have been sorry to see it relegated to the limbo of unsuccessful diplomatic efforts. Like much of the war-time diplomacy its language was loose and could not stand the test of reality. It was neither a Japanese victory nor an American defeat. It was simply unsatisfactory.

[89] Chinese Minister to Lansing, November 12, 1917, *ibid.,* p. 270.

[90] Reinsch to Lansing, April 30, 1918, *Foreign Relations, 1918,* p. 93.

[91] Morris to Lansing, November 16, 1917, *Foreign Relations, 1917,* p. 272.

CHAPTER VI

CHINA'S PARTICIPATION IN THE WAR

As a result of the outcome of the struggle for political supremacy which went on during the spring and summer of 1917 between the Kuomintang-dominated Parliament on the one side and the oligarchy of military tuchuns who controlled the Central Government on the other, a forced dissolution of Parliament was brought about. In the fall of 1917 a number of the members of the dissolved Parliament assembled in Canton as a rump Parliament, and a provisional government was set up under the nominal leadership of Sun Yat-sen. The actual control of the Southern government, however, soon became exercised by the military governor of the two Kwang provinces, Kwangtung and Kwangsi.[1]

The tuchuns of the northern provinces, no longer faced by the opposition of Parliament to a declaration of war against Germany, declared war on August 14. Their first concern was to strengthen their somewhat precarious hold upon the government and to receive the financial aid which the Entente Powers and the United States had hinted would be forthcoming once China was ranged on the side of the Allies against Germany.[2] Secondly, they saw in the declaration of a state of war an excuse to raise powerful military forces, ostensibly for the quixotic purpose of being sent to Europe to fight the white man's battles but actually to be used in a determined campaign to crush their hated Kuomintang opponents in the South.

The position, however, of the military tuchuns was by no means made secure by a mere paper declaration of war. Their financial needs forced them to share control of the government with the so-called Communications party under the leadership of Tsao Ju-lin. This party desired to work in close co-operation with Japan. When the expected financial aid from the European Allies and the United States did not materialize, Tsao Ju-lin and his associates were given the opportunity to turn to Japanese sources for funds.[3]

[1] Dispatch of the American Consul at Canton, of October 9, 1917, quoted in Lansing to Secretary of War, November 26, 1917, *Foreign Relations, 1917*, p. 111.

[2] *Supra*, pp. 104–13.

[3] See list of loans made to the Chinese government during 1917 and January

The league of the northern tuchuns was itself extremely unstable. The men composing it had inherited and divided among themselves the military power formerly exercised by Yuan Shih-k'ai.[4] Each man acted more or less independently, his influence in the coalition largely depending upon the size of the military forces he could muster. These forces were considered primarily as personal armies with no purpose other than to further their chiefs' own interests and were used largely with that end in view. The tuchuns were loosely divided into three factions: the Chihli group was nominally under the leadership of the Acting President, Fêng Kuo-chang; the Anhui group was under the leadership of the Premier, Tuan Chi-jui, who at the same time acted as spokesman for the military tuchuns as a whole; finally, there was the Fengtien group, dominated by Chang Tso-lin, who at this time was just beginning to play an important part in the affairs of China south of the Great Wall. This league of military chiefs shared no common interests other than a common hatred of Sun Yat-sen and his followers and the desire to enjoy whatever gain would come to them through the domination of the Central Government.

Not only was this makeshift combination threatened by continual factional and personal differences, but it was also threatened throughout the period of China's participation in the war by a strong military movement on the part of the provisional government which had been set up at Canton. The Canton Provisional Government, somewhat similar to the Peking government, was composed of two elements. One element was the Kuomintang under Sun Yat-sen. This group charged the Peking government with having violated the constitution in dissolving the Parliament and forcing the resignation of President Li Yuan-hung. It stood for the observance of the 1913 Constitution and the independence of Parliament. However, the Kuomintang possessed no military forces of its own and therefore was forced to rely upon the armies of Lu Yung-t'ing, the governor of Kwangtung and Kwangsi.[5] Lu Yung-t'ing was dominated by the same motives of self-aggrandizement that characterized the northern tuchuns and could only be relied upon to work with the Kuomintang

1918, in *Foreign Relations, 1918,* pp. 167–68. Most of these loans were from Japanese sources. It is estimated that, during 1917 and 1918, the Chinese government borrowed more than 320,000,000 yen from Japanese sources.

[4] See Tang L'iang-li, *The Inner History of the Chinese Revolution,* pp. 130–36, for a description of political events and persons following the death of Yuan Shih-k'ai.

[5] *Supra,* pp. 104–13.

to the extent to which such co-operation furthered his own interests. He gradually became the commanding force in the Canton government, and on May 9, 1918, his domination caused Sun Yat-sen to resign as head of the Provisional Government in despair of freeing the South of the militarists.[6] Sun's resignation was followed by the reorganization of the Canton government into a frankly military government.

The situation which thus came into existence shortly after war had been declared upon Germany was not one in which the Central Government of China could be expected to make any important contributions to the Allied cause. The poverty of the government was such that the Allies could expect no contribution whatsoever without extending a large loan to China, either through the Consortium, which had succeeded in getting its option extended beyond the date of its actual expiration in June 1917, or from the United States or Japanese interests acting independently of the Consortium. The Consortium Powers, however, hesitated to advance a loan to the Central Government because the proceeds would inevitably be used by the Northern military chiefs in efforts to crush their opponents in the South rather than for participation in the war.

The failure of the Allies to extend to the Chinese government the financial assistance which it had been seeking since early in 1915, and which after the declaration of war was pressed for with great vigor on the ground that funds were necessary if China was to render any assistance to the Allies, resulted in the Communications party's concluding a series of loans with a group of Japanese banks outside of the Consortium.[7] The result of this series of loans was that Japanese influence in Peking became paramount. The Bolshevik Revolution in Russia together with the supposed danger of Germany's forming a front in Siberia resulted in further increasing the influence of Japan over the Chinese government. The logic of the situation indicated that Japan would necessarily have to take the lead in meeting the German-Bolshevik danger in Siberia and Manchuria were it to arise. The Allies, therefore, could hardly refuse Japan the right to name the conditions under which the Chinese military and naval establishment should co-operate in this task. A military and naval agreement was concluded between Japan and China in May 1918 and later elaborated.

[6] Sun Yat-sen's letter of resignation, May 9, 1918, quoted from the *Peking Leader,* of May 26, 1918, in *Foreign Relations, 1918,* pp. 95–96.

[7] See note 3 of this chapter.

This agreement effectively placed any military movements the Chinese government attempted to take in defense of its Manchurian borders under the control of Japan.[8]

Despite the conclusion of the Lansing-Ishii notes in November 1917, the American government continued to oppose the ascendancy of Japan in Chinese affairs, and particularly in Manchuria. The American government now, however, was completely absorbed in defeating Germany. In this great task China became a secondary issue for which little time or attention could be given.[9] Disagreement arose between President Wilson and the Allies with regard to the character and extent of Allied military activities in Siberia and Manchuria. By and large, however, after the United States had entered the war, the Wilson administration adopted a rather quiescent policy in Chinese affairs, which indicated that it had been tacitly decided to postpone consideration of the Chinese situation until the Peace Conference or after.

While the outcome of the struggle between the Northern military group and the Kuomintang majority in Parliament was yet uncertain, the Allied governments adopted a policy of watchful waiting. Once, however, the military group had emerged victorious and had obtained complete control of the government, the Allied governments, led by Japan, threw their support to the Northern militarists. On September 4, 1917, the Japanese government sent a note to the American government in which it urged that "all the foreign Powers ought in their common interests to lend their sincere and effective support to that government [the government then in control in Peking] which represents the sole legal authority in China at present and that it is of the utmost importance for them to withhold any encouragement or material assistance to individuals or associations seeking to overthrow the Government at Peking."[10]

The British government had already communicated to the American government its belief that "the adoption by all the Allied Powers

---

[8] For texts of these agreements, see *Foreign Relations, 1918,* pp. 224–26. China was to act independently in defense of its western borders and Sinkiang.

[9] Minister Reinsch visited the United States in the summer of 1918. He found in Washington very little interest in China. "After many, many departments and boards were consulted I found they were not thinking of China. Their chief problem was to train the American army and to transport it to the western front." Reinsch, *An American Diplomat in China,* p. 356.

[10] Japanese Embassy to the Department of State, September 4, 1917, *Foreign Relations, 1917,* p. 103.

of a policy based on these lines affords the best prospect of the restoration of order in China."[11]

Secretary Lansing replied to the British and Japanese communication on September 6. He stated that "the American Government shares in principle the views expressed" and he added further that "the American Government is moreover of [the] opinion that the principal Powers at war with Germany ought at once to confer together and agree upon the best method of supplying that effective support to which the memorandum under acknowledgment refers."[12]

Having decided among themselves to support the combination of military chiefs and the Communications party who were in control at Peking, the Allied governments caused their representatives on September 8 to deliver to the Chinese government a joint note in which were set forth "the advantages the [Allied governments] were disposed to accord to China in recognition of its spontaneous entry into the war." At the same time there were set forth certain specific measures which, it was stated, "they [the Allies] will be glad to see taken by China in its own interests."[13]

The advantages which the Allies were disposed to accord to China were, briefly:

1. To agree to the postponement without interest of the annual installments of the 1901 Boxer indemnity during a period of five years.
2. To agree to the principle of the increase of the maritime customs duties to an effective five per cent.
3. To consent to the temporary access of Chinese troops to the reserve zone at Tientsin so far as may be necessary for the surveillance over German and Austrian subjects.[14]

The Italian government reserved its decision as to the portion of its amount of the indemnity which it was willing to postpone, giving as its reasons the necessary "internal administrative changes involved." The real reason, however, was that the Italian government was demanding that a portion of the Austrian concession in

11 Spring Rice to Lansing, September 3, 1917, *Foreign Relations, 1917*, p. 102.

12 Lansing to Sato, September 6, 1917, *ibid.*, p. 104; and Lansing to Spring Rice, September 6, 1917, *ibid.*, pp. 103–4.

13 Text of the Allies' joint note of September 8, 1917, *Foreign Relations, 1917, Supp. 2*, Vol. I, pp. 685–87.

14 *Foreign Relations, loc. cit.* The Boxer indemnity installments were postponed for five years, beginning with December 1, 1917, but the revised customs tariff was not put into effect until August 1, 1919.

Tientsin be ceded to them before they would consent to the fore-going concessions to the Chinese government.[15]

The Russian government consented to the postponement of such portion of the annual installments due to it as was equivalent to average sacrifice made by the other Allies.[16]

The measures which the Allied governments would "be glad to see taken by China in its own interests" were:

1. The promulgation by the Chinese convention of a general tariff for all countries without treaties.
2. Prohibition of Chinese from all trading with enemy subjects.
3. Internment or expulsion of the enemy subjects whose names will be indicated by the Allied Legations; suppression of the right of meeting for enemy subjects; interdiction of navigation and of the use of wireless telegraph apparatus and confiscation of all objects of contraband.
4. Putting under sequestration of German and Austro-Hungarian commercial firms, complete liquidation of which will be effected.
5. An understanding with the representatives of the Allied governments in interests of the foreign trade of China and with regard for the interests of the Allies to organize in the form of international concessions the former German and Austro-Hungarian concessions in the ports of Tientsin and Hankow.
6. Placing at the disposal of the Allies the enemy vessels seized by the Chinese government in Chinese ports.
7. Collaboration with the Allied Legations with a view to drawing up regulations similar to those which were in force in other countries at war with Germany and Austria-Hungary.
8. Co-operation as complete and effective as possible on the part of China in the operations of the Allies.[17]

The American government did not officially support the foregoing note because, as Mr. Lansing pointed out, "the United States is not at war with Austria-Hungary and because the law in this country makes it impossible to accede to some of the measures proposed."[18]

What was actually offered here, although disguised in the language of diplomacy, was a bargain. The Allies, on their part, agreed

[15] At the Paris Peace Conference in 1919 the Italian government laid claim to the former Austro-Hungarian concession in Tientsin. This claim was disallowed at a meeting of the Heads of Delegations of July 16, 1919, as being contrary to the principle of restoration to China of her full rights of sovereignty over the enemy concessions. *Peace Conference Documents,* Heads of Delegations, No. 500, July 16, 1919.

[16] *Foreign Relations, 1917, Supp. 2,* Vol. I, p. 686. Russia finally agreed to postpone one-third of her indemnity installments.

[17] *Ibid.,* p. 687.   [18] *Ibid.,* p. 690.

to lend their support to the group who were then in control of the Central Government and to grant to that group concessions which would relieve somewhat the extreme financial distress of the government pending the conclusion of the large Consortium loan which was then being considered. In turn, the Chinese government was asked to adopt certain measures the immediate effect of which would have been to place the control of enemy subjects in China under the direction of the Allied Ministers and the eventual design of which was to eliminate completely from China the extensive business enterprises which had been carefully built up by the Germans prior to the outbreak of the war.

Tuan Chi-jui and his fellow tuchuns never fully accepted the bargain thus proffered by the Allies, and, in consequence, the Chinese government was accused of being remiss in its support of the Allied cause. The bargain, however, was not a good one. In the first place the Allies and the United States were unable to reach an agreement until after the war as to the conditions upon which they would advance a large loan to the Chinese government.[19] Such a loan had been under discussion all during the period between China's break of diplomatic relations with Germany and her declaration of war, and every indication had been given that as soon as China was definitely ranged against Germany the loan would be forthcoming. Mr. Lansing plainly told the Chinese Minister in Washington that "if China should be among those engaged in war with our enemies she might have some reason to expect such financial assistance" (as contemplated under the provisions of the legislation passed by Congress on April 24, 1917, providing for financial assistance to those governments engaged in war with the enemies of the United States).[20] Secondly, the Chinese government, although dominated as it was at this time by self-seeking militarists and civil officials, refused to accede to the specific proposals of the Allies because they represented a direct interference with the Chinese government's administrative independence and a continued disregard for China's sovereign rights which the Chinese people had been led to expect the declaration of war upon Germany would partially overcome.

The reply of the Chinese government to the Allied joint note was

[19] The agreement for a new International Financial Consortium was not signed until October 15, 1920, but to date the Consortium has made no loans to China. See Carnegie Endowment for International Peace, *The Consortium*, p. 67.

[20] Lansing to Reinsch, April 23, 1917, *Foreign Relations, 1917, Supp. 1*, pp. 431–32.

delayed until October 6.[21] It was friendly in spirit, but it avoided committing the Chinese government to measures which were inconsistent with Chinese sovereignty. The evident intention of the Chinese reply was to avoid dictation on the part of the Allies in regard to the control of the persons and property of enemy subjects.

The Chinese note stated that a general tariff for countries without treaties had been drawn up and was about to be promulgated. In place of acceding to the Allied request that all trading between Chinese and enemy subjects be prohibited and that the Chinese government sequestrate and liquidate all German and Austrian commercial firms, the Chinese government stated that "it would promulgate special regulations on the subject of industrial enterprises and commercial establishments of enemy subjects . . . . closing those which a Chinese inspection had shown should be closed." The Allies had asked that the Chinese government intern or deport those enemy subjects whose names would be indicated by the Allied legations. The Chinese government avoided this attempt to dictate what it should do in the important question of controlling the persons of enemy subjects by merely stating that "if plots are discovered the plotters will be interned."[22]

The Allied representatives and communities in China had been somewhat disturbed by the independence shown by the Chinese government after the declaration of war in taking over the former Austrian and German concessions in Tientsin and Hankow without first consulting with the Allied Ministers in Peking. The Allies were reluctant to see these concessions revert completely to China. They therefore proposed in their joint note that these concessions be organized in the form of international concessions. Such a procedure, however, would have caused the Central Government to "lose face" and would have aroused adverse comment among the Chinese people, who since the incident of the Twenty-one Demands had evinced a growing determination to take every advantage to get rid of the unequal treaty arrangements between China and the Powers. The Chinese government therefore framed its reply to indicate that, entirely of its own accord, it was

arranging to have the old German and Austrian concessions at Tientsin and Hankow thoroughly reorganized, so as to enable nationals of the different powers residing therein to enjoy all commercial advantages as well as a system

[21] Text in *Foreign Relations, 1917, Supp. 2*, Vol. I, pp. 702–3.
[22] *Ibid.*

of local self-government, with the object of securing such a perfect organization as to constitute the said areas into model voluntarily opened Sino-Foreign trade marts.[23]

The direct transfer of the German and Austrian merchant vessels held in Chinese ports to the Allies was avoided by placing such vessels in the control of a private Chinese company, which in turn was to arrange special subleases with the Allies.[24]

The Allied governments were not satisfied with the reply of the Chinese government to their joint note of September 8. Attempts were made by the British and French governments to get the American government to join with them in pressing the Chinese government to accept the specific proposals of the Allies. The British and French notes to the American government relative to this question definitely revealed that their chief purpose was to influence the Chinese government to take measures which would completely destroy German business enterprise in China and which would result in the deportation of all German and Austrian residents from China. The note of the French government pointed out that

. . . . as military assistance from China can be but limited, the Government of the Republic holds that the Allies must strive to obtain effective aid from her on economic lines by putting an end to the injury inflicted on Allied commerce by the Germans. It further deems it imperative that measures be taken to intern or expel enemy subjects so as to prevent their carrying on intrigues that are as harmful to the maintenance of order in China as to the obvious interests of the Allies.[25]

The British government was more specific in stating its desires. The dangers of leaving the control of enemy subjects "under some loose form of supervision by the Chinese authorities" were pointed out, and it was suggested that "the only safe means of securing their allies and themselves from these dangers" was to "press the Chinese Government to consent to the general deportation of all enemy subjects now in China for internment in Australia." The British note concluded by stating:

. . . . if enemy subjects are permitted to remain in China . . . . they will certainly succeed in maintaining their trade relations with the Chinese and will, in all probability, be able to prevent the liquidation and sequestration of their businesses. The Allies will thus not only be deprived of one of the principal advantages, if not indeed the principal advantage, which they hoped to derive

---

[23] *Foreign Relations, loc. cit.*   [24] *Ibid.*
[25] Jusserand to Lansing, October 16, 1917, *ibid.,* p. 694.

from China's entry into the war, but Germany, on the conclusion of peace, will be enabled speedily to recover her trade and influence in China.[26]

These two notes plainly reveal that the chief motive of Great Britain and France for pressing China to enter the war was not the expectation that she would make any material contribution to their eventual victory but that by this means German competition in China would be eliminated and the business which the Germans had built up would fall into the hands of British and French merchants.

During the autumn of 1917 the Allies and the American government did discuss the possibilities of sending a large force of Chinese troops to Europe. However, this idea was soon given up, and thereafter French and British efforts were concerned chiefly with wholesale deportation of all Germans and Austrians and the destruction of their commercial enterprises in China. Enemy subjects were not deported, however, until after the armistice. In part the delay in deportation was due to the reluctance of the Chinese officials to take such drastic action against the nationals of a nation which might yet emerge victorious, and in part it was due to the fact that the threat of German reprisals caused the Allies to stay their hand until after the armistice.[27]

The difficulties of getting the Chinese government to co-operate effectively, that is, effectively from the Allied viewpoint, in the prosecution of the war lay not alone in the unwillingness of the Chinese authorities to accept the Allied proposals of September 8 but also in the inability of the Allies to agree among themselves or with the United States as to many of the details connected with the carrying out of those proposals. The position of the United States vis-à-vis China was at variance in many particulars with that of the Allied governments. Mr. Lansing informed Minister Reinsch in connection with the inability of the American government to subscribe fully to the joint note of September 8 that, "while desirous of cooperating in a general way with the Governments at war with Germany, it is not always possible for us to support their policies entirely since our situation as belligerents is not identical with theirs."[28] This inability of the Allies and the American government to agree among them-

[26] British Embassy to the Department of State, November 27, 1917, *ibid.*, pp. 703–4.

[27] *Infra*, p. 154.

[28] Lansing to Reinsch, September 20, 1917, *Foreign Relations, 1917, Supp. 2*, Vol. I, pp. 689–90.

selves as to the details of the arrangements they were to come to with the Chinese government with regard to China's participation in the war was in a great measure responsible for the final meagerness of her contribution.

One of the first questions which arose following China's declaration of war upon Germany was that of the disposal and allocation of the enemy ships seized by the Chinese government in Chinese ports. The Allies asked that these ships either be transferred directly to Allied flags or be chartered immediately to them. The request of the Allies disregarded the extreme dearth of ships which the war had brought about in the Far East. Despite the high prices which prevailed, Chinese exporters were barred from taking advantage of these prices or even of maintaining their normal volume of trade because of their inability to secure shipping space. The Shanghai Merchants' Association addressed an appeal to the government that "German and Austrian ships . . . . should be used to open a shipping line abroad, so that freight may become more reasonable and native products find an outlet."[29] The Chinese government evaded placing the ships at the disposal of the Allies for some time but eventually decided to charter the vessels to Chinese merchants who would then be permitted to subcharter only to the Allies.[30]

Following this decision of the Chinese government the question arose as to the allocation of the vessels among the Allies and the United States. The vessels totaled in all approximately 35,000 tons and included some fourteen vessels, of which only four were large enough for transoceanic purposes. The others were either tugs or river boats. Early in September the British government proposed to the American government that one-third of the above-mentioned tonnage be chartered to either a British firm or to the British government, leaving the other two-thirds to be divided between the American and Japanese governments.[31] Difficulties immediately

[29] *North China Herald*, October 6, 1917. The allocation of the enemy ships became mixed up with the question of the importation of tea into Great Britain. The importation of Chinese tea was prohibited in February 1917. This measure threatened disaster to the Chinese tea trade. Finally the British government agreed to admit the current crop of tea if it were sent in the seized enemy ships and if upon arrival these vessels would be turned over to the Controller of Shipping. *North China Herald*, December 11, 1917.

[30] *North China Herald*, December 22, 1917.

[31] Lansing to Reinsch, September 7, 1917, *Foreign Relations, 1917, Supp. 2*, Vol. I, pp. 687–88.

arose in connection with this proposal. The American government objected on the ground that three of the vessels, the largest and the best of them, had been sold previously to an American corporation before China entered the war and that, although the purchase price had not been paid, the corporation stood ready to pay it to China if delivery of the vessels were made. Mr. Lansing also expressed concern for American interests which he evidently felt had been disregarded in the arrangements which had been made by the British and Japanese governments with the Chinese government whereby the latter promised to give these two governments the first refusal to subcharter.[32] The American and British governments, after some negotiations, arrived at agreement as to the allocation of the enemy vessels, the American government acquiescing in the British view that the private claims should not be supported and agreeing to accept two out of the three vessels claimed by the American corporation.[33] The Japanese government, however, now raised objections to the proposed allocation of enemy vessels in China and Siam; Japan's purpose in seeking a share of enemy vessels was to supplement her merchant fleet devoted to Far Eastern trade, which had been depleted as a result of sale and charter of vessels to the Allies for service in European waters. She therefore desired to keep her share of the enemy vessels in Chinese ports in Eastern waters and not to devote them to direct war purposes. A plan was finally worked out whereby Japan renounced her claim to a share in the enemy vessels seized in Siamese ports in return for a one-third share of the vessels in Chinese ports and with the understanding that she should maintain absolute liberty of action in the use of her share.[34]

The Chinese government was greatly criticized by the Allied communities in China for the delay in placing the enemy vessels at the disposal of the Allies, but in this instance, as in many others connected with China's participation in the war, the delay was as much the result of petty differences arising among the Allies as it was of the reluctance on the part of the Chinese government to do something which in any case was obviously not in harmony with the best interests of China.

The Allied request that the enlistment of Chinese workmen for service in France be greatly increased raised no particular difficulties. The practice of hiring Chinese coolies for service in Allied countries

[32] *Ibid.*   [33] Lansing to Reinsch, October 13, 1917, *ibid.,* pp. 693–94.
[34] British Embassy to Department of State, November 7, 1917, *ibid.,* pp. 698–99.

had been originated by Russian contractors in Siberia early in the war. The Allied governments, however, did not begin using this source of labor until the summer of 1916, when the first shipment of Chinese laborers and artisans left for France.[35] In all, about 190,000 Chinese served behind the lines in France, 150,000 of them under British control and 40,000 under French. They rendered service of considerable value to the Allied cause and were the most significant contribution made by China to the final victory.[36]

The idea of using the war as a pretext to destroy German trade competition in China had animated the British merchant community in China from early in the war. Various proposals for getting rid of the Germans in China were championed and pushed forward by the British merchants in China long before the British government began to support such a procedure. Possibly because of fear of reprisals and because at the outbreak of the war under English law enemy status for belligerent purposes was determined by domicile rather than nationality, the British government was slow to take steps to restrict trading between Britishers and Germans in China. It was not until the Proclamation of June 25, 1915, that the prohibition against trading with the enemy was extended to China.[37]

These mild measures were not considered drastic enough by the British commercial community in China, and efforts were made to persuade the British government to take stronger action. Early in 1915 the China Association in London and the British Chamber of Commerce of Shanghai began agitating to force the British government to take measures designed to capture the former German trade in China and particularly the export trade which the Germans had fairly well controlled.[38] These two bodies were largely responsible for the Proclamation of June 25, and later on were responsible for urging that China become a belligerent in order to extinguish German trade in China completely. This was to be done by the simple expedient of causing the Chinese government to deport all Germans and to sequestrate their businesses.

[35] *Far Eastern Review*, August 1916.

[36] *North China Herald*, January 18, 1919.

[37] Great Britain, *British and Foreign State Papers, 1915*, Vol. 109, p. 629. The British Board of Trade announced on December 28, 1914, that "transactions between British traders in the United Kingdom and in China, and enemy subjects and firms domiciled in China are not expressly prohibited; but such transactions are undesirable."

[38] *North China Herald*, July 10, 1915.

When in February 1917 the prospect arose of China's severing diplomatic relations with Germany, the proposal that Germans resident in China be deported from China became a matter of discussion between the Allied governments. The French government, in communicating its promise to the Japanese government to support the Japanese claims at the Peace Conference, named as one of the conditions of its support that Japan press the Chinese government to break off diplomatic relations with Germany and that, among other things, the Chinese government be urged to give this act desirable significance by causing "all under German jurisdiction to leave Chinese territory."[39] The unexpected delay in China's declaration of war postponed any further action upon the deportation question until September 1917. In their joint note of September 8, the Allied governments asked that China intern or expel those enemy subjects whose names would be indicated by the Allied legations, and that all German and Austrian commercial firms be sequestrated and liquidated.[40] This moderate proposal, however, did not satisfy the British communities in Shanghai, Tientsin, etc. Under date of September 15, 1917, the editor of the *North China Herald* wrote:

There are only two ways of dealing effectively and as the welfare of China demands with the German and Austrian residents; internment and deportation. The former should be applied to those who are an actual or potential danger, notorious conspirators like Herr Knipping, men capable of bearing arms, wireless telegraph operators, engineers and the like. For the obviously useless, deportation.[41]

Mention has already been made of the dissatisfaction with which the Allies received the reply of the Chinese government in response to their note of September 8. They were particularly dissatisfied with the mild measures which it proposed to take in regard to the sequestration of enemy commercial concerns and the control of enemy subjects. The Chinese government proposed merely to sequestrate and liquidate those enemy concerns which it considered should be closed and to intern only those enemy subjects directly connected with anti-Allied plots.[42] The mildness of these measures prompted Great Britain to urge that all enemy subjects in China be deported and interned in Australia. France and the United States

[39] *Supra*, p. 97. See MacMurray, *Treaties and Agreements with and concerning China*, Vol. II, p. 1169.
[40] *Supra*, p. 145.
[41] *North China Herald*, September 15, 1917.   [42] *Supra*, p. 147.

supported this proposal.[43] Secretary Lansing, on December 18, 1917, instructed Mr. Reinsch to inform the Chinese government that

the American Government views with favor the suggestion of the British and French Governments that all enemy subjects in China, particularly those suspected by the Chinese government or Allied Legations of secret plotting should be deported and interned in Australia.[44]

Previous to this, the British Ambassador in Washington, on December 10, informed the American government that "the Japanese representative at Peking has now been instructed to give his full support to Allied representations to the Chinese Government, urging that all enemy subjects should be deported."[45]

Despite the unanimity on the part of the Allies and the United States with regard to the deportation proposal, the spring of 1918 passed without any definite measures being taken to deport the Germans and Austrians from China. The Allied communities became restive at this delay. On April 16, 1918, the *North China Herald* reported:

Sir John Jordan .... has just received from the Senior Consul in Shanghai an imposing petition signed by all the principal residents in Shanghai urging the Allied Diplomatic Representatives to put pressure on the Chinese Government to secure the deportation of enemy subjects from China.[46]

However, the delay was not alone due to the reluctance of the Chinese government to act, as on the surface it appeared to be. The execution of the measure offered more difficulties to the Allies than had been anticipated. These difficulties were indicated by the British Ambassador in Washington. In a note of June 10, 1918, he informed the American government that

.... the Allied Governments have come to the conclusion that a reexamination of the question of transporting German and Austrian subjects from China to Australia is necessary, owing to the threat of severe reprisals from the German Government and to a consequential request from the Belgian Government for a further consideration of the subject.[47]

---

[43] British Embassy to Department of State, November 27, 1917, *Foreign Relations, 1917, Supp.* 2, Vol. I, pp. 703–4; French Embassy to Department of State, December 7, 1917, *ibid.,* p. 705; Lansing to Reinsch, December 18, 1917, *ibid.,* p. 709.

[44] Lansing to Reinsch, December 18, 1917, *ibid.,* p. 709.

[45] British Embassy to Department of State, December 10, 1917, *ibid.,* p. 706.

[46] *North China Herald,* April 20, 1918.

[47] Reading to Lansing, June 10, 1918, *Foreign Relations, 1918, Russia,* Vol. II, pp. 199–200. The agreement of the Chinese government to the deportation measure can only be inferred from articles in the press, i.e., Chinese press reports in *North China Herald,* June 29, 1918.

A further reason which had caused the Allies to hesitate to deport enemy subjects in China to Australia was that during the summer of 1918 the British government was attempting to arrive at an agreement with Germany for the exchange of interned civilian prisoners.[48] One of Germany's conditions of ratification of the agreement was "a satisfactory arrangement of the position of the Germans in China."[49] Another reason for delaying the deportation project was that the development of the situation in Siberia and plans for intervention there necessitated the use in this enterprise of the ships which had been set aside for the transport of the enemy subjects to Australia.[50]

In the late autumn of 1918, the unmistakable signs of Germany's collapse and the approaching end of the hostilities in Europe caused the Chinese officials in Peking to attempt to make some sort of a last-minute war record in order to placate the Allies. At the end of October 1918 the Chinese government announced its intention to intern certain Germans in the Western Hills, near Peking, and the liquidation of the Deutsche Asiatische Bank in Shanghai, about which very little had been accomplished, was promised to be speeded up. Tuan Chi-jui and his military oligarchy realized that they would need the support of the European Allies if China were going to get any concessions from the coming Peace Conference.[51] They, therefore, began to show a great zeal for the Allied cause. On November 10, the day before the Armistice, the Peking correspondent could at last report that "Pro-Germanism in China is dead. Chinese officials here are enthusiastically devoting themselves to war work, in which all from President downward are taking part." He added, significantly: "The Powers have released over $5,000,000 of the Salt Gabelle surplus in order not to embarrass the Chinese Government."[52]

The certainty of victory also caused the Allied governments to be more outspoken in their dissatisfaction with the dilatory way in which the Chinese government had carried out its measures to control the enemy subjects and to sequestrate their property. On November 2,

---

[48] The agreement was concluded at The Hague, July 14, 1918, but was not ratified. Great Britain, *Parl. Papers, Commons, 1918*, Vol. 26, [Cd. 9147].

[49] Quoted from the semi-official communiqué of the German government in *North China Herald*, September 7, 1918. See account by the London correspondent of the same paper, *loc. cit.*, Aug. 24, 1918.

[50] Reading to Lansing, June 10, 1918, *Foreign Relations, 1918, Russia*, Vol. II, pp. 199–200.

[51] *North China Herald*, November 2, 1918, editorial.

[52] *Ibid.*, November 16, 1918.

1918, their representatives in Peking delivered a long note to the Peking authorities in which was pointed out the failure of the Chinese government to co-operate properly with its Allies, together with a bill of particulars with regard to its delinquencies. China was warned of "the results which a continuance of this condition would have upon public opinion among the Associated Powers, and, therefore, upon the standing of China after the peace is concluded . . . ."[53] Uncomfortable questions were being asked in the House of Commons as to the effectiveness of China's participation in the war. Mr. Stewart, on November 7, asked Lord Cecil "if due regard will be taken of the little assistance the Chinese Government have given us in this matter [deportation of the Germans in China and the sequestration of their property]." Lord Cecil replied that "undoubtedly we shall not forget the events of the case wherever they occur."[54]

The Armistice of November 11 removed any possibility of Germany inflicting reprisals upon her enemies. The Allied Powers, therefore, urged on by the Allied communities in Shanghai and Tientsin, moved to carry out the destruction of German trade in China. The temper of the Allied community in Shanghai was definitely set upon the deportation of all Germans and the complete liquidation of German enterprises. Fear was continually expressed in the columns of the *North China Herald* that if drastic measures were not taken there would be "nothing to prevent the German firms in China from re-opening business five minutes after the telegram announcing peace. . . . ." The usual measure of bringing pressure upon the Chinese government to act, that is, the stopping of the monthly payments of the Salt Gabelle surplus, was advocated, and it was proposed "to make it quite plain that no Chinese representative will be admitted to the Peace Conference unless full satisfaction is given on this and other points of China's dereliction."[55]

The Chinese government attempted to escape the blame which was somewhat unjustly falling upon it by issuing a *White Book,* the intent of which was to show that the Dutch Minister in Peking had prevented the Chinese government from taking action to deport the

---

[53] Allied Memorandum of China as a Co-belligerent in the War. Dated October 30, 1918, delivered November 2, 1918. In the *Peking Leader,* "Special Anniversary Supplement," February 12, 1919.

[54] Great Britain, *Parliamentary Debates,* 1918, Vol. 110, pp. 2269–70.

[55] *North China Herald,* November 2, 1918, editorial. Also *ibid.,* December 11, 1918, and December 19, 1918.

Germans by intimating that Germany would seek severe reprisals at the end of the war.[56] At the request of the Chinese government, Jonkheer Beelaerts van Blokland, the Dutch Minister, who had opposed the deportations upon the grounds that to deport enemy civilians was a violation of international law, was recalled.

The deportation to Germany of enemy subjects was finally carried out during March 1919. Exemptions were made for those above sixty years of age, those whose services were required by the Dutch Consul, certain physicians, and, temporarily, those too sick to travel. All together about 2,200 men, women, and children were deported, with about 200 finally exempted.[57] This cruel measure, designed purely to destroy the German trade in China and having nothing directly to do with the war, was carried through regardless of the fact that to deport German missionaries and doctors crippled many educational institutions and hospitals in the interior of China and that many Germans upon whom Chinese firms were dependent were deported. The British Consul General in Shanghai, Mr. E. H. Fraser, lent a fine touch of irony to the final act of deportation by engaging in a controversy with Mr. J. D. de Reus, Consul General for the Netherlands, over the accommodations provided by the British government in the deportation ships. The object of Mr. Fraser was to assure everyone that the accommodations provided were quite sufficient to assure the health of the deportees, etc.[58]

The British Chamber of Commerce of Shanghai, whose members had been active in pushing through the deportation of the Germans, was able to report with evident satisfaction at its annual meeting on March 19, 1919, that "The majority of German residents in China are now on the high seas . . . ." and added that "just as the Chamber has been largely instrumental in driving them out of this country, so too has it been instrumental in destroying their trade."[59]

Soon after China declared war upon Germany, M. Conty, the French Minister in Peking, brought forward the proposal that China should send a contingent of troops to France for active service on the Western Front.[60] The French government was at the same time

[56] Ibid., December 7, 1918, for a summary of the contents of the White Book.

[57] Ibid., March 15, 1919.

[58] North China Herald, March 15, 1919.

[59] Ibid., March 22, 1919.

[60] Reinsch to Lansing, December 30, 1917, Foreign Relations, 1917, Vol. I, pp. 720–21.

pushing forward a proposal among the Allied Powers that Japan be requested to send troops to the Western Front for service in the spring of 1918.[61] During the latter three months of 1917 the project of sending Chinese troops to Europe was seriously discussed by the United States and the Allied governments. On November 4, 1917, Mr. Reinsch reported that the "Prime Minister through the Vice Minister of War has just given me written assurances that the Chinese government has decided to send 40,000 soldiers to Europe as a beginning. The prime Minister trusts that on the basis of the assurances to the Chinese Minister at Washington, financial assistance will now speedily be accorded so that the above decision can be carried out."[62]

Despite the fact that the plan of the Chinese government to send troops to Europe looked suspiciously like a move on the part of Tuan Chi-jui and the other tuchuns to secure the loan from the United States which had been under discussion for some time, the American government received the proposal with sympathy and began working out a plan for financing the venture and transporting and arming the troops. The British government, however, was less enthusiastic. The British Ambassador in Washington informed Mr. Lansing that "the British War Office do not consider it advisable to proceed with the proposal of forming a combatant Chinese brigade until the programme of transporting Chinese labourers for the British Armies and pioneers for the French Armies has been completed."[63] By the latter part of December the State Department in co-operation with the War Department of the American government had worked out a plan whereby a Chinese expeditionary force was to be dispatched to France. On December 26, 1917, Mr. Lansing informed Ambassador Page, in London, that the

. . . . Chinese Government has offered to send troops to Europe. War Department is entirely in accord with the project provided the troops are organized as engineer corps and quartermaster corps under the leadership of a Chinese general officer and ordered to report to Pershing . . . . It is now pro-

---

[61] Phillips to Lansing, October 23, 1917, *Foreign Relations, 1917,* Vol. I, p. 696.

[62] Reinsch to Lansing, November 4, 1917, *Foreign Relations, 1917,* p. 698. The promise of financial assistance referred to in the foregoing dispatch was given to the Chinese Minister in Washington, at least by implication, following China's breaking diplomatic relations with Germany and prior to her declaration of war. *Supra,* p. 111.

[63] Spring Rice to Lansing, November 13, 1917, *Foreign Relations, 1917,* pp. 700–1.

posed to make the Chinese Government a loan in the form of credits in the sum of $50,000,000 . . . .[64]

Ambassador Page was instructed to lay this plan before the Inter-Allied Council for its consideration. However, by this time the situation which was developing in Russia and Siberia as a consequence of the Bolshevik revolution caused the United States and the Allies to give up all plans designed to draw Chinese and Japanese troops to the Western Front and caused them to consider ways and means to meet the danger of Germany's utilizing the great numbers of German and Austrian prisoners believed to be in Russian concentration camps in Siberia. Japan was looked to logically to bear the brunt of and to take the leadership in any military movement designed to meet this danger. As Manchuria would inevitably be involved, the necessity arose of Japan and China coming to some sort of definite military arrangement. Negotiations were entered into between the two governments in February 1918, and on May 16, 1918, there were signed two agreements providing for military and naval co-operation in order to meet "the steady penetration of enemy influence towards the East."[65]

The conclusion of these agreements came only after the Bolshevik revolution had profoundly modified the status quo in North Manchuria and after negotiations between the Allies and the United States had been initiated looking forward to intervention in Siberia. The immediate effect of the Bolshevik revolution in Manchuria was to cause the breakdown of the established Russian authorities in the zone of the Chinese Eastern Railway and to inaugurate a period of lawlessness and disorders in such places as Harbin and Changchun.[66] For some time, during the early and middle part of November, the consular representatives of the Allied nations in Harbin considered recommending that an international police force be sent there to protect the lives and property of foreigners.[67] The situation revolved around the person of General Horvat, the Russian governor in the zone of the Chinese Eastern Railway and manager of the railway. Under the Imperial regime he was subject to the direct orders of

[64] Lansing to Page, December 26, 1917, *ibid.,* p. 712.

[65] *Foreign Relations, 1918,* pp. 222–26.

[66] Moser (American Consul at Harbin) to Reinsch, November 17, 1918, *Foreign Relations, 1918, Russia,* Vol. II, pp. 2–4; also *North China Herald,* November 17, 1917, and December 1, 1917.

[67] Reinsch to Lansing, November 19, 1918, *Foreign Relations, 1918, Russia,* Vol. II, p. 4.

the Russian government, but with its overthrow by the Bolsheviks he was left with the choice of accepting the authority of the Soviet government or of assuming an independent position until the situation somewhat cleared up. The Russian Imperial Government, by liberally interpreting the clauses of the Chinese Eastern Railway Agreement of 1898, had gradually assumed complete authority within the railway zone and had exercised full powers of government there.[68] Cities such as Harbin had long been considered and treated as if they were Russian colonies. The fact that Chinese sovereignty had never been renounced within the railway area was conveniently forgotten. But with the breakdown of law and order there arose the possibility of China reasserting her sovereign rights. The logical course for China to take would have been to reassert her authority and to take over the policing and control of the railway zone pending the re-establishment of the former Russian regime or the recognition of the new Bolshevik government. The Chinese government, however, hesitated to take independent action to reassert its authority.

In the meantime, General Horvat became subjected to increasing pressure from Bolshevik elements in Harbin to submit to their control. The Allied Ministers in Peking became alarmed at this possibility, and on December 6 Minister Reinsch reported that "General Horvat [is] ready to conduct joint administration with the Bolsheviks" and then added that the "Allied Ministers to-day decided to call on Chinese Government to support with troops the authorities established under the treaties in Manchuria."[69] The Russian Minister in Peking, now that the authority of the representative of the Czar's government in the Chinese Eastern Railway zone was threatened by the Bolsheviks, suddenly remembered that "as Russia had no territorial possessions in Manchuria, the authority of Russian officials was dependent entirely upon treaties with China."[70] He, therefore, welcomed the plan to send Chinese troops to support General Horvat.

Acting on this request the Chinese government immediately dispatched troops to Harbin and by December 15 had three thousand troops on the ground to insure order and to support Horvat.[71] During

---

[68] See Houang Tchang-sin, *Le problème du Chemin de fer Chinois de l'Est,* especially pp. 313–43.

[69] Reinsch to Lansing, December 6, 1917, *Foreign Relations, 1918, Russia,* Vol. II, p. 5.

[70] *Ibid.*   [71] Reinsch to Lansing, December 15, 1917, *ibid.,* p. 8.

the following days the position of General Horvat became stronger owing, no doubt, to the presence of the Chinese troops. Meanwhile the Soviet authorities in Moscow, much as they differed in other respects from the old regime, accepted its notion that Harbin was to be considered Russian territory. The introduction of Chinese troops was resented. Trotsky, the Soviet Commissar for Foreign Affairs, sent instructions to a certain Captain Lutsky to arrest all those officials who "have succeeded in introducing foreign [Chinese] troops into Harbin" and to advise the foreign representatives that the "foreign troops must be withdrawn."[72]

Whether or not the Bolshevik leaders in Harbin attempted to carry out these instructions is not clear. On December 28, however, the Chinese troops under General Meng En-yuen, the tuchun of Kirin, disarmed two regiments of Bolshevik disaffected troops and deported them beyond the borders of Manchuria.[73] This action was evidently taken at the request of General Horvat, and after its fulfillment arrangements were made for the Chinese troops to occupy the Russian barracks along the line of the Chinese Eastern Railway.[74] In other words, by the end of December 1917 Chinese troops had successfully intervened to restore order in Harbin and to preserve the authority of General Horvat within the zone of the Chinese Eastern Railway, and Chinese troops had begun the task of guarding the railway. The question then logically arises why did not the Chinese authorities continue to assert their rightful sovereignty in the railway zone and to preserve order in northern Manchuria? Why was it that in the next few months the railway zone was permitted to become a hotbed of plots designed to overthrow the Soviet government which made Chinese territory liable to invasion by Soviet troops? The answer to these questions is that the Allied governments were not interested in seeing the Chinese bring about any modification of the existing treaty rights enjoyed by Russia with regard to the railway, and, further, that as long as Horvat was left in authority in the railway zone the Allies were able to foster and support the anti-Bolshevik movements of such White Russians as Semenov, Horvat, and Kolchak before they themselves declared openly against the Soviet government.

[72] Leon Trotsky, *The Lessons of October, 1917*, Vol. II, p. 151, reprinted from *Izvestia*, December 12, 1917.

[73] *North China Herald*, December 29, 1917, and January 5, 1918; *Utro Rossii*, January 18, 1918.

[74] *North China Herald*, January 5, 1918.

The desire of the Allies to avoid any reassertion by China of her sovereign rights in the railway zone and to avoid for the time being an open clash with the Soviet government was evidenced by a communication of the British government to the American government of December 28, the day that the Chinese troops disarmed the two Bolshevik regiments in Harbin. The note raised the question "as to whether it was desirable that the Bolshevik leaders and disaffected troops at Harbin should be arrested and deported by Chinese troops."[75] In answer to its own question the British government said:

> His Majesty's Government have instructed the British Minister [at Peking] that it would not, in their opinion, be wise for the Chinese troops to arrest the Bolshevik troops and leaders in present circumstances.[76]

The American government replied the following day to this communication and stated:

> The American government believes that it would be unwise for the Chinese Government to take any steps at Harbin which might lead to armed conflict . . . .[77]

Both governments agreed to instruct their ministers at Peking to persuade the Chinese government not to order the disarming of the Bolsheviks. This, however, had already been carried out.

A few days after this initial incident in the changed situation in Manchuria, the *North China Herald* correspondent in Harbin reported that "the Chinese troops are gradually leaving Harbin and only one regiment remains."[78] Evidently, once the authority of General Horvat had been restored, their presence was none too welcome in a town predominantly composed of white inhabitants.

Two other incidents mark the first effects of the Bolshevik revolution upon Chinese action in Manchuria. On January 2, 1918, Kuo Hsing-hsi, civil governor of Kirin, was appointed by mandate the president of the Chinese Eastern Railway, "thereby reviving the Chinese right, held in abeyance since 1900, to have a representative in connection with the affairs of the railway."[79] Toward the end of January 1918, the Chinese government "at the instance of the British

---

[75] British Embassy to the Department of State, December 28, 1917, *Foreign Relations, 1918, Russia,* Vol. II, p. 14.

[76] *Ibid.*

[77] Lansing to Spring Rice, December 29, 1917, *ibid.,* pp. 15–16.

[78] *North China Herald,* January 5, 1918.   [79] *Ibid.*

Minister . . . . prohibited every kind of exportation from Man-churia."[80] This measure caused serious losses to Chinese merchants and imposed considerable hardship upon the population of Eastern Siberia, who were dependent upon Manchurian wheat and other foodstuffs. The Soviet government threatened reprisals upon the many thousands of Chinese in Russia, but, nevertheless, the embargo, owing principally to the objections of the French government, was not lifted until June 20, 1918.[81]

From January, 1918 on, the Chinese government played a passive role in the development of the situation in Manchuria. Although its territory was involved, little consideration was given to the rights or interests of China in Manchuria. Its initial failure to assert its rights and to take over the control of the railway zone left General Horvat in authority. He was violently anti-Bolshevik and allowed the zone to become the rallying ground for movements against the Soviet government. The neutrality of China was thus compromised from the beginning, and eventually the continuance of anti-Bolshevik plotting in the railway zone had a considerable effect upon bringing on the Allied intervention in Siberia in the autumn of 1918. L. H. Grondijs in his *La Guerre en Russie* says:

In January, 1918, all resistance of the Russians against the Soviet régime seemed definitely extinguished. At this moment an unknown figure emerged from the chaos . . . . Captain Semenov organized in Manchuria a volunteer detachment who fought with intermittent success against the Reds.[82]

This Captain Semenov quickly secured the support of the British and French governments, who saw in him a means of combating the spread of Bolshevism.[83] The American government was approached by Great Britain to lend its support to him but refused to do so. Later on the Japanese, at British instigation, supplied him with arms and ammunition.[84] Simultaneously with the advent of Semenov, the Allied governments began seriously to consider intervening in Siberia, with what exact purpose in view it was never clearly stated. With the negotiations leading to the decision to intervene and the actual intervention we are here concerned only in so far as Chinese territory and Chinese rights in Manchuria were affected.

[80] Reinsch to Lansing, January 28, 1918, *Foreign Relations, 1918, Russia,* Vol. III, p. 172.

[81] Reinsch to Lansing, June 24, 1918, *ibid.,* p. 181.

[82] L. H. Grondijs, *La Guerre en Russie,* p. 491.

[83] See p. 164 and note 85, *infra.*   [84] Grondijs, *op. cit.,* p. 491.

As early in the year as February 6 the British government had communicated with the American government outlining in detail the plan of action Semenov proposed to carry out from his headquarters "on the Manchuria Railway at Hailar and Dauriya," both places being well inside the Chinese border. According to the British note, Semenov's plan was to seize control of the Trans-Siberian Railway at Karymskaya "which would enable Captain Semenov to control traffic on the former [Amur] railway, and to stop entry of munitions for the revolutionary party in the Primorsk and Amur Provinces." The note frankly stated that "the principal resistance in the Trans-Baikal Province is anticipated from a small force of some nine-hundred railway workmen at Chita who have been organized as Red Guards . . . ." The American government was informed that "steps are therefore to be taken through the British Consulate at Harbin to let Captain Semenov's followers know that the British Government propose to support him with money, and also with arms and ammunition . . . ." The note concluded by saying that "His Majesty's Government earnestly hope that the United States Government will concur in their views as to supporting Captain Semenov, and that they will be ready, if they agree with the course of the action proposed, to participate in this action . . . ."[85]

In other words, the British government early in February 1918 proposed to support a frankly anti-Bolshevik movement which would have its base of operations in Chinese territory and which would be designed to fight against a government with whom the Allies and China were still theoretically on friendly terms and with whom they were attempting to work out some basis of co-operation in order to limit German activities in Russia. The support of Semenov continued throughout the spring and summer until Semenov was severely defeated by the Red Army in June.[86] His defeat gave rise to the conviction on the part of Japan that northern Manchuria was in danger of being invaded by Bolshevik troops assisted by former German and Austrian prisoners of war.[87] This danger, whether real or imaginary it is difficult to say, provided a reason for the Japanese to bring into

[85] Barclay to Lansing, February 6, 1918, *Foreign Relations, 1918, Russia,* Vol. II, p. 38.

[86] For further evidence of British, Japanese, and French support of Horvat, see *ibid.,* pp. 38, 46, 73, 151, 156, 163.

[87] See Morris to Lansing, August 5, 1918, *ibid.,* p. 330; Same to Same, August 13, 1918, *ibid.,* pp. 343–44; Ishii to Lansing, August 14, 1918, *ibid.,* pp. 345–46.

operation the Sino-Japanese Military Pact of May 16, 1918, and resulted in the occupation of northern Manchuria by Japanese forces. The effect of the support of Semenov by the Allies was to prevent the Chinese troops in Manchuria from keeping the railway zone free from anti-Bolshevik movements as they possibly could have done if they had been allowed to take charge following the disarming of the Bolshevik regiments in Harbin at the end of December 1917.

At about the same time that the events described above were taking place, the Japanese government approached the Chinese government with a proposal of co-operation between the two governments in order to take common measures to meet the dangers arising on the borders of Manchuria.[88] The Chinese government sought the advice of the American government as to the course it should take. Mr. Lansing informed the Chinese Minister in Washington that "it would seem the wisest course, in case Japan deemed military occupation [of the Trans-Siberian Railways] a necessity, for the Chinese Government to take over and guard that part of the Trans-Siberian Railroad system which passes through Manchuria . . . ."[89] Negotiations continued between Japan and China, and on March 25, 1918, there were exchanged notes providing for military and naval co-operation. The formal agreements were signed the following May.[90] The articles of these agreements were couched in general terms, the time of their coming into operation and the details of military and naval co-operation being left to the military and naval authorities of the two countries.

On September 6, 1918, there was signed a supplementary agreement which provided for further details of the military action to be taken.[91]

Prior to the decision of the British government, later concurred in by the French and Japanese governments, to support the anti-

[88] Reinsch to Lansing, February 23, 1918, *ibid.*, p. 55.

[89] Lansing to Page, February 27, 1918, *ibid.*, p. 58.

[90] Text in *Foreign Relations, 1918,* pp. 224–26. The military agreement was modified again on February 5, 1919. This modification defined the time when the agreement would terminate as the time when both the Chinese and Japanese governments shall have approved the Peace Treaty concluded with the enemy countries by the European Peace Conference and when both Chinese and Japanese troops stationed outside Chinese territory shall have been withdrawn simultaneously with the troops of the various Allied countries stationed in the same territories (MacMurray, *op. cit.*, p. 1414).

[91] *Ibid.*

Bolshevik activities of Semenov, discussions had taken place between the Allied governments and the American government as to the possibilities of intervening in Siberia and as a part of this intervention to secure control of the Chinese Eastern Railway and the Trans-Baikal sections of the Trans-Siberian Railway. The idea of intervention in Siberia was first broached by the British government on December 14, 1917, when the British Minister in Tokyo discussed with the Japanese government, "what action ought to be taken by the Allies in Siberia to protect stores and ammunition at Vladivostok and to control in case of emergency the Amur and Trans-Siberian Railways."[92] No specific mention seems to have been made at this time of the Chinese Eastern Railway, but on January 17, 1918, Ambassador Morris in Tokyo reported the substance of a discussion with the Japanese Minister for Foreign Affairs in which the latter stated that "if, however, conditions should hereafter require occupation of Vladivostok and the lines of the Chinese Eastern and Amur Railways, Japan asks that this task be left to her alone . . . ."[93]

Further steps were taken in the plan to occupy the Siberian Railway when on January 28, and again on February 6, the British government approached the American government with the proposal that Japan be invited, as mandatory of the Allies, to occupy the Trans-Siberian Railway, including the Chinese Eastern.[94] To this proposal the American government replied on February 8, advising against intervention but concluding that if such intervention should become necessary in the future it should "be undertaken by international cooperation and not by any one power acting as the mandatory of the others."[95] From about the date of this last note on through 1918 the American and Japanese governments waged a diplomatic battle around the question of the control of the Chinese Eastern Railway. The American government desired to place the control and operation of the railway in the hands of the Russian Railway Corps and under the direction of the American engineer, John F. Stevens. The Russian Railway Corps was the official designation given to a group of 300 or so American railway men organized in the United States in the autumn of 1917 at the request of the

---

[92] Morris to Lansing, March 22, 1918, *ibid.,* p. 84.

[93] Morris to Lansing, January 17, 1918, *ibid.,* p. 30.

[94] British Embassy to Department of State, January 28, 1918, *ibid.,* pp. 35–36, and Same to Same, February 6, 1918, *ibid.,* p. 38.

[95] Department of State to British Embassy, February 8, 1918, *ibid.,* pp. 41–42.

Kerensky government to aid Russia to reorganize and operate its Trans-Siberian system, which was fast falling into a state bordering on chaos. Early in the spring of the same year the American government had sent to Russia, at the request of the Russian government, a small group of railway experts to advise the Russian government generally on the operations of its railways. John F. Stevens headed this group, while Colonel Emerson was in charge of the Railway Corps. Neither group had any relationship to the American military forces. Furthermore, the Corps was maintained from funds previously set aside by the Russian government, and their purpose was for services devoted exclusively to assist the Russian people.[96]

The Railway Corps sailed from San Francisco on November 18, 1917, and arrived at Vladivostok on December 14.[97] However, because of the delicate political situation which existed at Vladivostok, which was in the hands of the Bolsheviks, and because it was thought that the landing of such a large body of men might be misconstrued by the Soviet government as an act of intervention, the Corps did not land and shortly thereafter returned to Nagasaki to await developments.[98] As the weeks passed by with this group of valuable men, who had been withdrawn from the railways in the United States at a time when every railway man was greatly needed, lying idle at Nagasaki, Mr. Stevens, an exceedingly energetic man, began attempting to work out some plan with General Horvat whereby part of the Railway Corps could be used to assist in operating the Chinese Eastern Railway.[99] His efforts were successful, and during early March about one hundred men of the Railway Corps were sent to Harbin to work on the Chinese Eastern.[100]

Japan's interest in keeping the Chinese Eastern Railway out of the hands of the Bolsheviks was influenced presumably by the fact that in 1916 the Russian and Japanese governments entered into an agreement whereby Russia agreed to transfer that portion of the

[96] For a description of the Russian Railway Corps, see Lansing to Morris, May 22, 1918, *Foreign Relations, 1918, Russia,* Vol. II, p. 165.

[97] *Foreign Relations, 1918, Russia,* Vol. III, p. 208.

[98] Stevens to Lansing, December 17, 1917, *ibid.,* p. 212.

[99] Stevens to Lansing, February 1, 1918, *ibid.,* p. 218.

[100] Stevens and Moser, the American consul in Harbin, were both for controlling the Chinese Eastern Railway and the Trans-Baikal Railways in the interests of the White Russian forces. See Stevens to Lansing, February 1, 1918, *ibid.,* p. 218, and Moser to Lansing, February 3, 1918, *ibid.,* p. 219.

Chinese Eastern Railway between Changchun and the Sungari River to Japan in payment for military supplies. At the time the Sino-Japanese Military and Naval Agreements were signed, the Japanese government informed the Chinese government of this agreement and, according to Mr. Reinsch, stated that it would "be consummated when [a] stable government [was] established in Russia."[101]

During the early and late spring of 1918 the anti-Bolshevik activities of Horvat and other White Russians in the railway zone became more pronounced. Some time in April, Horvat went to Peking, where in collaboration with the Russian Minister, Admiral Kolchak, and others opposed to the Soviet regime there was formed a new board of directors for the Chinese Eastern Railway. This board was formed ostensibly to safeguard the existing rights of all parties in the railway, but actually its purpose was to be better able to provide means of fighting the Soviet regime.[102] For the time being this was to be accomplished by assisting Semenov and later by setting up an independent government in Eastern Siberia. Owing to the assistance granted by the Allies to Semenov, he was able to advance along the line of the Chinese Eastern Railway into Siberia; but in June he was definitely defeated by the Bolshevik forces and was forced to retreat back into Manchuria. His defeat was reported to have been brought about by the assistance given the Bolsheviks by large forces of German and Austrian armed prisoners under the command of General Taube, a Russian of German descent.[103] These forces, it was rumored, were preparing to invade northern Manchuria in pursuit of Semenov. Semenov's forces retreated into Manchuria, where the Chinese military forces guarding the border attempted to disarm them. Exactly what happened upon this occasion is still a matter of rumor. Minister Reinsch reported that the Chinese troops were prevented from disarming Semenov's men because of the encouragement given them to resist such action by Japanese officers attached to Semenov's command.[104] In any event, the retreat of Semenov into

101 Reinsch to Lansing, May 16, 1918, *Foreign Relations, 1918, Russia*, Vol. II, pp. 161–62. For confirmation of the negotiations of this agreement see *Un livre noir, diplomatie d'avant guerre et de guerre d'après les documents des archives russes*, 1910–1917, Vol. III, part 3, pp. 82–83, Isvolsky to Sazenof, June 26, 1916.

102 Stevens to Lansing, April 29, 1918, *Foreign Relations, 1918, Russia*, Vol. III, p. 231; Reinsch to Lansing, April 25, 1918, *ibid.*, Vol. II, pp. 137–38.

103 Stevens to Lansing, May 30, 1918, *ibid.*, Vol. II, pp. 181–82; Moser to Lansing, June 19, 1918, *ibid.*, pp. 216–17.

104 Reinsch to Lansing, June 26, 1918, *ibid.*, pp. 231–32.

Manchuria opened Chinese territory to invasion by Bolshevik troops bent upon destroying Semenov's forces.

The danger along the borders of Manchuria which arose because of the defeat of Semenov caused China and Japan to bring into effect the provisions of the Military Pact of May 16, and Japan prepared to move a considerable portion of its Kwantung garrison to North Manchuria. The American government showed its uneasiness at the first intimation that the Japanese were planning an expedition to the Manchurian border. On July 13 the American Ambassador in Tokyo reported to the State Department that he was "reliably informed that the General Staff is urging upon the Cabinet the immediate occupation of Manchuria by Japanese troops as this can be done now without offense to China because of the recent military agreement. The plan submitted includes taking over the control of the Chinese Eastern Railway."[105] The American government immediately stood out against this plan and, on July 19, instructed Ambassador Morris to inform the Japanese government that it "trusts that the Imperial Japanese Government shares its opinion that a military occupation of Manchuria would arouse deep resentment in Russia . . . ."[106] The Japanese government, however, resolved to proceed with its plan to occupy the railway zone. Its object was not only to meet the danger which threatened on the Manchurian border but also to protect the lines of communication of the Czechoslovak troops who were now moving from Vladivostok westward through Manchuria "to rescue their brothers in Siberia," who had clashed with the Red Army.[107]

In the meantime the American Department of State was suggesting to Japan and advising the Chinese government that China should guard the lines of the Chinese Eastern Railway within Manchuria and that she should act alone in so doing.[108] This advice was not followed, however, and on July 27 the Chinese government dis-

---

[105] Morris to Lansing, July 13, 1918, ibid., p. 281.

[106] Polk to Morris, July 19, 1919, ibid., pp. 297–98.

[107] General William S. Graves, commander of the American forces in Siberia at the time of the intervention, is of the opinion that the Czechs in Siberia were never in danger and could have easily reached Vladivostok, that they rather than the Bolsheviks were the aggressors. See Gen. William S. Graves, America's Siberian Adventure, chapter ii, and especially pp. 51–54.

[108] Polk to Morris, July 29, 1918, Foreign Relations, 1918, Russia, Vol. II, p. 314; Morris to Lansing, August 1, 1918, ibid., pp. 321–22; Long to Koo, July 26, 1918, ibid., p. 304.

patched a note to the Japanese legation in Peking formally acknowledging the existence of a condition which would necessitate bringing the Sino-Japanese military pact into force.[109] Shortly thereafter Japanese troops began to move from South Manchuria into North Manchuria and to take up positions in the neighborhood of Manchouli on the Manchurian-Siberian border. China already had a considerable force on the border, but it signified its intention to send 10,000 additional troops.[110]

The American government, having failed in its efforts, first to prevent the Japanese expedition into North Manchuria and, secondly, when this expedition was decided upon, to have the Chinese Eastern Railway patrolled by Chinese troops alone, turned its efforts for the remainder of the year to preventing Japan from assuming sole control of the railway.

It will be recalled that since March 1918 American railway men from the Russian Railway Corps had been helping the Russian administration to operate the Chinese Eastern Railway.[111] On July 9 General Horvat, the Russian manager of the railway, crossed the Manchurian border into Siberia and there issued a proclamation declaring himself head of an independent government for Eastern Siberia.[112] This action on the part of Horvat gave the Chinese an opportunity to attempt to assert control over the railway. On the day that Horvat declared himself head of the new government, the Chinese governor of Kirin informed the American Consul that the "Chinese wished to regain complete sovereignty and take over the railways as Horvat's departure constituted Russia's abandonment, but it was difficult to accomplish because the Chinese lacked money and operatives necessary." At the same time the Chinese governor hinted at the possibility of the American government helping China out financially with regard to the railway.[113] The American government, however,

[109] MacMurray to Lansing, August 8, 1918, *Foreign Relations, 1918, Russia*, Vol. II, pp. 334–35.

[110] MacMurray to Lansing, August 15, 1918, *ibid.*, pp. 348–49. The Chinese Minister in Washington informed the Department of State on August 21, that Japan had moved 12,000 troops along the Chinese Eastern Railway, and that China had about 40,000 troops in Heilungkiang province (Memorandum of a conversation between the Third Assistant Secretary of State and the Chinese Minister, Koo, August 21, 1918), *ibid.*, p. 353.   [111] *Supra*, p. 167.

[112] MacMurray to Lansing, July 9, 1918, *Foreign Relations, 1918, Russia*, Vol. II, p. 273.

[113] MacMurray to Lansing, July 12, 1918, *ibid.*, p. 278.

not only was unresponsive to this suggestion but instructed the American chargé in Peking to inform the Chinese government that it "would view with regret any attempt by China to take advantage of Russia's present distress to regain control of the Chinese Eastern Railway . . . ."[114] Shortly after this exchange of notes the Japanese movement of troops into North Manchuria took place and the representatives of the American government at Harbin and Tokyo and also Mr. Stevens became convinced that Japan was planning to take over control of the Chinese Eastern Railway.[115]

In order to meet this situation the American government, on August 30, expressed its belief that "further complications would not arise and best results would be had if Mr. Stevens for and in behalf of the Russian people were to have general direction of the Trans-Siberian and the Chinese Eastern Railways . . . ."[116] This proposal was made formally to the Allied governments and to China on September 13. The operation of the railways was to be undertaken by "the Russian Railway Corps in conjunction with Russian railway officials and personnel and in cooperation with the Allies . . . ."[117]

Negotiations were carried on in an attempt to settle the details of a plan for the operation of the Trans-Siberian Railways along the lines of the American suggestions. Unexpectedly, the main opposition to the plan for Mr. Stevens and the Railway Corps to take over the operation of the lines came not from the Japanese government but from the British government. The British wanted the railways to be operated by the Russian railway officials under the supervision of an Allied commission.[118]

The Japanese did attempt, however, to make the position of Mr. Stevens, who was to be in charge of the operation of the lines, one purely advisory to the Russian officials, who were to be retained.[119] Mr. Stevens refused to accept an advisory position and stood out for a position of real control of operations. The Japanese government

[114] Polk to MacMurray, July 18, 1918, *ibid.*, p. 292.

[115] See Morris to Lansing, July 13, 1918, *ibid.*, p. 281; Stevens to Morris, September 6 and 7, 1918, *ibid.*, Vol. III, pp. 242–43.

[116] Lansing to Morris, August 30, 1918, *ibid.*, Vol. III, p. 239.

[117] Lansing to Page, September 13, 1918, *ibid.*, p. 249.

[118] Morris to Lansing, September 20, 1918, *ibid.*, p. 262; Polk to Davis, December 24, 1918, *ibid.*, p. 299.

[119] Morris to Lansing, December 3, 1918, *ibid.*, p. 288.

accepted Mr. Stevens' views, and the British finally withdrew their alternative plan. The final plan of operation was accepted by Japan and the United States on January 9, 1919, and shortly thereafter there was set up an Inter-Allied Commission having on it representatives of each Power with military forces in Siberia, to supervise the railways in the zone in which the Allies were operating.[120] Under this Commission there was set up a Technical Board with Mr. Stevens at its head. This Board was entrusted with the actual operation of the railways.

The result of this plan as far as China was concerned was that the rights of the former Russian government were preserved by international action, which at the same time, temporarily at least, precluded the Chinese government from taking advantage of the situation to recover control of the Chinese Eastern Railway, which in effect meant control of North Manchuria.[121]

Shortly after the events described in this chapter took place, the Peace Conference met at Versailles to render to the Allied and Associated Powers the rewards of victory. Judging from the final decisions of that body, the war efforts of China were not regarded very highly. Her derelictions in failing to contribute materially to the victory of the Allies were no doubt held against her. But an examination of the facts indicates that the fault was not China's alone. True, her attempts to participate in the war were not pushed with energy or enthusiasm, but at the same time nearly every one of her attempts was hampered because it clashed with some interest of the Allies. China's declaration of war, which was hailed as her entrance into the family of nations as an equal, was followed by added humiliations rather than by the treatment due to a comrade in arms. Perhaps no nation entered the war on the Allied side and then did less to help win it, but then no nation was drawn into the war for such trivial reasons as was China. To drive out of China a thousand German traders and missionaries and their families was not a reason of which the white man could be proud for dragging into a white man's quarrel the Chinese nation.

[120] "Inter-Allied Agreement of January, 1919," *Conference on the Limitation of Armament, Sub committee, Washington, D.C.,* pp. 696–98.

[121] Early in 1920 the Chinese government, following the fall of the Siberian independent government at Omsk, took over the railway. For its subsequent history, see Houang Tchang-sin, *Le problème du Chemin de fer de l'Est,* pp. 334–434

CHAPTER VII

CHINA AND THE PARIS PEACE CONFERENCE
THE SHANTUNG QUESTION: FIRST PHASE

China was as unprepared for the sudden end of the fighting in Europe in November 1918 as she had been for the outbreak of the war in August 1914. There had been discussions from time to time in the native press as to what claims China should make at the Peace Conference. However, no definite program had been worked out, and in view of the chaotic state of internal conditions in China it was not to be expected that any reasonable program could be decided upon.

The southern provinces had been in open rebellion since early in 1918. The northern military clique and the Communications party, who had brought about the declaration of war upon Germany, had wasted their energy and the income of the Central Government in carrying on ineffectual campaigns against the Provisional Government at Canton. In consequence, China's contribution to the Allied victory was negligible, although the inability of the Allies to agree upon a common policy governing China's participation in the war in great measure frustrated any contribution China might have made.[1]

The Canton Provisional Government, which was actually as much under the domination of the military governors of the southern provinces as was the Peking government under those of the North, outwardly stood for constitutional government. The Provisional Government had been set up by Sun Yat-sen and the Kuomintang in protest against the dissolution of Parliament and the assumption of dictatorial power by the northern military group. The new president of China, Hsü Shih-ch'ang, who succeeded Fêng Kuo-chang in September 1918, sought to bring about peace between the North and the South. President Hsü's efforts in this direction received the strong moral support of President Wilson, who, in his message of congratulation upon the new president's assumption of office, stressed

[1] *Supra*, chapter vi *passim*.

173

the necessity China was under to compose her internal dissensions "before she can fulfil her desire to cooperate with her sister nations in their great struggle . . . ."[2]

President Wilson's message was followed shortly by a proposal advanced by Japan that "a serious attempt should now be made by the Governments of Japan, the United States, Great Britain, France, and Italy in the form of joint representation to the leaders both in the North and in the South to impress upon them the urgent and supreme importance of arriving at an amicable settlement of their differences . . . ."[3]

These powers fell in with the Japanese proposal, and representations in the sense indicated were presented to the Chinese government on December 2, 1918.[4] Prior to this event, the approaching end of the war had already caused the military leaders in the North and the South to take steps to compose their differences. They declared a truce toward the end of November, and delegates were appointed to a conference which assembled at Shanghai in February 1919. This internal peace conference was going on all during the sittings of the Peace Conference at Paris, and for many reasons its deliberations were of more importance to the political and military clique who ruled China than were the proceedings of the far more spectacular assembly in Paris.

Early in December the Chinese Delegation to the Paris Peace Conference left Peking for Europe. All during the time that the representatives of China were pleading China's case before the Paris Peace Conference, the Kuomintang and the Anfu clique, as the combination of military leaders and the Communications group began to be called, continued their political duel for the control of the Central Government.[5] This conference to adjust the differences between the Northern and Southern factions met at Shanghai on February 20, but it was soon found convenient to substitute private meetings for the public sessions. The Southern faction wanted the War Participation Army disbanded because they believed that the

[2] Message of President Wilson to Hsü Shih-ch'ang, October 10, 1918, *Foreign Relations, 1918*, p. 111.

[3] Japanese Embassy to the Department of State, October 25, 1918, *ibid.*, p. 114.

[4] Text of the representations in Reinsch to Lansing, December 2, 1918, *ibid.*, p. 134.

[5] For accounts of the domestic political situation in China at this time see *Foreign Relations, 1919*, Vol. I, pp. 270–358.

Northern tuchuns were building it up with the idea of crushing all opposition to their dictatorship. They also wanted the Peking government to refrain from drawing on the 17,000,000-yen balance of the War Participation Loan which had been extended by Japanese interests at the time the Sino-Japanese Military and Naval Agreements came into effect. Furthermore, the South wanted the Parliament which had been dissolved in 1917 to be reconvoked and the puppet Parliament, which had been created in 1918 as a screen for the oligarchic dictatorship of the Northern tuchuns, to be disbanded.

While the bargaining between the northern and southern factions over these points was going on at Shanghai, the attention of the Chinese people became focused upon the efforts of the Chinese Delegation at Paris to push through its idealistic program. In fact, one can hardly escape the conviction that the Chinese Delegation to the Paris Peace Conference was permitted to advance claims which had little chance of ever being realized but which appealed to the very vocal "Young China" elements in order to provide a convenient smoke screen for the realistic political maneuvering which was taking place at the Shanghai conference.

Undoubtedly, the military clique in Peking and the Communications party, having become progressively more dependent upon Japanese sources for the funds with which to maintain themselves in power, would have preferred to work with Japan in arriving at a settlement of the Shantung question rather than openly to defy her at the Paris Peace Conference. Evidence of the desire of the military leaders to work with Japan rather than against her was shown by the departure for Japan a few days before the Armistice in Europe of General Hsü Shu-cheng, the chief lieutenant of Tuan Chi-jui, and the spokesman of the military group. His mission ostensibly was to attend the military maneuvers in Japan, but it was rumored that his real mission was to arrange a Sino-Japanese Alliance, which, logically, would first presume a settlement of the Shantung question.[6]

The state of public opinion in China and the precarious political situation of all those who enjoyed power in Peking prevented this course, however, from being followed. The agitation which was raised against Japan at the time of the Twenty-one Demands and which had never completely subsided had inflamed public opinion,

[6] *North China Herald*, November 9, 1918.

especially among the student groups, against any co-operation with Japan. The merchant class had become thoroughly resentful toward the military oligarchy because of the interruptions to business which were caused by the continual marchings and countermarchings of the armies of the various tuchuns and because of the tremendous drain on the public revenues which these sham military movements entailed. Finally, the series of Japanese loans which followed each other in bewildering rapidity during 1918, together with the rumors of the secret military and naval pacts concluded with Japan in the spring of 1918, evoked the suspicion among all classes that the military and Communications cliques had completely sold out to Japan in order to perpetuate their own power.

This conviction was furthered by well-substantiated rumors concerning a series of secret agreements entered into toward the end of September 1918 by the Chinese minister at Tokyo and the Japanese Minister for Foreign Affairs which amounted to a recognition of Japan's claims in Shantung. The most important of these agreements, as they were subsequently revealed, had to do with the former German railway in Shantung. They provided for the eventual conversion of the railway into a joint Sino-Japanese concern and also granted Japanese capitalists the right to finance the construction of two important branches to this railway. The preamble of the agreement providing for the joint control of the railway included the significant statement that "the Government of Japan, being desirous of arranging matters in a spirit of harmony, has drawn up an agreement which it regards as a satisfactory settlement of all outstanding questions relating to the Province of Shantung."[7] The agreement for the construction of the two branch railways provided for a 20,000,000-yen advance which was paid over to the Central Government, or rather to certain of those men who at this time represented the Chinese government.[8] In bringing the agreement to the notice of the American government, the Japanese government pointed out that the "projected lines in Shantung are within the scope contemplated in Article 1 of the Sino-Japanese treaty respecting the Province of Shantung of 1915 . . . ."[9] It will be recalled that this article provided:

---

[7] For the text of these agreements see *Foreign Relations, 1919,* Vol. I, pp. 571–72 and pp. 574–76.   [8] *Vide* note 11, *infra.*

[9] Japanese Embassy to the Department of State, October 30, 1918, *Foreign Relations, 1918,* p. 205.

The Chinese Government agrees to give full assent to all matters upon which the Japanese Government may hereafter agree with the German Government relating to the disposition of all rights, interests and concessions which Germany, by virtue of treaties or otherwise, possesses in relation to the Province of Shantung.[10]

Clearly, it was the object of the Japanese government in this agreement to re-commit the Chinese government to the procedure set forth in the 1915 treaty whereby the former German rights in Shantung were to be transferred by Germany to Japan, who would thereupon restore the Kiaochow leasehold to China, retaining certain of the economic rights in Shantung formerly enjoyed by Germany. The existence of the agreements of September 1918 became important when the Chinese Delegation at the Peace Conference pleaded for direct restitution of Kiaochow to China and the abrogation of the 1915 Treaties and Agreements. The Japanese representatives argued that the 1918 agreements constituted a voluntary recognition by China of the validity of the 1915 Treaties and Agreements and therefore greatly weakened the Chinese argument that they should be abrogated as they were imposed upon the Chinese government by *force majeure*. The fact that the advance of 20,000,000 yen was accepted by officials of the Chinese government was particularly damaging to the Chinese case.[11]

Two other Sino-Japanese agreements signed in 1918 served to increase the uneasy suspicions of the Chinese people that China was being allowed to fall under the complete military and financial domination of Japan. One was the Arms agreement of July 31, 1918, whereby the Taihei Kumiai (Company) of Japan agreed to supply China with enormous supplies of arms and ammunition to the total value of 23,643,762 yen.[12] These arms were to be standard supplies of the Japanese army. The Arms agreement revived the fears which had been aroused at the time of the Twenty-one Demands by Article 4 of Group V, which had asked that Japan be allowed to supply the Chinese government with a considerable proportion of its armament needs. The second agreement was the so-called War Participation Loan, whereby Japan (a Japanese banking syndicate) agreed to loan

---

[10] The *Sino-Japanese Negotiations,* p. 40.

[11] See the statement of Baron Makino made before the Council of Four on April 22, 1919, *infra,* p. 214.

[12] MacMurray, *Treaties and Agreements with and concerning China,* Vol. II, pp. 1414–15.

to the Peking government 20,000,000 yen for the purpose of raising and equipping three divisions to form the War Participation Army.[13]

The so-called War Participation Army had been created at the time when the plan to send Chinese troops to Europe was under consideration. When this scheme fell through, the Army was continued and enlarged, supposedly for the purpose of defending China's western and northern frontiers against a German-Bolshevik invasion.

General Tuan Chi-jui, after his resignation as Premier in October 1918, became head of the War Participation Bureau and commander of the War Participation Army. The Southern Federation believed that this was merely a move on the part of the military clique to keep the control of the government in the hands of Tuan and that the army was to be used against the South rather than in defense of China's borders.

Rumors of these events gradually engendered a feeling of resentment and suspicion against the Peking government which after the Armistice turned into a torrent of criticism. Much of this criticism was directed against Japan, creating a situation whereby it became politically impossible for the military and Communications groups to work directly with Japan in effecting some sort of solution of the Shantung question and other problems which the war had brought about. The native press and the student class, buoyed up by the hope that President Wilson and Wilsonian idealism would enable the Chinese nation to escape paying for the misdeeds of the corrupt rulers who had claimed to represent China from 1914 to 1919, vociferously demanded that Japan be defied at the Paris Peace Conference. This course was followed while, at home, the northern and southern factions were settling their differences at Shanghai.

The Chinese Delegation to the Peace Conference left Peking for Europe at the beginning of December 1918. At Mukden, Mr. Lu Chêng-hsiang, senior member of the Delegation, gave to a group of press correspondents the first official intimation of the claims which China proposed to make at the Peace Conference. The conditions of peace which China would demand, as given by Mr. Lu, were: (1) the abolition of extraterritoriality; (2) the revision of the tariff; (3) the Chinese government to assume control and management of the railways of Eastern China; (4) the return of Tsingtao; (5) on the part of China, the opening of Mongolia and Tibet to international

[13] Text in *Foreign Relations, 1919*, Vol. I, pp. 342–43.

traffic.[14] The program outlined by Mr. Lu indicated that the opportunity offered by the Paris Peace Conference was to be used to attempt to arrive at a broad solution of China's difficulties arising from her inferior position as a sovereign state rather than to confine the Chinese claims to questions directly arising out of the war.

In addition to the senior delegate, Lu Chêng-hsiang, the Chinese Delegation consisted of V. K. Wellington Koo, at that time Chinese Minister to the United States, Alfred Sze, Chinese Minister in London, and C. T. Wang, who joined the Delegation in Washington, where he had been sent by the Canton government in an effort to get the United States to recognize it.[15] The Delegation, having once arrived in Paris, seemed to act quite independently of the authorities in Peking and to pursue the course which in their judgment seemed best. Whether this was due to lack of instructions from the Chinese government or to the fact that the younger members of the Delegation, Koo and Wang, soon assumed the lead in matters pertaining to the claims of China, leaving the more conservative and older Lu and Sze in the background, it is impossible to say. In any event the character and background of the members of the Chinese Delegation undoubtedly influenced the course which was adopted at Paris and therefore must be taken into consideration in order to understand the eventual outcome of the ambitious program which the Chinese Delegation formulated.

Lu Chêng-hsiang was born in Shanghai in 1870, some twelve years before the birth of C. T. Wang and some seventeen years before Wellington Koo. He was older by six years than Alfred Sze. The difference in ages between Lu and the other members of the Delegation, which ordinarily would not have been of any great significance, in this particular instance was of great importance. For this short span of years separated by an almost impassable gulf the last of the Chinese officials of the old regime, who had prepared for public service by the formal classical learning and the rigid examination system, from the first crop of young Chinese officials who had been educated in the West and had become thoroughly imbued with Western ideology. Whereas Lu Chêng-hsiang was a typical representative of the old scholar type of official, Wellington Koo and

[14] France, Ministry of Foreign Affairs, *Bulletin périodique de la presse japonaise*, No. 20, March 11, 1919, p. 5.

[15] Later Mr. C. C. Wu, prominently identified with the Canton government, joined the Delegation.

C. T. Wang were outstanding representatives of the American-educated, returned-student type which became prominent in public life with the advent of the Republic.

After passing through the prescribed course of formal study and examinations, with the variation of attending a government language school, Lu Chêng-hsiang entered the service of the Empire in 1890 as an interpreter to the Chinese legation in St. Petersburg. He rose through the regular diplomatic ranks until in 1911 he was appointed Chinese Minister to Russia. With the establishment of the Republic he was recalled to Peking and served as Foreign Minister in the first Republican cabinet. He resigned in 1913 but returned to office in 1915 and was Foreign Minister at the time of the Twenty-one Demands negotiations. He later resigned but again returned to office in December 1917, and was serving in this capacity at the time of his appointment to the Peace Delegation.[16]

Alfred Sze was born in 1876; but this difference of six years between his age and that of Lu Chêng-hsiang made his education and general experience quite different from that of his senior colleague. After receiving the fundamentals of a Western education in China he came to the United States in 1893. From 1893 to 1896 he was enrolled at Washington High School, and in 1897 he entered Cornell University. He received his A.B. degree from Cornell in 1902 and shortly thereafter returned to China. In 1906 he was appointed Junior Secretary of the Board of Communications. In 1908 he served as Customs Taotai at Harbin, and in 1910 he entered the Wai Chiao Pu as Junior Councillor. In 1912 he entered the first republican cabinet as Minister of Posts and Communications, but soon resigned. In 1914 he was appointed Minister to Great Britain, at which post he was serving at the time of his appointment to the Chinese Delegation. Sze, therefore, was not in China during the political disturbances of 1914 to 1919 and thus escaped becoming entangled in the welter of party politics which characterized Chinese public life during this period.

The careers of Wellington Koo and C. T. Wang are typical of many of the Western-educated young Chinese who came into prominence with the Republic. Koo was born at Shanghai in 1887. His education was entirely along Western lines. He attended St. John's

---

[16] In 1928 Lu Chêng-hsiang entered a monastery in Belgium, where he has since died. It is said that the complete defeat of the Chinese program at Paris influenced him to take this strange course.

College in Shanghai and in 1904 came to Cook Academy in New York State. He did not return to China until 1912, all these years in America being spent in completing his education. He entered Columbia University in 1905 and left there in 1912 after having passed through the successive academic grades to the degree of Doctor of Philosophy. His career at Columbia followed the usual pattern of a successful American college youth. He was elected to Phi Beta Kappa, distinguished himself as a member of the varsity debating squad, and was the editor of several magazines, including the *Chinese Students' Monthly*. He did his graduate work in international law under the direction of John Bassett Moore, and he became thoroughly imbued with the latter's idealistic-legalistic conception of international politics.

Upon his return to China he served as Secretary to Yuan Shih-k'ai and also as Councillor of the Wai Chiao Pu. During the Twenty-one Demands negotiations he acted as a liaison agent between the Chinese Foreign Office and the American Minister, Dr. Paul Reinsch.[17] He was appointed Minister to Mexico in 1915, but later in the same year was transferred to Washington. He was serving in Washington at the time of his appointment to the Chinese Delegation.

C. T. Wang was born in 1882 and therefore was a few years older than Wellington Koo. He was the more radical of the two and, despite Koo's superior gifts of eloquence, dominated the Chinese Delegation at Paris. He received his education at Peiyang University and from there went as teacher to the Anglo-Chinese college at Tientsin. In 1903 he went to Japan, where for four years he was Secretary of the Y.M.C.A. in Tokyo. With the financial aid of his friends he came to the United States in 1907 to study law, and graduated from Yale University in 1911. In 1912 he returned to China and became Vice-Minister of Commerce and Industry in the first Republican cabinet. Later he became Vice-President of the Senate, but along with the rest of the Kuomintang he was forced out of politics by Yuan Shih-k'ai's purge of November 1913. When Parliament was reconvoked after Yuan's death, he returned to office. He was forced out of office again in 1917 when the military tuchuns gained the upper hand in their fight with the Kuomintang over the question of declaring war upon Germany. He thereupon joined the independent government set up at Canton in the spring of 1918. He

[17] *Supra*, p. 54, n. 14.

was appointed to the Peace Delegation in order to give the southern provinces representation at Paris and to impress the Powers with an outward show of the solidarity of the Chinese republic.

Upon the two younger delegates fell, or rather by them was assumed, the responsibility of formulating and presenting China's case to the Peace Conference at Paris. If older men and men more deeply steeped in Chinese rather than Western learning had been given this responsibility, perhaps the Chinese program would not have aroused the extraordinary fervor among the idealists of America and the youth of China which was evoked by the eloquent pleadings of Wellington Koo and C. T. Wang. On the other hand, perhaps a more modest program and one based upon the realities of China's treaty and financial obligations to Japan would have prevented the Chinese Delegation from leaving the Peace Conference empty-handed and the Chinese people from being sorely disappointed in all their high hopes.[18]

Wellington Koo preceded the other members of the Chinese Delegation to Paris, and upon his arrival late in December 1918 he immediately got in touch with the members of the American mission who were there preparing the American program. David Hunter Miller, the close adviser of President Wilson during the Conference, noted in his diary under date of December 27, 1918, that Wellington Koo called on him and said that "he would wish to consult with me informally from time to time in advance of formal communications between our respective Governments, which I told him would be entirely agreeable to me."[19]

Miller describes a luncheon meeting on January 22, 1919, with C. T. Wang during which they discussed "a paper . . . . which was the Chinese idea as to the Treaty so far as relations between China and the enemy Powers were concerned."[20]

[18] Liang Ch'i-ch'ao, one of the most influential men in China, arrived in Paris during the Peace Conference. He, however, not being an official member of the Delegation, could not influence the Chinese program. His presence resulted in many protests being sent to President Hsü demanding that he be recalled, as he was suspected of wanting to deal directly with Japan (*Bulletin périodique de la presse chinoise*, No. 14, July 14, 1919, p. 1).

[19] David Hunter Miller, *My Diary at the Conference of Paris, with Documents,* Vol. I, p. 60. Mr. Miller's diary consists of twenty-one volumes. The first volume contains his day-to-day personal observations of the Conference; the other twenty volumes consist of documents, minutes, etc., pertaining to the Conference. Hereafter cited as Miller, *Diary.*

[20] *Ibid.,* p. 88.

These two meetings were indicative of the close consultation which thereafter took place between Koo and Wang and certain of the members of the American Delegation who were acting in an advisory capacity to the American representatives at Paris. Support and encouragement were given by these American advisers to the Chinese program, and much of the responsibility for its broad and idealistic character must rest on them.

The paper which Miller discussed with Mr. Wang on January 22 revealed the method of approach by which the Chinese Delegation hoped to get its claims recognized. It provided for the renunciation by Germany and Austria-Hungary and the denunciation by China of all treaties and agreements between China and the other two governments. These treaties were to be denounced because they were "the offspring of acts of war" and were "contrary to the spirit of the note of September 6, 1899, of the Secretary of State of the United States," i.e., the Open Door note.[21]

This provision was followed by a statement the very evident intention of which was to get the Powers to guarantee the retrocession *directly* to China of all rights enjoyed by Germany and Austria-Hungary in China. In other words, the Chinese Delegation wanted the Powers to stand between China and Japan and to nullify the Sino-Japanese Treaties and Agreements of 1915 and 1918 by ignoring them in so far as these treaties and agreements applied to Shantung.[22]

The most important of the list of desiderata with which the Chinese statement concluded and which the Powers were asked to guarantee were: (1) The restoration of the leased territory of Kiaochow and cancellation of all German railway, mining, and other rights in Shantung; (2) The annulment of extraterritorial rights hitherto enjoyed by the subjects of Germany and Austria-Hungary;

[21] Miller, *Diary*, Vol. III, p. 527, Doc. 215.

[22] The statement, in part, said: "For the purpose of giving full effect to this article of the protocols of peace, the Allied and Associated Powers do hereby assure to the Government and the people of China their rightful place in the family of nations, complete and actual preservation of Chinese sovereignty and of the entirety of the domain of China, and full and complete retrocession of all rights, claims, concessions or undertakings whatsoever obtained by the Governments and nationals of Germany and Austria-Hungary, which are hereby declared to be subversive of universal interest in world peace. Such assurance must and shall provide for complete recognition of the sovereign rights of China in accordance with the expressed will of the Government and people of the Republic of China and of the associated interest and sympathy of enlightened humanity" (*ibid.*).

(3) The abrogation of all treaties and agreements between China and Germany and Austria-Hungary.[23]

This statement revealed that the core of the Chinese program at Paris was the claim for the direct return of the Kiaochow leased territory and the transfer to China of the German economic rights and properties in Shantung. In effect, this would have meant not only the return of the Kiaochow leasehold to Chinese jurisdiction but the transfer to China of the valuable railway and mining properties which the Germans had developed in the province. Such a claim directly conflicted with that of Japan, as set forth in the Sino-Japanese Treaty of May 24, 1915, with regard to the disposition of the German rights in Shantung, wherein Japan had expressed her willingness to return Kiaochow to China but on condition that she be compensated for her efforts in dislodging Germany from the China coast by having certain of the German economic rights transferred to her.

A few days after C. T. Wang and David Hunter Miller had discussed the Chinese program, the opportunity arose—much earlier than had been anticipated—for the Chinese and Japanese representatives to present their claims to the Council of Ten. The Chinese statement with regard to Shantung opposed at every point the claims presented by the Japanese delegates, thus closing any opportunity which had existed heretofore to negotiate directly with Japan.[24] The sympathy with which the Chinese claims for the direct restitution of the German rights were received and the optimistic press reports of the impression made by the eloquence of Mr. Koo upon the Council of Ten gave Chinese everywhere a feeling of confidence as to the final outcome of the Chinese program. The Chinese Delegation immediately was deluged by telegrams and messages[25] from Chinese student organizations and merchants' associations and pro-

---

[23] Miller, *Diary*, Vol. III, p. 527, Doc. 215.　　　　[24] *Infra*, pp. 198–99.

[25] See "Telegrams Received by the Chinese Delegation in Support of Their Stand on the Shantung Question," *The Chinese Delegation to Paris Peace Conference*, Paris, Impre. de Vaugirard, 1919. The following is a typical example of these telegrams, for they nearly all reiterated the arguments and pleas set forth in this:

"(Received Feb. 9, 1919)　　　　　　　　　　　　　PEKING, Feb. 3, 1919

Ministers Hoowieteh, Loutsengtsiang, Kooweichun,
Wangchengting, Weichengthu, Szeaoke,
Chinese Legation, Paris

"Peace Conference being pledged to respect people's rights, universal Chinese demand all German privileges Shantung restored China direct. Nation will unrecognize secret agreements, understandings between powers since opening war

vincial assemblies from all over China and from organizations of Chinese outside of China. These telegrams were unanimous in support of the stand taken by the Chinese Delegation, and they urged the Chinese representatives to continue to oppose the Japanese claims and to demand the direct restitution of Kiaochow. In most cases President Wilson's Fourteen Points were cited as the basis for the Chinese claims. Such realists as Tuan Chi-jui and Tsao Ju-lin would have preferred, in all probability, to adopt a less intransigent attitude toward Japan. Their political position at home, however, was too precarious to overcome the wild enthusiasm for Wilsonian idealism which swept "Young China" at the apparent success of Wellington Koo's first encounter with the Japanese representatives. Wilsonian idealism held not only the Chinese but the entire world in a spell at this moment. People everywhere had implicit faith in President Wilson's power to fashion a new world to his liking. His sympathy for China was well known. The future looked full of promise for the young republic. It was decided to cast aside "Old China's" well-known ability to compromise and "to take arms against a sea of troubles and by opposing end them."

The so-called Shantung question, which was the essential feature of both the Chinese and Japanese programs at the Paris Peace Conference, was intrinsically one of the least important questions which the Conference was called upon to decide. Stripped of all the complex of Sino-Japanese-American rivalries and cross purposes which it symbolized, the problem resolved itself into the choice of transferring the former leased territory of Kiaochow directly to China or of transferring it to Japan in the expectation that she would carry out her solemn promise to re-transfer it to China.

However, there was much more to the Shantung question than such a simple decision as this. In the first place, Japan was determined to insist upon the method by which she desired to effect the transfer, not alone because she wanted the transaction to be solely one between China and Japan without any outside interference but also because she was determined that the validity of the 1915 and 1918 treaties with China should not be questioned. Upon these treaties rested her position in Manchuria, the protection of which

---

making China pawn. All Sino-Japanese contracts agreements since 1914 being extorted abrogation demanded   Show Conference this telegram.

"PROVINCIAL ASSEMBLIES, CHAMBERS COMMERCE,
EDUCATIONAL ASSOCIATIONS AND OTHER BODIES."

was the cardinal aim of Japan's foreign policy. Furthermore, Japan had shown every indication of wanting gradually to establish a situation in the Far East whereby the Occidental powers would refrain from coming between her and China. In fact, Japan's foreign policy since the Russo-Japanese War had been moving toward the gradual reduction if not elimination of the political interference of the Occidental powers in the affairs of China. By this policy, it was argued, Japan could better preserve the peace of the Far East in the same manner that the Monroe Doctrine of the United States protected the Americas from being drawn into the quarrels of the European powers. Furthermore, the recent history of Japan had made the Japanese people extraordinarily sensitive with regard to the position which Japan occupied among the Great Powers. Theoretically Japan was considered a Great Power, but actually she had not been accorded the status. Even her ally, Great Britain, when it came time for Japan to declare war upon Germany, had attempted to get Japan to limit her sphere of action in accordance with the interests of Great Britain in a way which the British government would never have suggested to any of the leading powers of Europe.[26] At the opening of the Peace Conference, M. Clemenceau revealed that the reluctance to accord Japan the status of a Great Power still persisted.[27] In view of this situation, the determination with which the Japanese government insisted at Paris that the letter of its agreements with China relative to Shantung must be accepted without any modification whatsoever is best explained by its determination to use this opportunity to establish beyond question Japan's status as a Great Power.

President Wilson was in a great measure responsible for the prominence which the Shantung question received at Paris. He had shown great sympathy and interest for China throughout his administration[28] and, like Mr. Bryan and Mr. Lansing, he was exceedingly

[26] *Supra,* pp. 11–14.

[27] M. Clemenceau, when discussing the numbers of delegates to be accorded the Powers at the Conference, said: "We have agreed that Japan should have five delegates like Great Britain. Japan participated in the war in the Far East, but who can say that in the war she played a part that can be compared for instance to that of France. Japan defended its interests in the Far East, but when she was requested to intervene in Europe, everyone knows what the answer of Japan was." Notes of a Meeting of the Supreme War Council, January 12, 1919, B.C.A. 1a. (For and explanation of the official designation of the various councils, see p. 190, n. 36.

[28] *Vide* p. 203 for an indication of the deep suspicion with which President Wilson regarded Japan.

suspicious of Japan's good intentions toward China. Furthermore, America had a traditional policy toward Chinese territorial integrity which gave President Wilson a recognized basis for his approach to the claims of China. Perhaps, however, the most important factor which explains President Wilson's concern for the outcome of the Shantung question was that he quickly realized how a decision in favor of Japan could be used by his opponents in the United States to discredit him and to help defeat the acceptance of the Treaty and the League Covenant. This opposition had already assumed considerable proportions when, at the end of April, the Shantung question came before the Council of Four for final decision. Mr. Wilson more than once expressed his concern for the effect that the outcome of this question would have upon the American public.[29] As Ray Stannard Baker says, "the Japanese crisis . . . . troubled the President more than any other and the result of none, finally, satisfied him less."[30] Mr. Baker, himself, is of the opinion that "the exact record of what was done at Paris regarding the Japanese controversy, chiefly relating to the Chinese province of Shantung, is more important, at least to Americans, than any other."[31] From a distance of fifteen years, Mr. Baker's statement seems somewhat exaggerated, but we must remember that the Shantung decision was pictured by the political opponents of President Wilson as the betrayal of his own principles. In no small measure this argument was responsible for the defeat of the Treaty in the United States. It is this which makes the decision important for the American people.[32]

In China the Shantung controversy aroused tremendous enthusiasm. That indefinable group often called "Young China" believed that the Peace Conference offered the opportunity to wipe the slate clean. China was to enter the new world order, which the world fondly believed was being created at Paris, free of the unequal engagements which made her a pawn of the selfish interests of other

---

[29] *Infra,* pp. 224, 226, Statement of President Wilson to the Council of Four.

[30] Ray Stannard Baker, *Woodrow Wilson and World Settlement,* Vol. II, p. 223.

[31] *Ibid.,* p. 224.

[32] The extraordinary importance with which the Shantung decision was endowed in the United States is well illustrated in the stenographic report of the famous breakfast meeting of August 19, 1919, between President Wilson and the Senate Foreign Relations Committee when the Senate was considering the Versailles Treaty. At this critical meeting, the outcome of which greatly influenced the Senate's final decision not to ratify the Treaty, almost one-half of the time was spent by questioning President Wilson upon the Shantung decision. See *United States Senate Document 76,* 66th Congress, 1st session, Vol. 13, pp. 22 ff.

nations. The "old gang" in Peking were to be discredited because of their dealings with Japan, and Japan could be defied because it was believed that under the protection of Mr. Wilson she could be defied with impunity. President Wilson's power seemed irresistible, and he was on the side of China. His Fourteen Points were to be China's new charter of liberty, and the acknowledgment of China's Shantung claims would place the seal of authenticity upon that charter.

The successful outcome of the Chinese case depended entirely upon Woodrow Wilson's power actually to create a new world order on the basis of his Fourteen Points. If Wilson had held at Paris the power which the world believed he did in those buoyant days of early 1919, the faith with which the Chinese people believed that Japan could be pushed aside and the inconvenient commitments of China's first crop of Republican rulers could be rendered null and void would perhaps have been justified. Only gradually did the world perceive that which quickly became apparent to the privileged few who were inside the Conference room at Paris: President Wilson was not the dictator of the proceedings there. At most, he was *primus inter pares,* with all the necessity of making concessions to those around him that this position always entails.

The weak point in Wilson's armor was soon discovered by those who were seeking particular advantages and were only secondarily interested in the more idealistic aspects of his program. What President Wilson wanted above all things was a league of nations covenant framed in harmony with his ardent ideals. To attain this objective, he was willing to sacrifice immediate good for what seemed to him to be a vastly greater ideal. Once this situation was comprehended by those who were more interested in getting their special claims granted than they were in a league of nations, the bargaining power it gave them was fully utilized. Furthermore, when the Shantung question came up for final settlement at the end of April, almost upon the eve of the delivery of the peace terms to the German delegates, President Wilson's influence had been greatly weakened by the necessity of advocating reservations to the Covenant which a suspicious Senate forced upon him but which the European powers were reluctant to accept.

The Chinese Delegation, excluded from the inner sanctum of the Council of Ten, remained unaware of the steadily weakening position of President Wilson as the months of the Conference proceeded.

Encouraged by their first passage at arms with the Japanese representatives, at the time the Shantung question was first presented to the Council, Wellington Koo and C. T. Wang extended rather than modified their original claims. While in January they had asked that the Shantung Treaty and Agreements of 1915 be abrogated, toward the end of April they were asking that all the 1915 and 1918 Treaties and Agreements be abrogated, including those applying to Manchuria and Inner Mongolia.[33]

Through a series of unforeseen circumstances, the Japanese claim for a transfer to her of the German leasehold and German rights in Shantung and the Chinese counterclaim asking for a direct restitution of these rights were brought before the Council of Ten on January 27 and 28, just two weeks after the opening meeting of the Conference. They were not directly discussed again until the latter part of April and were among the final questions disposed of before the preliminary draft of the Versailles Treaty was presented to the German delegates. The Shantung question was finally disposed of by the Council of Three, consisting of President Wilson, Lloyd George, and Clemenceau, Signor Orlando, the Italian senior representative, having temporarily withdrawn because of President Wilson's objections to the proposed Fiume settlement. The Council of Three assented *in toto* to the Japanese claims, and the articles covering the disposal of the German rights in Shantung were incorporated in the final Treaty essentially as they had originally been proposed by the Japanese representatives.

In order to understand the complete defeat of the Chinese claims, it is more necessary to understand those factors which affected President Wilson's position at Paris than to follow in detail the activities of the Chinese Delegation. Any hope of a favorable outcome of the Chinese program rested almost entirely upon the influence President Wilson could exert toward this end. It was President Wilson who remained the unknown factor in the situation, and therefore it is to him that attention must be directed between the end of January, when the Chinese claims were first presented, and on April 22, when the Shantung question came before Wilson, Lloyd George, and Clemenceau for final settlement.

[33] Compare "The Claim of China for direct restitution of the leased territory of Kiaochow, etc.," dated Paris, February 1919, with "The Claim of China submitting for Abrogation by the Peace Conference the Treaties and Notes . . . . of May 25, 1915, etc.," dated Paris, April 1919. Texts in Miller, *Diary*, Vol. VI, pp. 115 and 213, Docs. 449 and 450.

The Paris Peace Conference, met to decide upon the "preliminary terms of Peace" to be presented to Germany, began its actual labors with the meeting of the Supreme War Council on the afternoon of January 12, 1919.[34] The representatives of all the Great Powers were present with the exception of those of Japan, because it had not yet been decided whether or not Japan was to have representation on the Council of Ten.[35]

At this initial meeting and at the following one on the morning of the 13th, questions were discussed which directly affected China and which laid the basis for the presentation of the Shantung claims some two weeks later. At these opening meetings President Wilson's ideas for a new world order received their initial encounter with the cold realities of world politics, while Premier Hughes of Australia and Premier Massey of New Zealand revealed themselves as the first of those many opponents who were to arise in the next few months to challenge President Wilson's conception.

The first question discussed by the Conference concerned the general procedure to be adopted in regard to the peace discussions. After it had been decided that the Great Powers should have five representatives each, Lloyd George brought forward the suggestion that the British Dominions be accorded independent representation. He based his proposal on the ground that the Dominions were autonomous states and that they would have a special interest and point of view with regard to such questions as the disposal of the former German colonies.[36] The French, in the tentative program which they

[34] *Vide,* note 36, *infra,* for a description of the several Councils and the official designation given to the minutes of their meetings.

[35] It was decided at this meeting to accord Japan representation at the Conference equal to that of the other Great Powers.

[36] B.C.A., 1a–1b, January 12, 1919. The minutes of this meeting and the meeting held on the following day were designated as B.C.A., because these were meetings of the Supreme War Council. With the formal commencement of the Peace Conference proceedings the Council of Ten was created, and the minutes of its sessions were designated in the American records as B.C., followed by the chronological number and date.

At the time of the opening of the Paris Peace Conference in January 1919 the Supreme War Council was the chief inter-Allied co-ordinating organ. Pending the formal organization of the Peace Conference several meetings of this body took place at which the chief delegates of Great Britain, France, the United States, Italy, and Japan were present and matters having to do with the Peace Conference were discussed. The minutes of these meetings were given the designation of S.W.C. 1a, S.W.C. 1b, etc.

With the formal organization of the Peace Conference, the Supreme Council became the chief organ of the Conference. It consisted at first of two representa-

had prepared, proposed that each of the smaller belligerent powers should have three representatives.[37] Mr. Lloyd George suggested cutting this down to two representatives each in order to make places for separate Dominion representation. President Wilson opposed Lloyd George's suggestion. He felt that it would look as if the Great Powers were "running the Conference." The question of Dominion representation was not settled at this meeting; but it was decided, in accordance with Mr. Lloyd George's suggestion, to cut the representation of the smaller belligerents to two representatives each.[38] The effect of this decision was to reduce the representation accorded China to two representatives, although the Chinese Delegation had asked for five on the basis of China's huge population.

The problem of representation was settled at the following meet-

tives from each of the five Great Powers. This body soon became known as the Council of Ten. The Council of Ten met regularly from January 15 to March 15; thereafter its meetings became infrequent. Its minutes were designated by the American Secretariat as B.C. followed by the chronological number of the meeting and the date. Beginning with March 27 and continuing until some time in June, the Council of Foreign Ministers, more popularly called the Council of Five, began to meet in place of the former Council of Ten. Its minutes are designated by the symbols F.M., plus the chronological number of the meeting and the date. Finally, from March 24 to June 24, the Council of Four, consisting of Lloyd George, Premier Clemenceau, President Wilson, and Signor Orlando, met separately. Until April 19 the minutes of the meetings of the Council of Four were kept somewhat fragmentarily, but from this date on, and therefore all during the Shantung crisis, full minutes were kept by the Secretary, Sir Maurice Hankey. These minutes are designated in the American records as C.F., plus the chronological number of the meeting and the date. After President Wilson left Paris, the principal organ of the Conference became known as the Heads of Delegations. The minutes of its meetings are designated as H.D., plus the number and date.

For the following two chapters the collection of the official minutes of the foregoing Councils of the Paris Peace Conference in the Hoover War Library at Stanford University has been used. The collection, however, does not include the minutes of the Council of Four. Recourse, therefore, was made to the Annotation by H. C. Nixon, of the United States States Department, of the minutes of the Council of Four in regard to the Shantung Articles of the Treaty of Versailles. The text of this annotation is found in David Hunter Miller, *My Diary at the Conference of Paris,* Vol. XIX, pp. 171–201. Occasionally I have referred to Ray Stannard Baker, *Woodrow Wilson and World Settlement,* particularly where he has quoted directly from the minutes of the Council of Four or where he has quoted more fully minutes that are only annotated by Mr. Nixon. (See Miller, *Diary,* Vol. XIV, prefatory note on the minutes of the Supreme Council at the Paris Peace Conference.)

[37] Miller, *Diary,* Vol. 2, pp. 4–16, Doc. 4, French tentative plan for the organization of the Conference.

[38] Brazil was granted three representatives at the special request of Mr. Wilson. Serbia also was accorded three representatives.

ing on the basis of a proposal by President Wilson whereby the Dominions and India were allotted two representatives each, with the exception of New Zealand, which received one.[39] Lloyd George in the meantime had discussed this allotment with the Dominion premiers, who had expressed their "disappointment at the smallness of the representation allotted to them."[40] Thus, at the outset of the Conference President Wilson provided grounds for the hostility toward himself which later was so markedly manifested by Premier Hughes of Australia and Premier Massey of New Zealand.

After the question of Dominion representation had been settled, President Wilson brought up a proposal which was to be of great significance for the subsequent history of the Peace Conference. He suggested a list of questions "to be discussed by the present Conference in the order given."[41] First on this list stood the "League of Nations," and the last item was "Colonies." In other words President Wilson wanted the Conference first to draw up and accept the Covenant for the League of Nations as the foundation for the new world order. The particular problems and special claims of the several nations could then be considered in relation to the Covenant. This program was bound to bring President Wilson into sharp conflict with those who were primarily interested in territorial adjustments, distribution of the former German colonies, and reparations. No action was taken on President Wilson's proposal at this meeting, but the order in which the various questions were to be considered was taken up at the meeting of the Council of Ten on January 23. At this meeting, in discussing the arrangement of the agenda, Lloyd George proposed bringing up Oriental and Colonial questions first.

Mr. Lloyd George said . . . . European conditions were so complicated that it would take a long time for such peoples as the Czecho-Slovaks and Poles to set forth a reasoned case. On the other hand Oriental and Colonial questions were less involved and to economize time he suggested that these matters be tackled at once. . . . .

President Wilson observed that the world's unrest arose from the unsettled condition of Europe, not from the state of affairs in the East or in the Colonies, and that the postponement of these questions would only increase the pressure on the Delegates of the Peace Conference. He would, therefore,

[39] B.C., 1 plus, January 13, 1919.

[40] *Ibid.* The Dominions were given separate representation on the Supreme Council only in the sense that the Dominion premiers were allowed to take the places of an equivalent number of representatives of Great Britain whenever a question concerning them was under discussion.

[41] B.C., 1 plus, January 13, 1919.

prefer to set in process immediately all that was required to hasten a solution of European questions. . . . .[42]

It was finally decided that "the Secretary General should ask all Delegations representing Powers with territorial claims to send to the Secretariat their written statement within ten days."[43]

The result of this decision had an important bearing on the success of President Wilson's program. It brought the disposal of the former German colonies immediately to the fore, and it placed the question of territorial settlements ahead of the League of Nations Covenant rather than after it, as Wilson desired.

It did not take the Dominion premiers long to respond to the general invitation to present territorial claims. At the meeting of the Council on January 24, the very next day, the Dominion premiers presented their claims for complete annexation of the former German islands in the Pacific south of the Equator and to German West Africa.[44] These claims, in effect, were the first direct challenge to the Wilson program for the creation of a new world order. Mr. Hughes of Australia demanded the direct annexation of German New Guinea and the adjacent islands under no form of mandate; Mr. Massey of New Zealand made the same claim for the annexation of German Samoa; and Mr. Smuts asked that German West Africa be granted to British South Africa.[45]

If President Wilson fully acceded to these claims, it would mean the immediate abandonment of the mandate principle which he believed should be a vital part of the League. Lloyd George was between two fires. He wanted to support Wilson, and yet he had to please the Dominions. Clemenceau was committed to the French claim to Togoland and Cameroon. Therefore, President Wilson, with some support from Mr. Balfour, had to bear alone the brunt of this first attack upon his Fourteen Points.

After it had been generally agreed that none of the former German colonies should be returned to Germany, Mr. Lloyd George explained, rather than advocated, the application of the mandate principle. He concluded by saying that as far as Great Britain was concerned he saw no objection to the mandatory principle in so far as it was applied to those territories captured by troops from the United Kingdom.[46] This, of course, would not include the Pacific

---

[42] B.C., 8, January 23, 1919, 10 : 30 A.M.   [43] *Ibid.*

[44] B.C., 10, January 24, 1919, 3 : 00 P.M.   [45] *Ibid.*   [46] *Ibid.*

islands claimed by the Dominions, as these were captured by Australian and New Zealand troops.

The next meeting of the Council of Ten occurred on January 27, at which time the claims made by the Dominion premiers on January 23 were discussed. At this meeting, President Wilson was directly responsible for raising the question of the claims of Japan to the former German islands in the Pacific north of the equator. This in turn raised the question of the disposal of the former German leasehold of Kiaochow and the German rights in Shantung. President Wilson referred to the claims presented by Premiers Hughes and Massey for outright annexation of German New Guinea and German Samoa.

President Wilson . . . . asked whether it was wise to deal with the Pacific piecemeal. He asked whether the Japanese case should not be heard before any partial decision was taken. If ready, he suggested that it should be heard first.

M. Clemenceau agreed.[47]

A discussion followed as to whether the Dominion representatives should be present to hear Japan. This discussion led to the question of whether or not the Chinese delegates should be invited to be present and whether Kiaochow should be included with the Pacific islands.

Mr. Lloyd George was of the opinion that the Chinese as well as Australian and New Zealand Delegates should be present at the Japanese statement.

Mr. Balfour thought that if his Japanese colleagues would agree, the case of the Japanese acquisitions in this war would fall into two categories—first, the Pacific islands, second those parts of China conquered from the Germans. In the first Australia and New Zealand were concerned. In the latter they were not at all concerned. He hoped, therefore, that the two cases would be dealt with separately.

Baron Makino said that he had no objection to the presence of the Dominion representatives, but he had prepared a statement including both Kiaochow and the Pacific islands, as the capture of both had been the result of one campaign. He would therefore not be able in his statement to follow the distinction laid down by Mr. Balfour . . . .

Mr. Balfour thought that great difficulties would be encountered if the discussion on China and the Pacific Islands was treated as one.

President Wilson suggested that even if the case for both were presented at one time and in one document the discussion might afterwards be held separately on each question.

Baron Makino asked whether the question would be discussed at once

[47] B.C., 11, January 27, 1919, 10:30 A.M.

after his presentation of the Japanese case, or whether all statements of Colonial claims would be awaited. . . . .

President Wilson then suggested that the question of the Pacific should first be taken up and a decision reached as to whether the mandatory principle should, or should not, apply in that area . . . . He, therefore, proposed that the Japanese case should be heard in the presence of the Chinese delegates and that after the statement, that part of the case concerning the Pacific should be discussed in the presence of the Dominion delegates. At a later meeting the other portion might be taken up in the presence of the Chinese delegates. . . . . Baron Makino said that he had another point to make. The presentation of the Japanese case concerning Kiaochow would be made with reference to Germany only. Japanese relations with China on these questions were on a different footing. The claim he would put forward was addressed to Germany alone, not to China. He did not wish to discuss in the presence of the Chinese delegates Japanese relations with Germany.

President Wilson said that he did not understand Baron Makino to contend that the disposition of Kiaochow did not affect China.

Baron Makino said that he was not very well versed in the procedure of the Conference. He asked whether he was to conclude that third Powers interested were to join in the discussion.

It was pointed out by the Chairman that this had been so decided in the regulations. It was therefore decided that the Japanese statement should be heard both by the Chinese and the Dominion delegates and that in the discussion to follow, the Dominion delegates should participate with regard to the Pacific Islands, and the Chinese delegates with regard to Kiaochow.[48]

President Wilson was thus the cause of precipitating the Shantung question before the Conference very early in its proceedings. It would seem from the record quoted, however, that at first he had in mind only the Japanese claims to the Pacific islands north of the Equator and not their claim to Kiaochow. Baron Makino succeeded, over Mr. Balfour's attempt to separate the two questions, in getting them presented together. President Wilson's suggestion that they be presented together and then discussed separately was the procedure that was followed.

These first remarks by Baron Makino revealed the basis of Japan's program relative to the settlement of the Shantung question. The contention of the Japanese government was that its claim to the former German leasehold was one which concerned Japan and Germany only. After Germany had transferred the leasehold to Japan, it would then be re-transferred to China in accordance with the provisions of the Shantung Treaty of May 25, 1915. According to the Japanese contention, China was a third power as far as the settlement between Japan and Germany was concerned and had no

[48] *Ibid.*

right to interfere or interpose herself in the transaction. In this preliminary discussion, however, President Wilson successfully asserted the right of the Chinese to be heard and to present their case. On the afternoon of the same day, January 27, the Japanese were given the opportunity to present their claims to the Pacific islands and to the leased territory of Kiaochow and other German rights in Shantung. It is obvious, however, from the record of Baron Makino's speech that it was the Shantung claim that was really being advanced. The claim to the Pacific islands was, to use a slang phrase, already "in the bag." Mr. Clemenceau having declared the meeting open, Baron Makino read the following statement of Japan's claims:

The Japanese Government feels justified in claiming from the German Government the unconditional cession of:

(a) The leased territory of Kiaochow, together with the railways and other rights possessed by Germany in respect of Shantung province.

(b) All of the Islands in German possession in the Pacific Ocean north of the Equator with the rights and properties in connection therewith.

Baron Makino then went on to state the circumstances which had obliged Japan to take the leased territory of Kiaochow and to occupy the Tsingtao-Tsinan Railway.

. . . . The Japanese Government, in consultation with the British Government, conformably with the agreement of 1911, gave notice to the German Government to surrender the leased territory of Kiaochow with a view to its restoration to China . . . . By the reduction of the German stronghold, the base of her military as well as political offensive in the Extreme Orient has been completely destroyed . . . . Now that the primary object for which Japan entered the war . . . . has been successfully achieved, Japan cannot view with equanimity anything that may tend to revive German activities in the Far East to the undoing of all that has been achieved at no small sacrifice, and is compelled to advance the claims under item A.

He concluded his statement by saying:

In conclusion, it may be stated that, in view of the extent of their efforts and achievements in destroying German base in the Extreme Orient and in the South Seas, and in safeguarding the important routes in the Pacific and Indian Oceans and in the Mediterranean waters, to say nothing of their contribution in other respects, the Japanese Government feels confident that the claims above advanced would be regarded as only just and fair.[49]

Upon Baron Makino concluding the reading of his statement, Mr. C. T. Wang, of the Chinese Delegation, asked that "the Great Powers would reserve decision until the views of the Chinese had been heard." This was agreed to.

[49] B.C., 12, January 27, 3 : 00 P.M.

The remainder of the meeting was devoted to a discussion of the mandatory principle. President Wilson defended the application of the mandatory principle to the former German colonies in the Pacific. It became evident as the discussion proceeded that the Dominion premiers were inclined to push their claims for outright annexation despite the eloquence of President Wilson. Lloyd George, in an attempt to find a middle ground, proposed that the meeting adjourn to examine this "new principle before its application in particular cases came under consideration."[50]

The discussion of the mandatory principle was renewed the next morning, January 28. Lloyd George, while willing to agree to the application of the principle "to territories conquered by troops from the United Kingdom . . . . did not think that a special exception in favor of the Dominions would spoil the whole case . . . ."[51]

During the discussion the important question arose as to whether or not the secret treaties concluded during the war should be brought before the Conference and should be taken into consideration in making territorial adjustments. This question came up in the following manner:

M. Clemenceau pointed out that there were certain Franco-British conventions relating to the German colonies; for instance Togoland. He asked whether these conventions should be produced before the Council.

Mr. Lloyd George was of the opinion that any arrangements made during the war should be placed before the meeting.

Mr. Clemenceau undertook to produce them, and asked whether the Japanese delegates would do likewise.

Baron Makino said that he had no objection to doing so, and would send all such agreements to the Chairman. He would point out, however, that the Japanese conventions were in the form of an exchange of ideas rather than formal conventions.

Mr. Balfour asked whether Baron Makino alluded to the agreement reached in 1917.

Baron Makino assented.

M. Orlando said that Italy also had a convention with France and Great Britain concerning German colonies.

M. Pichon asked if M. Orlando referred to the Pact of London.

M. Orlando replied in the affirmative.

President Wilson asked that if the drafts were submitted to the Council, no sense of finality should be attached to them.

Mr. Lloyd George entirely agreed. He was much influenced by what the President had said on former occasions, and quite agreed that any proposal submitted should be provisional.[52]

[50] *Ibid.*   [51] B.C., 13, January 28, 1919, 11 : 00 A.M.   [52] *Ibid.*

Thus it was by the action of M. Clemenceau that the Secret Agreements of 1917 between Japan and her Allies were officially brought before the Conference as a factor to be considered with regard to granting the Japanese claims.[53] The Japanese case had been advanced, so far, without the necessity of direct action upon the part of the Japanese representatives. M. Clemenceau brought up the Secret Agreements of 1917 presumably in order to justify and lend support to the Franco-British secret convention with regard to the French claims to the former German colonies of Cameroon and Togoland in Africa.

This discussion was followed by further discussion of the claims of Australia and New Zealand for outright annexation of the former German colonies. Mr. Massey prefaced his restatement of New Zealand's claim to German Samoa by rather ominously referring to the failure of the Congress of Vienna to create a League of Nations. "He hoped that this Congress would not end in the same way, but it was well to remember that history repeated itself."

With this not altogether pleasant prelude, the Chinese delegate, Mr. Wellington Koo, was asked to present China's claim in regard to Kiaochow and Shantung.

> Mr. Koo said that . . . . the Chinese Delegation would ask the Peace Conference for the restoration to China of the leased territory of Kiaochow, the railway in Shantung, and all other rights Germany possessed in that province before the war . . . . The territories . . . . were an integral part of China. They were part of a province containing 36 million inhabitants, of Chinese in race, language and religion . . . . [The lease to Germany] had been extorted by force . . . . On the principles of nationality and of territorial integrity . . . . China had a right to the restoration of these territories. The Chinese delegation would feel that this was one of the conditions of a just peace. If, on the other hand, the Congress were to take a different view and were to transfer these territories to any other Power, it would, in the eyes of the Chinese Delegation, be adding one wrong to another. The Shantung Province . . . . was the cradle of Chinese civilization, the birthplace of Confucius and Mencius, and a Holy Land for the Chinese . . . . The density of the population . . . . rendered it quite unsuitable for colonization. The introduction of a Foreign Power could only lead to the exploitation of the inhabitants, not to genuine colonization. Strategically, Kiaochow commanded one of the main gateways of North China . . . . China was fully cognisant of the services rendered to her by the heroic Army and Navy of Japan in rooting out German power from Shantung. China was also deeply indebted to Great Britain for helping in this task . . . . China also

[53] See *supra*, pp. 95–97, for a discussion of the circumstances under which these treaties were concluded.

was not forgetful of the services rendered her by the troops of the other Allies in Europe which had held in check an enemy who might otherwise have easily sent reinforcements to the Far East . . . . But, grateful as they were, the Chinese Delegation felt that they would be false to their duty to China and to the world if they did not object to paying their debts of gratitude by selling the birthright of their countrymen, and thereby sowing the seeds of discord for the future. The Chinese Delegation therefore trusted that the Conference, in considering the disposal of the leased territory and other rights held by Germany in Shantung, would give full weight to the fundamental and transcendental rights of China, the rights of political sovereignty and territorial integrity.[54]

The Chinese plea was based upon two considerations. The first one was that in justice to China and, by implication at least, in conformity with the Fourteen Points, the leased territory of Kiaochow and the former German rights in China should be restored directly to China. The second consideration was the appeal to the Great Powers based on the fact that they had all at one time or another pledged themselves to preserve Chinese sovereignty and territorial integrity.

Upon Mr. Koo's finishing his statement, Baron Makino arose and read the Japanese ultimatum to Germany of August 15, 1914. The record of his remarks and those which followed continues:

Since the occupation of Kiaochow, Japan has been in actual possession. In view of all that had passed between the Governments of China and Japan, Baron Makino thought that China fully realized the importance of Japanese occupation. The friendly interchange of views on this subject had been entered into, and Japan had agreed to restore Kiaochow as soon as Japan had free disposal of the place. Agreements had also been reached with regard to the leased railway.

As notes had been exchanged, he thought that a statement of these engagements might be worth a consideration of the members of the Council.

President Wilson asked Baron Makino whether he proposed to lay these notes before the Council.

Baron Makino said that he did not think the Japanese Government would raise any objections, but as the request was an unexpected one he would be compelled to ask its permission.

President Wilson asked on behalf of China if Mr. Koo would do likewise.

Mr. Koo said that the Chinese Government has no objection to raise.

Mr. Clemenceau asked both the Japanese and Chinese Delegates to state whether they would make known to the Council the conditions of the restoration agreed between them.

Baron Makino said that he would do so provided his Government would make no objection. He did not think it would. If it were within his power,

---

[54] B.C., 13, January 28, 1919, 11 : 00 A.M.

he would produce these documents as soon as possible. There was, however, one point he wished to make clear. Japan was in actual possession of the territory under consideration. It had taken it by conquest from Germany. Before disposing of it to a third party it was necessary that Japan should obtain the right of free disposal from Germany.

President Wilson pointed out that the Council was dealing with territories and cessions previously German without consulting Germany at all.

Baron Makino said that the work now in hand was one of preparation for the presentment of the case to Germany. It followed therefore that the cession of Kiaochow would have to be agreed upon by Germany before it was carried out. What should take place thereafter had already been the subject of an interchange of views with China.

Mr. Koo said that the Chinese Delegation did not adopt quite the same view as Baron Makino. He was well aware that Japan after her undertaking in 1914—which he was glad to note had just been renewed by Baron Makino—would not retain the territory.

But there was a choice between direct and indirect restitution. Of the two China would prefer the first . . . . They had always considered all the Conventions made with Japan as provisional and subject to revision by the Peace Conference. Before becoming a belligerent China had agreed to accept all the conditions made to Germany by Japan.

China's entry into the war, however, had completely altered her status. None of the previous arrangements precluded China either from declaring war on Germany, or from being represented at the Peace Conference. Nor could they preclude her now from demanding from Germany direct restitution of her rights. China's belligerency had itself put an end to the leases obtained by Germany in Chinese territory. Furthermore, there was a clause in the lease to the effect that Germany could not transfer her rights to another power.[55]

The foregoing interchange between Baron Makino and Mr. Koo well defined the Japanese and Chinese positions.

It was clear that Japan was going to hold China to the 1915 and 1918 agreements. The Japanese argument implied—although Baron Makino did not state it in so many words—that Japan's promise to return Kiaochow was contingent upon China's acceptance of the procedure outlined in the Shantung Treaty of 1915.[56]

The Chinese claim, on the other hand, was based on the assumption that China's entrance into the war abrogated these 1915 agreements and gave China the right to demand directly from Germany the restitution of the German rights in Shantung. In other words, China claimed that her declaration of war gave her the right to ask

[55] B.C., 13, January 28, 1919, 11 : 00 A.M.

[56] This was definitely required in Article I of the Sino-Japanese Treaty of May 25, 1915, relating to Shantung.

the Peace Conference (actually the United States, Great Britain, France, and Italy, the latter three pledged to support Japan's claims) to restore directly to her all rights possessed by Germany in Shantung, that the Powers in order to do this should disregard the agreements that China had made with Japan before and after her entrance into the war, and furthermore that the latter three Powers should disregard the pledge each had given in the Secret Agreements of 1917 to support Japan's claims.

According to the rules of the so-called "old diplomacy," the Chinese claim stood no chance against the strong position of Japan, both in the fact of Japan having wrested the German rights in China from Germany by an act of war and in the fact that China agreed by treaty and agreement to accept the procedure proposed by Japan. But the "old diplomacy" was supposedly gone forever. President Wilson's Fourteen Points were to be the constitution of the new world order. World opinion was demanding that the settlements of the Peace Conference be in harmony with this new world order. However, the foregoing recital of the conversations and discussions that were taking place among those chosen few who had been elected to decide the problems of the peace and to bring the new world order into being showed that it was the realities of the "old diplomacy" which were being applied to these settlements rather than President Wilson's Fourteen Points.

With the closing statement by Mr. Koo, at the meeting of January 28, the Shantung question faded into the background of the discussion at Paris until it dramatically reappeared at almost the very end of the work of drawing up the peace terms to be presented to Germany. It reappeared in the Council of Four on April 22, there to occupy a goodly part of the time of that esoteric body until its final settlement on April 30. It seems quite evident that as long as Japan was going to insist upon the settlement of the question along the lines Baron Makino had outlined on January 27 and 28 Lloyd George and Clemenceau were prepared to hold to the pledges of Great Britain and France given in 1917 and to support the Japanese claims. President Wilson was the sole hope of the Chinese, and the influence he could exert in their favor remained, as yet, unpredictable.

Lloyd George, regardless of his personal convictions, was under too much pressure to resist the demands of the Dominions for representation, and with the admittance to the Council of the Dominion premiers Wilson's ideal of trusteeship for the former German colonies under a system of mandates received a brusque challenge. Such men as Hughes and Massey knew what they wanted and were not going to be put off by one who, no matter with what awe the world regarded him, was probably to their way of thinking no more than a particularly fortunate politician whom the accident of time and circumstance had placed where he was.

The apparently impregnable position of Wilson was rapidly being weakened by the resistance that was being offered to his cherished mandatory principle, and this resistance in turn also revealed the serious divergence between the French conception and his conception of a League of Nations.[57]

It began to look as if the Japanese delegates had merely to sit quietly by while Hughes and Massey and Clemenceau established by inference the Japanese case for them.

The Chinese delegates approached the Conference with great hopes. To them it must have seemed, as it surely did to most of the world, that President Wilson by the sheer power of his position was about to fashion a new world out of the fragments of the old—a world based upon justice, upon self-determination, and upon protection of the weak by the strong. All these phrases the Chinese interpreted to mean the direct restitution of Kiaochow together with the other German rights in Shantung.

Meanwhile, as the Conference progressed the Japanese enjoyed the considerable advantage of being able to follow the trend of events from inside the Conference room, whereas the Chinese delegates had to depend upon the fragmentary information that drifted from the Council chamber and upon the advice of their friends in the American and British delegations.

The mandates question was settled at the meeting of the Council of Ten, January 30, in the compromise form in which it finally appeared in the Covenant.[58] Mr. Lloyd George said that "the decision had not been wholly accepted by the Dominions. The Dominions, however, were prepared to accept the conclusions reached in the docu-

[57] E.g., the remarks of M. Clemenceau at the meeting of the Council of Ten on January 28: "The League of Nations, he [Clemenceau] thought, was to be a League of Defence. But it appeared they had now gone beyond that limit when they proposed to create a League of Nations with governmental functions to interfere in internal affairs, with trustees in various places sending reports to—he did not know whom" (B.C., 14, January 28, 4:00 P.M.).

[58] That is, the classification of the mandates into A., B., and C. mandates, the latter class embracing the former German islands in the Pacific.

ment as a compromise . . . . But three classes of mandates would have to be recognized . . . ."[59]

David Hunter Miller reports a conversation which President Wilson had with him immediately after the meeting at which the compromise on the mandates was reached. It reveals Wilson's deep distrust of the Japanese, and it also reveals that he had other than purely idealistic motives for advocating the application of the mandate principle to the former German islands in the Pacific.

He [President Wilson] then spoke of the limitation in the resolution to the islands in the South Pacific and asked me to consider this question in respect of the islands in the North Pacific which Japan held. He said that these islands lie athwart the path from Hawaii to the Philippines and that they were nearer to Hawaii than the Pacific coast was, and that they could be fortified and made naval bases by Japan; that indeed they were of little use for anything else and that we had no naval base except Guam.

The President said that he did not trust the Japanese; that he had trusted them before,—in fact they had broken their agreement about Siberia. We had sent 7,000 troops to Siberia and they promised to send about the same number but had sent 70,000 and had occupied all the strategic points as far as Irkutsk, and that he would not trust them again.[60]

With the meeting of January 30, the first phase of the Shantung question comes to an end.

[59] B.C., 17, January 30, 1919.

[60] Miller, *Diary*, Vol. I, p. 100. Wilson refers here to the wording of the resolution when it did not specifically mention the islands north of the Equator. The wording was subsequently changed between February 11 and February 13 from "certain islands in the South Pacific" to "the South Pacific islands," and it appears thus in the final Covenant. At whose suggestion this change was made is not clear from the documents available (Miller, *Diary*, Vol. V, Doc. 396, p. 279).

The documents are now available to indicate whether or not Japan made any such promise as President Wilson's remark indicated to limit the size of her expeditionary forces sent to Siberia. From the correspondence published in the United States' *Foreign Relations* relative to this question, it appears that the Japanese government consistently refrained from committing itself to any limitation on the number of troops it would send to Siberia. In its memorandum of August 2, 1918, to the American government it spoke of having decided to "dispatch suitable forces for the proposed mission" (*Foreign Relations, 1918, Russia,* Vol. II, p. 324). On the following day Viscount Ishii, the Japanese Ambassador in Washington, specifically informed Mr. Polk, the Acting Secretary of State, that the Japanese government, in view of the necessity for immediate action, accepted the proposals of the American government but it reserved the right to dispatch additional troops to Vladivostok or elsewhere if circumstances made it necessary (*ibid.*, p. 325). The situation of the Czechs in Siberia became almost immediately critical, as did the situation on the North Manchuria border, as a result of the defeat of Ataman Semenov by the Red forces. The Japanese government, therefore, began to enlarge the forces it already had in Siberia and Manchuria.

CHAPTER VIII

CHINA AND THE PARIS PEACE CONFERENCE
THE SHANTUNG QUESTION: SECOND PHASE

During the three months which elapsed between the presentation of the Chinese and Japanese claims to the Council of Ten and the final settlement of the Shantung question at the end of April the Chinese Delegation at Paris seemed to grow increasingly confident of the successful outcome of its case. The older and more conservative members of the Delegation, Mr. Lu Chêng-hsiang and Mr. Sze, fell more and more into the background.[1] In consequence, the management of the Chinese program fell almost exclusively into the hands of Wellington Koo and C. T. Wang. Their long stay in America and their American education made them very congenial with certain members of the American Mission. David Hunter Miller's *Diary* contains enough information to show that there was a close liaison between some of the American advisers and the two younger Chinese delegates and that on more than one occasion Koo and Wang were advised by them as to the course to adopt.[2] None of the members of the American Mission seem ever to have made a move to persuade or warn the Chinese Delegation to modify its claims, although it must have been evident as the months passed that the Chinese program had little chance of success. On the contrary, as the Conference proceeded, the Chinese program was expanded and made even more intransigent toward Japan.

In January and February the Chinese Delegation limited its claims to the direct restitution of Kiaochow and the former German rights in Shantung. Early in April, the Chinese Delegation circulated a pamphlet in which it asked the "Abrogation by the Peace Conference of the Treaties and Notes made and exchanged by and between China

---

[1] Mr. C. C. Wu, a prominent member of the Canton government, was added to the Delegation but seems not to have taken an active part in the deliberations of the Conference.

[2] See, e.g., Miller, *Diary*, Vol. I, pp. 88, 151, 159, 160–61; Vol. V, p. 484; and Vol. VII, pp. 145–46.

and Japan on May 25, 1915, as a transaction arising out of and connected with the war . . . ."[3]

This latter claim presented a far more defiant attitude toward Japan than did the former claim of direct restitution. It challenged the entire position of Japan in Manchuria. It offered no opportunity for compromise, and it placed the Great Powers, if they had wished to grant the Chinese claims, in the awkward predicament of having to repeat the situation of 1895 and again humiliate Japan by attempting to force her to declare her treaties with China null and void.

The explanation of the increasing intransigence of the Chinese Delegation is to be found partly in the tremendous enthusiasm with which the Chinese people received the reports of Wellington Koo's open defiance of Japan at the meeting of the Council of Ten on January 28. His apparent success in this first encounter with the Japanese representatives and the sympathy with which the American press reported this event created an ardent belief among the Chinese that the Peace Conference would grant the Chinese claims.[4] Early in February, the Peking correspondent of the *North China Herald*, reporting on the optimism prevailing in Peking despite the financial difficulties of the government, said:

Probably Peking also reflects the hopes based upon the Peace Conference in Europe. About the middle of the week [ending January 31] Government circles were very much depressed, fearing that the Chinese representatives would be overcome by the weight of the Japanese Delegation ranking with the Big Five. Later telegrams reporting that Dr. Wellington Koo and Mr. C. T. Wang had crossed swords successfully with the Japanese delegates inspired the Chinese with greater confidence because it showed that China was receiving a hearing from the Powers independently of Japanese tuition or influence. Moreover, it demonstrated a united China which was, perhaps, more apparent than real. The entire effect was distinctly good. Again, the statement that this is the Year One in the matter of all treaties is very encouraging to Chinese, who naturally hope that the many secret conventions which have been entered into between Japan and China will henceforth become null and void.[5]

At the same time that the news of Wellington Koo's success at Paris raised the hopes of the Chinese to great heights, an incident

[3] Miller, *Diary*, Vol. VI, p. 213, Doc. 450. Abrogation of the Manchurian Treaty and Agreements of 1915 were asked, as well as those relating to Shantung.

[4] See the report of Minister Reinsch, for the quarter ending June 30, 1919, for confirmation of the general confidence held by the Chinese that the Peace Conference would grant China's claims. *Foreign Relations, 1919*, Vol. I, p. 364.

[5] *North China Herald*, February 8, 1919.

occurred in Peking which greatly increased the existing hostility of Chinese public opinion toward Japan and made it all the more insistent that Japan be defied at Paris.

As a result of the presentation of the Japanese and Chinese claims before the Council of Ten on January 27 and January 28, Mr. Obata, the Japanese Minister at Peking, called on Mr. Chen Lu, Acting Minister for Foreign Affairs, on January 31, to discuss the speech made by Wellington Koo at that time. The accounts of the interview as given by Mr. Chen and Mr. Obata differed considerably. Mr. Chen claimed that Mr. Obata, referring to the attitude taken by the Chinese delegates at Paris at the meeting of January 28, demanded that the Chinese government promise not to reveal the secret Sino-Japanese Treaties of 1918 without the permission of the Japanese government and that the Chinese government should telegraph immediate instructions to the Chinese Delegation to modify its attitude toward the Japanese claims. Mr. Obata promptly denied this version of the interview, and in a public statement to the press said that he had merely called to the attention of Mr. Chen that, in accordance with international law, the revelation of secret treaties was usually done with the consent of both parties.[6]

Regardless of what actually took place at this interview, the incident was reported in the Chinese press in such a manner as to arouse Chinese public opinion to the belief that Japan was attempting to bring pressure upon the Chinese government to make Koo and Wang adopt a more conciliatory attitude. The result was that sentiment was inflamed against Japan to a degree that the military chiefs, who still dominated the Peking government, dared not instruct the Chinese Delegation to modify its program. The Chinese press clamored for the publication of all secret Sino-Japanese treaties entered into during the war, and the publication of these secret agreements one by one over the months of March and April served to keep Chinese public opinion greatly wrought up against Japan.

Meanwhile, at Paris, the task of completing the treaty to be presented to Germany was being accomplished without anything further being done about the Shantung question. It began to look as if the Germans would be called to Paris without the Japanese having attained either of the two major points in their program, namely, their Shantung demands and their desire to see some sort of definite ex-

[6] For Mr. Obata's and Mr. Chen Lu's statements, see *North China Herald*, February 8, and February 15, 1919.

pression of the equality of races incorporated in the Covenant of the League of Nations.

The Japanese first presented the latter proposal on February 7, at a meeting of the League of Nations Commission.[7] The text of their proposal was:

> The equality of nations being a basic principle of the League of Nations, the High Contracting Parties agree to accord, as soon as possible, to all alien nationals of States members of the League equal and just treatment in every respect, making no distinction, either in law or in fact, on account of their race or nationality.[8]

The difficulties which such an article might raise with regard to the legislation of certain American states directed against land-ownership by Orientals or upon the "White Australia" policy of Australia raised doubts in certain quarters as to the wisdom of including it in the Covenant. These doubts were expressed by Lord Cecil on February 13, when the Japanese proposal was formally presented to the Commission. In support of it, Baron Makino made a splendid speech couched in language which made it difficult to refuse the Japanese amendment without at the same time seeming not to accept the fundamental ideals upon which the League was to be based. He stressed the obligations which would fall upon the citizens of all nations regardless of race, color, or creed to defend any member of the League against aggression. "Seeing these new duties arising before him as a result of his country's entering the League, each national would like to feel and in fact demand that he should be placed on equal footing with the people he undertakes to defend even with his life."[9]

Lord Cecil's reply left no doubt that the British were opposed to the proposal and that if it were raised again in the future they would resist its inclusion in the Covenant. Among other things he said:

> This matter has been the subject of long and difficult discussions throughout the world and in the British Empire. It is a question which deserves profound and serious consideration. But since it is essentially a controversial matter, I believe that it would be wiser not to go into an examination of it at this juncture.[10]

---

[7] David Hunter Miller, *Drafting of the Covenant*. The minutes [English and French] of the League of Nations Commission are given in these two volumes. Hereafter cited as Miller, *Covenant*.

[8] Miller, *Covenant*, Vol. I, p. 183.

[9] *Ibid.*, Vol. II, p. 325.

[10] *Ibid.*, Vol. I, p. 268.

The Japanese representatives accepted for the time being Lord Cecil's views, but they reserved the right to bring up the racial equality proposal at some time in the future. The Japanese did not exercise this right until April 11, at the final meeting of the League of Nations Commission when it completed its task of drafting the Covenant. Their proposal was brought forward immediately following the closing discussion upon the American Monroe Doctrine reservation to the sanctions of Article X. The discussion upon the American reservation, which had been presented on the previous day by President Wilson, had been long and at moments exceedingly bitter.[11] The French members of the Commission had shown marked reluctance to accept a reservation to Article X which they felt sure would weaken the ability of the United States to come to the support of the League in any European difficulty. They particularly had in mind the possible violation of the Covenant by Germany. The Brazilian delegate expressed doubt as to the wisdom of including a reservation of the Monroe Doctrine without stating exactly what the Doctrine was. The British would have preferred not to see the Monroe Doctrine expressly mentioned but would have liked to see the American reservation broadened to include all generally accepted international agreements. Wellington Koo objected to the British proposal because he feared that such an all-inclusive statement would include the Anglo-Japanese Alliance and therefore would prevent China at some future time from calling into question such occurrences as the Japanese claim to the former German leasehold of Kiaochow, whose capture had been undertaken by Japan under the terms of the Anglo-Japanese Alliance. Despite the fact that these objections indicated that the Commission was by no means unanimous in its support of the Monroe Doctrine reservation, it was finally incorporated in the draft of the Covenant. It was in this atmosphere of dissatisfaction over the American reservation that Baron Makino and Viscount Chinda again brought forward their proposal to place a statement in the Covenant definitely confirming the League's acceptance of the principle of racial equality.

The racial equality proposal was introduced by Baron Makino and Viscount Chinda toward the very end of the last meeting of the League of Nations Commission. It was the final item which was considered by the Commission before the draft Covenant was presented to the Conference as a whole. Warned somewhat by the oppo-

[11] See Miller, *Covenant*, Vol. I, pp. 442–49, 457–60.

sition of Lord Cecil at the February meeting, the Japanese had carefully modified their proposal so that they now merely asked that one of the general statements in the Preamble to the Covenant, which set forth the principles upon which the Covenant was based, be amended so as to include the phrase, "by the endorsement of the principle of equality of nations and just treatment of their nationals."[12]

David Hunter Miller reports upon the discussion of the proposal as follows:

The presentation of this proposal by the Japanese delegates was very admirably done. Baron Makino read a carefully prepared statement . . . . Viscount Chinda also spoke. It seemed as if they were supported by the feelings of almost everyone present. Lord Robert Cecil refused to accept the amendment and stood on his refusal . . . . Orlando, Bourgeois, Larnaude, Veniselos, Kramár and Koo all spoke in favor. Indeed the form of the proposal was such that to formulate any objection to its language was not an easy task . . . . but however unobjectionable the words might be their very vagueness could only mean that they were a sort of curtain behind which was the question of White Australia and of immigration of Eastern peoples into countries which regarded the possibility of such immigration as impossible to discuss.[13]

At the conclusion of Baron Makino's speech, Lord Cecil pointedly remarked that

. . . . either the points which the Japanese Delegation proposed to add to the Preamble were vague and ineffective, or else they were of practical significance. In the latter case they opened the door to serious controversy and to interference in the domestic affairs of States members of the League.[14]

President Wilson spoke on the proposal, not directly against it but rather suggesting the inadvisability of putting the amendment into the Covenant. Among other things, he said:

The trouble is not that anyone of us wishes to deny the equality of nations or wishes to deny the principle of just treatment of nationals of any nation. The trouble is not with our decision here, but with the discussion which would certainly be raised in the Plenary Council if the words suggested were introduced into this Covenant . . . . It is in my own mind for the purpose of quieting these prejudices, of letting them play no part in the discussion connected with the establishment of this League, that I am looking at this whole matter . . . .[15]

Finally, upon the insistence of the Japanese representatives, an affirmative vote was taken upon the proposal, but it failed to secure the unanimous support of the members of the Commission, and

---

[12] *Ibid.*, p. 465.
[14] Miller, *Covenant*, Vol. II, p. 389.

[13] *Ibid.*, p. 461.
[15] *Ibid.*, Vol. I, p. 462.

therefore President Wilson, acting in his capacity as chairman, declared that the amendment was not adopted.[16]

President Wilson was subsequently criticized for ruling against the Japanese amendment, and at the time his ruling must have seemed arbitrary. This may have seemed all the more so because it followed the adoption of the Monroe Doctrine amendment over the expressed dissatisfaction of several members of the Commission. In view of the fact that President Wilson has been generally held responsible for the defeat of the Japanese proposal, a statement which appears in David Hunter Miller's *My Diary at the Conference of Paris* is particularly illuminating. Under date of April 17, he notes:

I went to Colonel House's office and saw a secret dispatch going to Ambassador Morris at Tokyo, from Washington, regarding the interview which Hughes gave to the Japanese press. Hughes' interview was to the effect that Australia was not responsible for the rejection of the Japanese amendment, whereas the dispatch stated that the Americans would have accepted it but the British flatly refused it. Unquestionably, it was Hughes' opposition that killed it.[17]

Regardless of just where the responsibility lay for the refusal of the Japanese amendment, the immediate consequence of defeat in this direction was to cause the Japanese Delegation to press for a settlement of the Shantung question in their favor before the Covenant was presented to the Conference and before the Germans were handed the Treaty. Whether or not the necessity of refusing the Japanese amendment inclined President Wilson to be more amenable to the Japanese views in regard to Shantung, when a few days later they came before the Council of Three, it is difficult to say. It was obvious, however, that the Japanese could not be defeated on both of their major issues without endangering their adherence to the Covenant. In fact, Viscount Chinda, in answering Lord Cecil's objection to the racial equality proposal, had uttered a scarcely veiled threat that Japan might reject the Covenant. He closed his rejoinder to Lord Cecil's objection by remarking:

Public opinion in Japan was very much concerned over the question and certain people had even gone so far as to say that Japan would not become a member of the League of Nations unless she were satisfied on this point.[18]

---

[16] Those voting in favor of the amendment were Japan, France, and Italy, with two votes each, and Brazil, China, Greece, Yugo-Slavia, and Czecho-Slovakia, with one vote each. This made the vote eleven out of the seventeen present, two members being absent. (Miller, *Covenant,* Vol. I, p. 464.)

[17] Miller, *Diary,* Vol. I, pp. 257–58.   [18] Miller, *Covenant,* Vol. II, p. 390.

Shortly after this incident, Viscount Chinda and Baron Makino took steps to have incorporated in the Treaty their draft articles providing that the German rights in Shantung be transferred to Japan. However, this did not take place until one more attempt was made to sidetrack a consideration of the Shantung question until after the Treaty was given to the Germans. This arose through a suggestion made by Mr. Lansing, the American Secretary of State, in the Council of Foreign Ministers (more popularly known as the Council of Five). He suggested that, in order to avoid delay in the preparation of the Treaty, which would be involved by an attempt to settle the claims of the Allies to the various German colonies, a "blanket clause" be included in the Treaty whereby Germany would be required to renounce all of her former colonies in favor of the Allied and Associated Powers who would act as trustees pending the final disposal of these territories. The suggestion of Mr. Lansing arose out of the discussion of two draft articles designed to recognize the new British position in Egypt created by the war and the similarly created new situation for the French in Morocco.[19]

Mr. Lansing expressed his inability to accept the draft articles relating to these two questions, for the reason that, in his opinion, a "blanket" clause should in the first place, be prepared to cover all German interests outside the actual territory of Germany in Europe. . . . .

M. Pichon thought . . . . in his opinion it was essential that the renunciation of Germany's claims and privileges should be made in favour of some one party or other. . . . . Mr. Lansing expressed the view that all questions relating to the renunciation of territorial rights and privileges and the abandonment of claims by Germany should be decided en bloc. In his opinion the question of Morocco could not be given special treatment. He enquired whether France and Great Britain would be prepared to discuss the Chinese question and other German territorial rights in China.

M. Pichon pointed out that the latter constituted a territorial question, whereas Morocco and Egypt dealt purely with a matter of status. . . . . Baron Makino said that if Mr. Lansing's proposal was adopted it would be necessary to make a reservation in the case of Kiauchau since that formed the subject of a special treaty and could not therefore be included in a general clause.[20]

The question was referred to the Drafting Committee, which was instructed to draw up a general renunciation clause and at the same time to make provisions for special clauses to cover the matters not to be included in the general clause.

[19] Minutes of the Council of Foreign Ministers, April 15, 1919 (hereafter cited by the abbreviation F.M. See *supra*, p. 190, n. 36.

[20] F.M. 4, April 15, 1919.

At the meeting of the Council of Foreign Ministers of April 17 the draft article embodying a general renunciation clause as drawn up by the Drafting Committee was before the meeting. Baron Makino spoke at some length opposing the inclusion of the German rights in Shantung in the proposed "blanket" renunciation clause.

Baron Makino observed that he must insist on the reservations made by the Japanese Delegation in respect to Shantung and Kiau Chau. He had on a previous occasion drawn attention to the fact that Japan claimed all rights acquired by Germany from China.

Mr. Lansing enquired whether these rights were claimed by Japan from China or from Germany.

Baron Makino replied that they were claimed from Germany.

Mr. Lansing said that in the event of special treatment being required for Shantung, he would ask the Japanese Delegation to propose a special clause. Once a precise text was before the meeting, it would be possible to debate upon the reservation made. At present he was not aware of its purport.

Baron Makino reminded the meeting that towards the end of January, he had presented the Japanese claims in a general statement. He had then declared that the claims would subsequently be presented in such a form as to be introduced into the treaty. He proposed, therefore, to bring forward a few articles embodying these claims. All he meant by recalling his reservations was to give notice that . . . . he was engaged in certain pourparlers which he thought might lead to an early settlement of the question.

Mr. Lansing then suggested that the General Renunciation clause be accepted, with the proviso that any Power wishing to put forward special cases should do so as early as possible.

Baron Makino agreed, with the reservation previously stated.[21]

The Japanese thus were successful in keeping the Shantung question on the basis which they originally had set forth on January 27, before the Council of Ten.[22]

[21] F.M. 5, April 17, 1919.

[22] It is not exactly clear just when Kiaochow was set aside as not coming under the provisions of the Mandate resolution of January 30. D. H. Miller in his comments on President Wilson's Second Paris Draft of the Covenant of January 10, 1919, reports advising the President as follows: ". . . . attention is called to the fact that one of the German colonies is Kiau-Chau, which, according to reports, Japan is willing to give up to China. The suggestion, therefore, is that an exception to the general language regarding the German colonies should be made as to Kiau-Chau" (Miller, *Drafting of the Covenant*, Vol. II, p. 87). These comments were in the hands of the President by January 20. Miller states further with regard to the scope of the Mandates Resolution that "Kiau-Chau, for example, was an entirely separate question" (*ibid.*, Vol. I, p. 103). At the meeting of the League of Nations Commission of February 8, it was decided that "Kiaochow is not deemed as one of the German Colonies" (Miller, *Diary*, Vol. V, p. 169).

The treatment of the Shantung question as a special question apart from any general territorial clause was a cardinal point in the Japanese program, for upon this point depended the success of maintaining their far more important contention that the arrangements to be made, as far as the Peace Treaty was concerned, were arrangements between Japan and Germany, and did not involve China. They did not want the Shantung question to be treated in any way which would cast reflections upon the validity of the 1915 and 1918 Sino-Japanese agreements. The Japanese were greatly helped in maintaining their position that the Shantung question was a special question requiring special treatment by the fact that the British and French were making the same claims for special treatment of the Egypt and Morocco clauses of the Treaty. Baron Makino's statement that he was engaged in pourparlers "which he thought might lead to an early settlement of the question" meant that he was engaged in negotiations which would bring the Shantung question directly before President Wilson, Lloyd George, and Clemenceau. The Japanese Delegation and the Japanese people were getting nervous. The Germans had already been called to Paris, and the Japanese had so far succeeded in getting none of their claims recognized.

A few days after the meeting described above, Viscount Chinda and Baron Makino called upon President Wilson in order to press for an early solution of the question. On the afternoon of the same day, April 12, President Wilson gave an account of this meeting to Clemenceau and Lloyd George. He described to them a number of modifications of the Japanese demands which he had proposed to Chinda and Makino, but he reported that Viscount Chinda and Baron Makino were firm in their refusal to agree to any modification of the Japanese claim for the transfer to Japan of the leased territory of Kiaochow.[23] The modifications which President Wilson had proposed were:

1. That the suggestion of Mr. Lansing that all claims in the Pacific should be ceded to the Allied and Associated Powers as trustees, leaving them to make a fair and just disposition of these territories, should be adopted.

2. That, although it had been understood that Japan was to have a mandate over the islands in the North Pacific, that he [Wilson]

---

[23] See Ray Stannard Baker, *Woodrow Wilson and World Settlement*, Vol. II, pp. 247–49, for an account of this meeting, based upon the minutes of the meeting.

made a reservation in the case of the island of Yap, which he considered should be international.

3. That all spheres of influence in China, including the Japanese, British, and French, should be abrogated.

On the next day, Baron Makino met with President Wilson, Clemenceau, and Lloyd George (Orlando had withdrawn from the Council of Four because of Wilson's stand on Fiume) and offered two draft articles embodying the Japanese claims in regard to Shantung. These draft articles, with only one slight change, became Articles 156 and 157 of the final Treaty.[24]

Baron Makino accompanied the presentation of the draft articles with a statement in which he reiterated the arguments supporting the Japanese claims. He reviewed the Sino-Japanese agreements of 1915 and 1918 pertaining to the former German rights in Shantung, and he summarized the exchange of notes between Japan and the Allies in 1917. He concluded by stating:

First. That Japan has undertaken to restore Kiaochow to China on conditions, none of which can be regarded in any sense as unjust or unfair, considering the part Japan took in dislodging Germany from Shantung.

Secondly. That the declaration of war by China against Germany could have no relation whatever to the validity of the treaty and the appended agreement which were concluded between Japan and China more than two years prior to the declaration of war, nor could it alter or affect in any wise the situation in connection with which the aforesaid treaty and agreement were made.

Thirdly. That the arrangements of September, 1918, which were made more than one year after China's declaration of war, could not have been entered into without presupposing the existence and validity of the Treaty of May, 1915. Some of the provisions of the former dealt with the subject-matters or furthered the claims, set forth in the latter. In fact, the arrangements of 1918 were intended to be, and are, a supplement and sequel to the treaty of 1915. It is to be noted that China has actually received the advance of 20 million yen according to the terms of the above arrangements.

To these summaries and deductions, I may add that as between Japan and China there is a well defined course laid out, for effecting the restitution. Any other course could [would?] be against the definite arrangements which have been agreed to between the two governments concerned. What Japan now seeks is to obtain from Germany the rights of free disposal of the leased territory and Germany's rights, privileges and concessions in relation to Shan-

---

[24] The following account of the discussions in the Council of Four is based on the annotation of H. C. Nixon (United States State Department) of the Minutes of the Council of Four in regard to the Shantung Articles of the Peace Treaty. Text in Miller, *Diary*, Vol. XIX, pp. 171–201.

tung for carrying out the provisions of the treaty of 1915 as well as the arrangements of 1918.

. . . . I feel firmly convinced that full justice will be done to the claims of Japan based upon her sacrifices and achievement and upon the fact of actual occupation, involving the sense of national honor.[25]

Baron Makino then handed around the following draft articles embodying the Japanese claims:

ARTICLE 156. Germany renounces in favour of Japan, all her rights, title and privileges—particularly those concerning the territory of Kiaochow, railways, mines and submarine cables—which she acquired in virtue of the Treaty concluded by her with China on March 6, 1898, and of all other arrangements relative to the Province of Shantung.

All German rights in the Tsingtao-Tsinanfu Railway, including its branch lines, together with its subsidiary property of all kinds, stations, shops, fixed and rolling stock, mines, plants and material for the exploitation of the mines are and remain acquired by Japan, together with all rights and privileges attaching thereto.

The German State submarine cables from Tsingtao to Shanghai and from Tsingtao to Chefoo, with all the rights, privileges and properties attaching thereto, are similarly acquired by Japan, [free and clear of all charges and encumbrances].[26]

ARTICLE 157. The movable and immovable property owned by the German State in the territory of Kiaochow, as well as all the rights which Germany might claim in consequence of the works or improvements made or of the expenses incurred by her, directly or indirectly, in connection with this territory, are and remain acquired by Japan, [free and clear of all charges and encumbrances].[27]

Discussion of these draft articles followed, relative parts of which are given:

President Wilson said he had already described as well as he could to M. Clemenceau and Mr. Lloyd George what had happened in his conversation with Baron Makino and Viscount Chinda.

Mr. Lloyd George said that so far as Great Britain was concerned they were in the same position towards Japan as towards Italy. They had a definite engagement with Japan, as recorded in the note of the British Ambassador at Tokio, dated February 16, 1917. . . . .

Viscount Chinda said the Japanese Government had a duty to perform to China in this matter, and they could not carry out their obligation to China unless Kiaochow was handed over to them. The Japanese delegates were

---

[25] Miller, *Diary,* Vol. XIX, pp. 178–79.

[26] Phrases in brackets were subsequently added.

[27] These draft articles became Articles 156 and 157 of the Treaty of Versailles. See the *Treaty of Peace with Germany,* Government Printing Office, Washington, D.C., 1920.

under an express instruction from their Government that unless they were placed in a position to carry out Japan's obligation to China, they were not allowed to sign the Treaty. They had no power to agree to postponement of this question.[28]

At this point President Wilson made a long statement setting forth his ideas as to the desirability of freeing China from the complex engagements which fettered her free determination. He concluded by saying that he wanted to see Japan take the lead in freeing China, but he feared that Japan, by standing on her treaty rights, would create the impression that she was thinking more of her rights than of her duties to China.[29]

Before the meeting ended Baron Makino said that

He wished to say a word about the form of restitution of Kiaochow to Japan. The Japanese Government attached supreme importance to the form which had been submitted that morning [draft articles]. Today fresh instructions had been received from the Government, and he could not too much stress the matter.[30]

Three decisive points were brought out at this meeting. In the first place it was made quite clear by the Japanese representatives that the Japanese government was unwilling to accept any modification of its Shantung claims. Secondly, Viscount Chinda's remark revealed that unless Japan's desires were met the Japanese delegates were instructed not to sign the Treaty. Finally, it was clear that as long as the Japanese government insisted upon the direct transfer to her of the former German rights in Shantung, Mr. Lloyd George and M. Clemenceau would uphold the promises Great Britain and France had given in 1917 to support such a claim.

One detail more is to be noted about the meeting of April 22; that is the tendency of President Wilson to introduce the larger aspects of the Chinese situation into the discussion. He went as far as to propose that all the Powers give up their spheres of influence in China. Lloyd George and Clemenceau, however, were very noncommittal about these larger aspects of the problem.

The Chinese representatives were invited before the Council on the afternoon of the same day, April 22. The official minutes of the meeting reveal best the substance of the discussion and are therefore quoted quite fully.

[28] Miller, *Diary*, Vol. XIX, pp. 179–81.
[29] *Ibid.*, pp. 183–84.
[30] *Ibid.*, p. 186.

President Wilson mentioned the conference he had had with the Japanese on the previous day and the meeting with the Japanese in the morning . . . . He mentioned the exchange of notes between Japan and China, in which Japan had laid down certain conditions, which the Chinese Government had accepted. Great Britain and France . . . . had entered into a similar but not identical agreement with Japan that they would support the claims of the Japanese Government on the Continent and in the islands north of the Equator. In the case of the British Government it had been on the understanding that Japan supported her claims to German islands south of the Equator. Great Britain and France were in much the same position in the matter.

Mr. Lloyd George explained that at the time the submarine campaign was very formidable. There was a shortage of torpedo-boat destroyers in the Mediterranean. Japanese help was urgently required, and Japanese had asked for this arrangement to be made. We had been hard pressed and had agreed.

President Wilson, after reading extracts from the notes exchanged between China and Japan, said that the Chinese Delegation would see the embarrassing position which had been reached. Mr. Lloyd George and M. Clemenceau were bound to support the claims of Japan. Alongside of them the Chinese had their exchange of notes with Japan. Mr. Koo, before the Council of Ten, had maintained that the war cancelled the agreement with the German Government. It did not cancel the agreement between China and Japan, made before the war. He had urged upon the Japanese that the leased territory of Kiaochow, as in the case of the Pacific Islands, be settled by being put into the hands of the Five Powers as trustees. He did not suggest the breaking of treaties, but it might be possible to modify the treaty and bring about an agreement. He had also proposed that all Governments renounce the special rights they had acquired in China. The Japanese were not willing to have Kiaochow handed over to the Five Powers; the British and French Governments were bound by treaties. . . . .

Mr. Koo explained that the Treaties of 1915 and the subsequent exchange of notes were the outcome of 21 demands which Japan had made on China and all were part and parcel of one transaction. He felt that the treaties and notes which had been exchanged after Japan had delivered an ultimatum stood outside of the regular procedure and course of treaties. They dealt with matters arising out of the war . . . . On the 7th of May (1915) the Japanese sent China an ultimatum in regard to the majority of the demands giving China 48 hours within which to accept. . . . . This caused absolute consternation to the Chinese Government which eventually had to submit to *force majeure*. . . . .

Mr. Lloyd George said it looked that, by the Treaty with China, Japan would get more than the Germans had had. He asked Mr. Koo which he would prefer, the Treaty with Japan or the transference to Japan of the German rights. . . . .

Mr. Koo, after consulting his colleague, said he could make no choice, because both alternatives were unacceptable; he would merely compare them; the Treaty and Notes with Japan provided for restoration of the leased territory to China upon certain conditions, but such restoration would be only nominal. Between the two he thought that the German rights were more limited.

President Wilson, after emphasizing that he had put the Chinese case as well as he could to the Japanese Delegation, said what he asked now was only a means of getting out of a position that was extremely difficult. In this Conference the United States was the only Power entirely unbound. Great Britain, France, China and Japan were all bound by treaties; bound to keep these treaties because the war had largely been fought to show that treaties could not be violated.

Lloyd George said he would like to have the two positions examined by British, French and American experts.

President Wilson read extracts from the Treaty and from Groups IV and V of the 21 demands, recalling that there were demands designed to exclude other powers from the commercial and industrial development. Then he asked if the following point of view would appeal to the Chinese plenipotentiaries. Hereafter, whatever arrangements were made both Japan and China would be members of the League of Nations, which would guarantee their territorial integrity and political independence. China would receive a kind of protection she had never had before and other nations would have a right they never had before to intervene. He, himself, was prepared to advocate at the Council of the League of Nations and at the Body of Delegates that the special positions occupied by the various nations in China should be abandoned. Japan declared she would support this. There would be a forum for advocating these matters. The interests of China would not be overlooked. . . . . While there was doubt as to the Treaty and Notes between China and Japan, there was no doubt as to the agreements entered into by France and Great Britain. Even if the agreements between China and Japan were abandoned, these Governments were bound to support Japan in getting whatever rights in Shantung Germany had. The question for the Chinese to consider was, would they prefer to retain the rights secured by the latter in treaty with China or would they prefer Japan should inherit the German rights in Shantung.

Mr. Koo said the Chinese people were at the parting of the ways. The policy of the Chinese Government was one of cooperation with Europe and the United States as well as with Japan. If, however, they did not get justice, China might be driven into the arms of Japan. There was a small section of China which believed in Asia for the Asiatics and wanted the closest cooperation with Japan. If the Government, believing the justice of the West and that their future lay there, failed to get justice there, the consequential reaction might be very great. . . . . .

President Wilson said these were serious considerations, but he would not like Mr. Koo to entertain the idea that there was injustice in an arrangement based on treaties which Japan had entered into. He emphasized the sacredness of treaties, and said the unjust treatment of China in the past had not by any means been confined to Japan. He hoped the quandary in which the Powers were would be stated to the Chinese people, that it would be shown to them that the undoing of the trouble depended on China uniting in reality with other nations, including western nations. The heart of the world went out to China's 400 millions of people. Any statesmen who ignored their fortunes were playing a dangerous game. But it would not do to identify justice with unfortunate engagements that had been entered into.

Mr. Koo thought that it would be better to undo unfortunate engagements now if they endangered the permanence of future peace.

Mr. Lloyd George said that the object of the war was not that. It had been fought as much for the East as for the West, China had been protected by the victory that had been won, the doctrine of the mailed fist had been propounded in relation to China. The engagements had been entered into with Japan at a time when support of that country was urgently needed . . . . Kiaochow could not have been captured without Japanese support. It was a solemn treaty and Great Britain could not turn around and say the treaty was a bad one and should not be carried out . . . .

M. Clemenceau said Mr. Koo could take every word Mr. Lloyd George had said as if he had said it also.

Mr. Koo made an additional remark that the engagements just considered had been made to meet a European situation, not one in the Far East, while President Wilson and Mr. Lloyd George emphasized [the] idea that they were to meet a world situation, to prevent German domination of the Far East as well as to save Europe . . . .[31]

The question was postponed pending the report of the Far Eastern experts attached to the American, British, and French Delegations. The question put to the experts was

whether it would be more advantageous for China if Japan were merely to inherit the rights possessed by Germany in Shantung and Kiaochow or if she were to accept the position created by the Sino-Japanese Treaties and Agreements of 1915 and 1918.[32]

The foregoing record of the interview with the Chinese Delegation on the afternoon of April 22 clearly shows that President Wilson had accepted the Japanese position. It is doubtful if either Lloyd George or Clemenceau had ever held any other intention about the question. It is obvious that President Wilson did not like the situation in which he found himself, but he recognized the force of circumstances and bowed to it. His concern in his conversations with the Chinese was to get them to see the inevitableness of accepting the Japanese claims. He later repudiated the idea that the final decision on the Shantung question had implied any recognition by him of the 1915 and 1918 Sino-Japanese Treaties and Agreements. Yet, during this interview, he did not hesitate to use the fact of their existence to persuade the Chinese representatives that the difficult situation in which China found itself was in part due to the Chinese themselves. President Wilson attempted to induce the Chinese to accept the Japanese claims by promising that he would advocate

[31] Miller, *Diary*, Vol. XIX, pp. 186 ff.
[32] *Ibid.*, p. 192.

before the League of Nations that the special position occupied by the various nations in China should be abandoned.

Mr. Koo did the best that he could under what must have been almost crushing circumstances. The Chinese delegates believed that they were going to get a chance to advocate their claims before a tribunal which would give them full consideration before rendering a final decision. On the contrary they found that the case had already been decided and that they were merely being consulted as to the best way of carrying out the verdict. It must have been a bitter moment for them.

From here on, President Wilson's efforts were directed toward getting the Japanese promise to restore Kiaochow to China set forth in such a manner as to give some sort of international sanction and supervision of the transfer. He had attempted in his conversation with Chinda and Makino on April 21 to get the Japanese to accept some such arrangement. But, as he had reported to Lloyd George and Clemenceau on the same afternoon, "the Japanese were too proud to accept this solution . . . . to be perfectly fair to the Japanese he thought they would interpret this as a challenge of their good faith."[33] There was one other thing left for President Wilson to attempt to do, in addition to getting the Japanese more definitely committed to the Powers as to the transfer of Kiaochow to China. This was to attempt to get more explicitly defined the conditions of the proposed joint Sino-Japanese control of the Tsingtao-Tsinan Railway. President Wilson wanted to be sure that Japan did not get any more rights than the Germans had possessed. The discussions which took place between April 22 and April 30, when the final decision was rendered, concern themselves largely with these two matters of detail. The real decision to transfer the German rights to Japan if not already taken was at least assumed.

The Far Eastern experts of Great Britain, France, and the United States, in accordance with the suggestion made at this meeting, examined the question of which course would be more advantageous to China; whether Japan should inherit the rights possessed by Germany in Shantung or whether the 1915 and 1918 treaties should be carried out.

They found that either alternative presented serious disadvantages for China. But they were of the opinion that it would be more advantageous for China to accept the first alternative and to agree to Japan succeeding to the

[33] Baker, *Woodrow Wilson and World Settlement*, Vol. II, p. 248.

rights and the position which Germany possessed in Kiaochow and the province of Shantung in 1914 on the outbreak of the war, provided that Japan's rights, both in the leased territory and in the province, were confined strictly to those secured to Germany by the Treaty of March 6, 1898, and by subsequent Sino-German agreements in regard to mines and railways. They noted that those treaties and agreements did not confer right to establish outside the leased territory any form of civil administration in the province of Shantung, or maintain troops in any district or town in the province, or to employ German troops or police to guard the Kiaochow Tsinanfu Railway . . . .[34]

This report was before the Council of Four on April 24, together with a new Chinese statement. The Chinese representatives found neither alternative proposed acceptable and in the place of either of them submitted the following four propositions as a settlement:

1. Germany renounces to the Five Allied and Associated Powers her holdings, rights and privileges in Shantung for restoration to China.
2. Japan, being in possession of the said holdings, rights and privileges, engages to effect the said restoration to China within one year after the signature of the Treaty of Peace with Germany.
3. China agrees to make a pecuniary compensation to Japan for the military expenses incurred in the capture of Tsingtao, the amount of the said compensation to be determined by the Council of Four.
4. China agrees to open the whole of Kiaochow Bay as a commercial port, and to provide a special quarter, if desired, for the residence of the citizens and subjects of the Treaty Powers.[35]

Both the recommendation of the Far Eastern experts and the new proposals of the Chinese representatives implied that the Shantung settlement should be carried out without reference to the Sino-Japanese Treaties of 1915 and 1918 and therefore would tend to impair the whole complex of treaties and agreements which had resulted from the Twenty-one Demands of 1915. The essence of the Japanese contention was to confirm the legality of the 1915 and 1918 Shantung agreements by insisting that the final transfer of Kiaochow to China should be carried out in accordance with their provisions. These last-minute proposals of the Chinese representatives, in fact, threatened to undermine the entire Japanese case.

On April 25, the Council of Four discussed the latest Chinese proposal and the report of the Far Eastern experts. President Wilson continued to exhibit dissatisfaction with the Japanese proposals for settling the question. After some discussion, in which Lloyd George suggested that the terms under which Japan would hand the

[34] *Ibid.*, pp. 192–93.
[35] *Ibid.*, pp. 193–94.

German rights in Shantung and Kiaochow back to China should be discussed, President Wilson

....commenting on Mr. Lloyd George's suggestion that the best plan would be for some one to sound the Japanese before they saw the Supreme Council, said they should be told that the Allied and Associated Powers could not consent to the return of Kiaochow and Shantung on the terms on which they had agreed with China. He suggested that Mr. Lloyd George and Mr. Balfour should see Baron Makino and Viscount Chinda.

Mr. Lloyd George undertook that Mr. Balfour should see the Japanese representatives.[36]

The following day, April 26, the President held a conference with the other American Commissioners about the situation in which the Council found itself with regard to the Shantung question. The concern which Wilson felt over this question and the firm attitude of the Japanese toward it can be judged by Mr. Lansing's account of this meeting. Mr. Lansing states:

On April 26th the President, at a conference with the American Commissioners, showed deep concern over the existing state of the controversy, and asked me to see the Japanese delegates again and endeavor to dissuade them from insisting on their demands and to induce them to consider the international trusteeship proposed. The evening of the same day the two Japanese came by request to my office and conferred with Professor E. T. Williams, the Commission's principal adviser on Far Eastern affairs, and with me. After an hour's conversation Viscount Chinda made it very clear that Japan intended to insist on her "pound of flesh." It was apparent both to Mr. Williams and to me that nothing could be done to obtain even a compromise, though it was on the face favorable to Japan, since it recognized the existence of the German rights, which China claimed were annulled.[37]

Mr. Balfour, following instructions from the Council of Four, met with the Japanese delegates, and at the meeting of the Council on the morning of the 28th a written summary of his conversation with them was discussed. There was need for definite action as the final draft of the League of Nations Covenant was to be presented to the Plenary Session of the Conference on the afternoon of the same day and the Japanese had reserved the right to bring up their "racial equality" proposal at this meeting. It has already been pointed out that any attempt on the part of the Japanese to push this amendment would greatly embarrass the British representatives. Yet the Japanese Delegation was in the position of every other delegation

[36] Miller, *Diary*, Vol. XIX, p. 194.
[37] Robert Lansing, *The Peace Negotiations*, pp. 254–55.

at the Conference: it could not return home empty-handed. If the Japanese Delegation were not to get their much-desired "racial equality" clause in the Covenant, they had to get their Shantung claims recognized or the government then in power in Japan would have to face the severe censure of Japanese public opinion. It must not be forgotten that Japan's experience of being negotiated out of what she considered her just reward for military victory had been a bitter one. The Treaty of Shimonoseki of 1895 had been followed by international action on the part of Germany, Russia, and France which forced her to give up the fruits of her victory over China. The Treaty of Portsmouth had resulted in Japan's finally emerging with very little to show for her victory over Russia. Now again, with the end of a Peace Conference in sight, Japan had nothing to show for her participation in the war except the unsatisfactory mandateship (which had not yet been granted) over the former German islands in the North Pacific. If the "racial equality" proposal was not to be accepted and along with it the frank and full acceptance of Japan's status as a Great Power, then Japan simply had to get the Shantung question decided her way or once again suffer the humiliation of being "put in her place." Times had changed since 1895 and 1905, and Japan fully recognized this fact. Her task now was to make the other Powers recognize that she had finally arrived as a "Great Power."

The substance of Mr. Balfour's report of his conversation with the Japanese delegates was that "the Japanese strenuously denied either that they intended to modify in their own favour the conditions which the Germans had imposed upon the Chinese in connection with the Shantung Peninsula, or that, in fact, their treaties with China would have had that effect . . . . the provisions that appear in the Treaty of 1918, with regard to maintaining a garrison at Tsinan and guarding the railway with Japanese troops, are purely provisional . . . ."[38]

In connection with the Balfour memorandum, President Wilson asked what would be the effect of saying to the Japanese:

We transfer to you the German rights but we do not confirm any arrangement you made with the Chinese earlier in the war and we do this provided that you give a definite assurance that you will not exercise your provisional rights for employing military forces in Shantung.

[38] For text of Mr. Balfour's memorandum, see Baker, *Wilson and World Settlement*, Vol. III, pp. 311–12.

President Wilson remarked further:

There was nothing on which public opinion in the United States was firmer than on this question that China should not be oppressed by Japan. Public opinion expected him to take the same line for Japan as he had taken for Italy. There was some difference between the two cases inasmuch as there was a definite understanding by China to transfer territory to Japan.[39]

Later in the meeting Mr. Balfour was introduced and gave an account of the circumstances of the memorandum and of a conversation he had had subsequently with Baron Makino.

Mr. Balfour said Baron Makino had come to see him on Sunday evening. With great delicacy but perfect clearness he had indicated that Japan wanted a decision on the Japanese claims as a whole, [he] had pointed out that Japan was asked to agree to the League of Nations although she could not obtain recognition of her claims for equality of treatment. He had said that public opinion in Japan was much concerned on this question, that if Japan was to receive one check as regards Shantung and another check as regards the League of Nations the position would be very serious. Consequently, it was very important to obtain a decision on the question of Shantung before the Plenary Meeting to be held the same afternoon on the subject of the League of Nations.

He [Balfour] understood that if Japan received what she wanted in regard to Shantung, her representatives at the Plenary Meeting would content themselves with a survey of the inequality of races and move some abstract resolution which would probably be rejected. Japan would then merely make a protest. If, however, she regarded herself as ill-treated over Shantung, he was unable to say what line the Japanese Delegates might take.[40]

At the conclusion of this meeting Mr. Balfour was instructed to write to Baron Makino outlining the settlement as it had been agreed upon. In part, Mr. Balfour wrote:

I was authorized to tell you that if . . . . the view which I represented to them as being yours was held by you, they were quite satisfied as regards the permanent arrangements come to between Japan and China on the question of Shantung.[41]

Mr. Balfour's letter to Baron Makino indicates quite clearly that the settlement, at least as he understood it, recognized the Sino-Japanese arrangements entered into by the treaties of 1915 and 1918 as being the basis upon which the transfer of the leasehold to China would be carried out.

President Wilson was still perturbed by the provision in the Sino-

---

[39] Miller, *Diary*, Vol. XIX, p. 196.   [40] *Ibid.*, pp. 196–97.

[41] *Ibid.*, p. 198. Text of his letter is given also in Baker, *op. cit.*, Vol. III, pp. 312–14, Doc. 42. This is the full text of Mr. Balfour's letter.

Japanese Treaty of 1918 with regard to maintaining a garrison at Tsinan and guarding the railway with Japanese troops. The Japanese had stated in their conversation with Mr. Balfour that such provisions "were purely provisional and refer only to the period of transition immediately following peace, and this period it is their intention to make as short as possible." Mr. Wilson, evidently, could not bring himself to trust the promised word of the Japanese government in this regard and visualized these "military clauses" as being the entering wedge by which Japan would force its control over the entire province of Shantung. Mr. Balfour, on the other hand, took the view that the Japanese should be taken at their word, particularly as there was nothing else much that could be done about it at this time.

The Japanese representatives, as Mr. Balfour had predicted, moved a mild "racial equality" amendment at the Plenary session of April 28, when the Covenant was accepted by the representatives of all the Powers. They refrained from pushing it, however, and it was quietly dropped.[42]

The conclusion inferred in some quarters that the Japanese representatives used the "racial equality" proposal as a means of bringing pressure upon President Wilson to overcome his last-minute objections to the Shantung settlement seems difficult to accept.[43] It is true that it was a critical moment for the Japanese representatives. President Wilson had just overridden the Italians on their Fiume demands, and it was not difficult to believe that he might do the same with regard to the Shantung claims of Japan. The Japanese, therefore, could not afford to overlook any pressure which they could bring to bear upon President Wilson. There can be no doubt that the Japanese did not hesitate to use the threat not to sign the Treaty as a means of forcing the issue, but it is difficult to see what they would have gained by pushing the "racial equality" amendment at the Plenary session of the Conference. Lloyd George and Clemenceau had already signified that they were going to hold to the promises made by Great Britain and France in 1917 to support the Japanese claims. Furthermore, the record seems to show that it was not President Wilson but the British who would have been chiefly em-

[42] Miller, *Diary*, Vol. XX, pp. 111–14, excerpts from the speech of Baron Makino relative to the Japanese "racial equality" amendment, Plenary Session, April 28, 1919.

[43] Lansing, *The Peace Negotiations*, pp. 243 ff.

barrassed if the Japanese had pressed their demand for an expression of "racial equality" in the Covenant. The true situation seems to have been that President Wilson, left alone to resist the Japanese demands and convinced that they would carry out their threat not to sign the Treaty, saw no alternative but to accept the Japanese claims and then to see that the rights in Shantung which the Japanese would get were strictly limited to those formerly enjoyed by Germany.[44] Therefore, on the day following the acceptance of the substance of the Japanese claims, President Wilson inquired closely into what form the policing of the Shantung Railway by Japanese troops and the stationing of a Japanese garrison at Tsinan would take.

President Wilson made strong objections to any arrangements by which the Japanese Government might exercise any such rights as being in excess of rights exercised by Germany and being an infringement of Chinese sovereignty. It was difficult for him to face public opinion in the United States on the question, and it would greatly increase his difficulty if the transfer of rights to Japan was greater than those exercised by Germany; he was not willing to admit the right of the Japanese Government to exercise supervision over the police force.

After considerable discussion, President Wilson made the following proposal:

Surrender to China of all right of sovereignty and retention with regard to the railway and the mines only of the economic rights of a concessionaire, retaining, however, the privilege of establishing a non-exclusive settlement at Singtau [sic].[45]

Clearly President Wilson's idea here was to modify certain of the clauses in the Sino-Japanese Treaties and Agreements of 1915 and 1918 relating to Shantung.

In the exchange of notes, dated May 25, 1915, supplementing the 1915 Treaty of the same date relating to Shantung, the Chinese government had agreed to the Japanese proposal, as one of the necessary conditions of the restoration of the leased territory of Kiaochow, that "a concession under the exclusive jurisdiction of

---

[44] See statement of President Wilson at the White House Conference of August 19, 1919, confirming his belief that Japan would have refused to sign the Treaty if their Shantung claims had not been granted, in *United States Congress, Senate Committee on Foreign Relations, Treaty of Peace with Germany*, Vol. I, p. 529. Secretary Lansing in his testimony before the Senate Foreign Relations Committee's hearing on the Treaty stated his belief that Japan would have signed regardless of the outcome of the Shantung question (*ibid.*, p. 182).

[45] Miller, *Diary*, Vol. XIX, p. 199.

Japan [was] to be established at a place designated by the Japanese Government."

Article 3 of the same note somewhat modified the foregoing by stating that "if the foreign Powers desire it, an international concession may be established."[46]

President Wilson's proposal would modify the first clause by making the concession a "non-exclusive" one regardless of whether the Powers had expressed their desires one way or the other.

The Sino-Japanese exchange of notes of September 24, 1918, stated with regard to the policing of the railway:

> With regard to the Japanese troops stationed along the Kiaochow-Tsinan railway, all the troops shall be concentrated at Tsingtao except for the stationing of a detachment at Tsinan.
>
> The guarding of the Kiaochow-Tsinan railway is to be undertaken by your Government [China] by the organization of a police force for the purpose. . . . .
>
> Japanese shall be engaged for the headquarters of this police force, at the principal railway stations and at the police training school.[47]

President Wilson finally accepted the Japanese statement that the provisions of the 1918 agreement for the retention of a garrison at Tsinan and Tsingtao were only temporary arrangements "referring only to the period of transition after peace."[48]

On the following day, April 30, the Japanese met with the Council of Four and presented their comments on the proposal made on the day before. They declared:

> The policy of Japan is to hand back the Shantung Peninsula in full sovereignty to China, retaining only the economic privileges granted to Germany and the right to establish a settlement under the usual conditions at Tsingtao.
>
> The owners of the railway will use special police only to ensure security for traffic. They will be used for no other purpose.
>
> The police force will be composed of Chinese, and such Japanese instructors as the directors of the railway may select will be appointed by the Chinese Government.[49]

This declaration substantially met the objections of President Wilson. The discussion, however, developed into a more general one with regard to the validity of the 1915 and 1918 Treaties and Agreements.

Viscount Chinda made it clear that in the last resort, if China failed to carry out the agreements—if, for example, she would not assist in the

---

[46] Carnegie Endowment for International Peace, *Shantung, Treaties and Agreements,* pp. 87–88.

[47] *Ibid.,* p. 91.   [48] Miller, *Diary,* Vol. XIX, pp. 199–200.   [49] *Ibid.*

formation of the Police Force or the employment of Japanese instructors, the Japanese Government reserved the right to fall back on the Agreements of 1915 and 1918.

President Wilson pointed out by that time Japan and China would be operating under the system of the League of Nations and Japan would be represented on the Council of the League. In such an event, he asked why should not the Japanese voluntarily apply for the mediation of the Council of the League of Nations. . . . .

Viscount Chinda said the difficulty was that President Wilson on his side did not admit the validity of these Agreements, but Japan did. He only mentioned the fact so as not to be morally bound not to invoke these Agreements . . . .

President Wilson said that frankly he must insist that nothing he said should be construed as an admission of the recognition of the notes exchanged between Japan and China.[50]

At this meeting, the Council accepted the text of the Shantung draft articles to be inserted in the Treaty as offered by Baron Makino and ordered them to be sent to the Drafting Committee. They underwent no change, however, and appeared in the final text of the Treaty in the form originally offered on April 22 and approved at this meeting.[51]

---

[50] From the Secret Minutes of the Council of Four for the meeting of April 30. Quoted in Baker, *Wilson and World Settlement*, pp. 263–64. Baker is cited for the meeting of April 30, rather than Miller, because he quotes directly and fully from the secret minutes of the Council of Four for this meeting.

The last remark of President Wilson is interesting in the light of the sharp exchange of views which took place in August 1919 between the State Department of the American government and the Japanese Chargé d'Affaires in Washington. The question arose as to whether the Japanese delegates to the Paris Peace Conference had agreed that Japan should give up the right to invoke the 1915 and 1918 Agreements in coming to a final settlement with China relative to the former German rights in Shantung. The Japanese Chargé d'Affaires denied that the Japanese delegates had agreed to renounce this right. Secretary Lansing, in his reply, stated:

"The Government of the United States has no doubt that the representatives of the Japanese Government at Paris clearly understood that a condition precedent to the assent of the President to Articles 156, 157 and 158 of the Treaty of Versailles was that the Japanese Government should agree that the Sino-Japanese agreements of 1915 and 1918 should not be relied upon or referred to in negotiations for the return to China of Kiaochow and the German rights as dealt with in the Japanese statement to the Council of Allied and Associated Governments at Paris. . . . . The President further directs the Secretary of State to say, that, since his assent to the Articles of the Treaty depended upon the acceptance of this condition precedent, the non-compliance by the Japanese Government may oblige him to consider the necessity of discontinuing his support of the Articles in question. . . . ." (See *Foreign Relations, 1919*, Vol. I, pp. 716–22, for the correspondence relative to this exchange of views.)

[51] That is, with the slight addition mentioned. Articles 128 to 134 (except 129) were accepted at this meeting also.

Thus ended the Shantung question, as far as the settlement of it by the Peace Conference was concerned. The Japanese obtained complete satisfaction of their claim to the former German leasehold and mining and railway properties in Shantung, and to the general economic privileges enjoyed by Germany by virtue of the Sino-German Treaty of March 6, 1898.

In the meantime the members of the Chinese Delegation were without any precise information as to the progress of events since their interview with the Council of Four on April 22. The task of officially informing them of the decision reached by the Council on April 30 fell to Ray Stannard Baker. They, however, had learned of the decision and Mr. Baker "found them bitterly disappointed." They did not, however, accept the decision as final, and there followed through the month of May attempts on their part, first, to get the decision re-examined, then, failing this, to be permitted to sign the Treaty with reservations to the Shantung articles. Upon being refused this request, they then asked that they be allowed to make a statement of reservations outside the Treaty while at the same time accepting the Treaty as it stood. This too was refused them, and at the last moment they decided not to sign at all. On June 28, when the Treaty was signed by all the Allied and Associated Powers and Germany, the Chinese representatives alone absented themselves from this final ceremony.[52]

[52] The actual steps taken by the Chinese Delegation to get the decision modified were as follows: On May 4 they addressed a letter to M. Clemenceau, as president of the Council, protesting the Shantung decision and again advancing the arguments originally used by Mr. Koo at the Plenary Session of January 28. On May 6 the Chinese delegates made a formal reservation to the Shantung articles before the Plenary Meeting of the Conference. On May 26 they again addressed a letter to M. Clemenceau in which they said that the Chinese representatives would sign the Treaty with the reservation made on May 6. On June 25 the Council of Four considered this communication but decided that the Treaty must be signed without any reservations or not signed at all. (See MacMurray, *Treaties and Agreements with and concerning China*, Vol. II, pp. 1494-98.)

M. Clemenceau said that "he had replied [to the Chinese communication] that they must either sign the Treaty with the intention of abiding by it or not sign. They were just as much bound to honor their signatures as the Germans were" (Miller, *Diary*, Vol. XVI, p. 458).

On June 28, the morning the Treaty was signed, the Chinese Delegation addressed a letter to the Supreme Council informing it that "The Supreme Council ....having established a rule of admitting no reservation of any kind whatever, either in the text of the Treaty or outside of it, and having refused to accept.... even a declaration to the effect that the signature of the Chinese Plenipotentiaries could not be considered as preventing China from asking at an opportune time for a new examination of the Shantung question, the Plenipotentiaries of the Chinese

The claim advanced by the Chinese Delegation for the abrogation by the Peace Conference of all the Sino-Japanese Treaties and Agreements of 1915, together with some of the larger questions that China had hoped to get settled at the Peace Conference, met with no more success than had their claim for direct restitution of the German rights in Shantung.

On May 14th the Council of Four decided that the Peace Conference should not take up certain proposals forwarded by the Chinese Delegation. These included a claim for abrogation by the Conference of the Treaties and Notes between Japan and China of May 25, 1915, and among other questions, "the withdrawal from China of Foreign Troops and Police, the withdrawal of Foreign Post Offices and the Abolition of Consular Jurisdiction." The Council of Four at this meeting accepted a proposal by Mr. Lansing that a statement be sent to the Chinese, informing them that it would be impossible for the Peace Conference to consider these important matters, and suggesting that they be brought to the attention of the Council of the League of Nations as soon as that body is able to function.[53]

The outcome of the Shantung controversy well illustrates the basic struggle which was going on at Paris between the idealism of a new world order, of which President Wilson was the most eloquent but by no means the only exponent, and the forces of *real politik,* who wanted the peace settlement to be made upon the traditional basis of national aggrandizement. The entire effort of Japan to establish her hegemony in Far Eastern affairs was involved in this intrinsically unimportant issue. The economic privileges which Japan gained in Shantung were trivial and her promise to return Kiaochow to China at an early date rendered the transfer of the leasehold meaningless from the standpoint of territorial gain. The essential motive of Japan in demanding that her views as to the settlement prevail at Paris was to more firmly establish the principle that the Western powers should cease interfering in Japan's political relations with China.[54]

Japan had come to the Conference fully prepared upon this issue. With the exception of the United States she had every one of the parties to the dispute, including China, committed to her claims. Furthermore, she had given her word to restore Kiaochow to China

---

Republic have the honor of informing you that they do not consider themselves qualified to sign the Treaty of Versailles today...." (Miller, *Diary,* Vol. IX, pp. 461–64).   [53] Miller, *Diary,* Vol. XIX, p. 152.

[54] It is of interest to note that it was the action of the League of Nations in the Sino-Japanese controversy of 1931 which caused Japan to withdraw from the League.

but only on condition that the German rights were unconditionally transferred to her first. Lloyd George and Clemenceau declined to withdraw their war-time promises to support Japan's claims. This left President Wilson with the choice of resisting the Japanese claims at the risk of Japan's defection from the League of Nations before it had even come into being or of bowing to the immediate situation with the hope that the League would be instrumental in eventually freeing China of the entire web of one-sided engagements which hampered her national growth. His views on the settlement are best portrayed in his own words. On the day of the Shantung decision he prepared a statement for the American press. Among other things he said:

> The Japanese-Chinese matter has been settled in a way which seems to me as satisfactory as could be got out of the tangle of treaties in which China herself was involved . . . . Japan thus gets only such rights as an economic concessionaire as are possessed by one or two other great powers and are only too common in China, and the whole future relationship between the two countries falls at once under the guarantee of the League of Nations of territorial integrity and political independence. I find a general disposition to look with favor upon the proposal that at an early date through the mediation of the League of Nations all extraordinary foreign rights in China and all spheres of influence should be abrogated by the common consent of all nations concerned. I regard the assurances given by Japan as very satisfactory in view of the complicated circumstances . . . .[55]

President Wilson quite evidently believed that the League would become the guarantor of China's territorial integrity and that the existence of the League would make impossible in the future such international bargaining with Chinese territory. This belief gave him some solace for consenting to a settlement which he felt to be not only unjust but contrary to his ideal of a new world order. He also recognized that the Shantung settlement would be used against him when the time came to persuade the American Senate to accept the Treaty. President Wilson's fears in this direction were amply justified. The Shantung settlement was seized upon by his political opponents to discredit him and to discredit his work at Paris. An insignificant piece of territory in far-off Asia became one of the important factors in defeating the acceptance of the Versailles Treaty by the Senate and of keeping the United States out of the League of Nations.[56]

[55] Text in Baker, *Wilson and World Settlement*, Vol. III, pp. 315–16.

[56] For an account of attacks upon the Treaty through the Shantung settlement made by President Wilson's opponents in the Senate, see D. F. Fleming, *The United States and the League of Nations, 1918–1920*, pp. 252–58, 426.

The program formulated by the Chinese Delegation at Paris finds its explanation in the general situation existing in China at the end of the war. The Military clique and the pro-Japanese Communications clique were thoroughly discredited. If they had occupied a strong position, they would undoubtedly have preferred to work out some sort of compromise with Japan rather than to defy her. But this was impossible. The temper of the Chinese people would not permit it. The surest way for their opponents in the southern provinces to discredit the group who came into control of the Peking government when China declared war upon Germany was to accuse them of betraying the country into the hands of Japan. "Young China" saw its chance to wrest power from "Old China" by defying Japan. Japan was now defied because it was believed that she could be defied now with impunity.

Finally, the talk of a new world order was in the air. Weak and oppressed peoples everywhere believed that a new day had come for them and that they were at last to be freed of the shackles which the old diplomacy had fastened upon them. The idealistic character of the Chinese program was greatly influenced by the atmosphere of Wilsonian idealism in which the Peace Conference met. Furthermore, the responsibility for its formulation fell into the hands of men who were outstanding representatives of the new China. The American education of Wellington Koo and C. T. Wang made them particularly sympathetic toward President Wilson's idealistic conceptions of international politics. Finally, in view of the comparative strength of the Japanese position, the appeal to international justice was the only ground upon which the Chinese could base their case.

The Chinese stand at Paris, however, was not completely without results. It no doubt influenced the prominent place given to a consideration of China's international position at the Washington Conference and the formulation of the Nine-Power Treaty which attempted to mitigate the worst features of the restrictions imposed upon China's sovereignty by the Treaty Powers. The Washington Conference also offered auspicious surroundings for Japan and China in which to arrange a final settlement of the Shantung question, which was carried out by Japan in faithful observance of the promises she had given at the Paris Peace Conference.

CHAPTER IX

RETROSPECT AND CONCLUSIONS

The complete defeat of the Chinese program at the Paris Conference came as a rude shock to the Chinese people. Following Wellington Koo's challenge to the Japanese position at the beginning of the Conference, the confidence of the Chinese people in the successful outcome of their demand for the direct retrocession of the German rights in Shantung grew until it became a conviction. The final decision, therefore, was received with deep disappointment and a feeling of humiliation. Criticism of the Military clique in Peking became exceedingly outspoken. In the past such outbursts of public indignation had been lightly treated by those in power, and there was an attempt in this instance so to treat the general dissatisfaction. However, a series of events soon occurred which indicated that a new and potent element had entered Chinese life. Public indignation found expression in a spontaneous mass movement which took the oligarchic masters of Chinese politics completely by surprise, and within a few months forced them to give up their hold upon the Central Government.

This movement received its initial impulse from the events of May 4, 1919. On that day several thousand students drawn from the colleges and universities of Peking gathered to make an orderly and peaceful protest against the Shantung settlement. They carried banners demanding that the three most markedly pro-Japanese officials, Tsao Ju-lin, the Minister of Communications, who had been chiefly responsible for the huge loans from Japan, Lu Tsung-yu, the head of the Currency Bureau, and Chang Tsung-hsiang, the Minister to Japan, who had signed the Sino-Japanese Naval and Military Agreements of 1918 and the Shantung Agreement of 1918, be dismissed from office. The student demonstration was quite peaceable until it reached the residence of Tsao Ju-lin, when, to quote one observer, "they went wild." Tsao Ju-lin's house was broken into, but he managed to make an ignominious escape over the rear wall. His colleague, the Chinese Minister to Japan, who happened to be there, was not so fortunate. The students severely beat him and then set fire to the house. Some time later the police arrested thirty-three of the students. This action caused a great sensation, particularly in Peking and at Shanghai and in the commercial cities of the Yangtze Valley. Merchants' associations in these centers protested against the detention of the students, and student demonstrations occurred in many cities. The students in Peking, now thoroughly aroused, prepared to lead a great public demonstration which was to take place on May 7, the anniversary of the presentation of the Japanese ultimatum to China in 1915. In view of this threat the authorities released the arrested students, but agitation increased rather than subsided. On May 15 the merchants of Shanghai showed their sympathy with the students by beginning a boycott on Japanese goods, which soon spread to other cities. On May 19 a nation-wide student strike began, and in the next few days it became evident the Peking soldiery had become disaffected and could no longer be relied upon to suppress these public demonstrations. The government, however, persisted in its attempt to whitewash the three officials accused of pro-Japanese dealings. The students' response to this was to organize larger and more vehement demonstrations. As a consequence, on June 3 and 4, one thousand students were arrested. But by this time public indignation could not be suppressed. A general strike upon the part of the merchants took place throughout the Yangtze Valley and in Shanghai and Tientsin. This merchant strike was accompanied by a similar strike upon the part of coolies engaged in dock and transport work. On June 7 the students were released but refused to leave their confinement until adequate apologies had been made for their detention. Finally, on June 10, the government capitulated by dismissing the three officials whose resignations the students had first demanded. Shortly afterward the entire cabinet resigned. Thus, this spontaneous public outburst, led by students, who heretofore had been completely ignored by the lordly tuchuns, was able to break the hold of the Military clique upon the government and bring to account the officials who had bartered away valuable national interests. For the first time in the life of the Republic, public opinion had been able to call a halt to the dictatorial and irresponsible rule of the tuchuns and the unscrupulous politicians.

The famous Chinese liberal, Hu Shih, writing shortly after these events, remarks upon the profound change which took place in the thought and ideas of the people during the year 1919.[1] He points out that at the commencement of the year the National University in Peking was being severely attacked for its liberal teachings but that the success of the student movement resulted in the University's being acclaimed as the center of intellectual leadership of the new China. Significantly enough, 1919 marked the year when the Chinese spoken language or *pai hua,* which, heretofore, had been despised by the literati as a means of expression, "triumphed as the recognized instrument for journalistic and literary composition as well as for popular education."[2] Hu Shih also remarks upon the tremendous stimulation the events of the year gave to the movement of the younger scholars who were trying to free themselves from the restrictions of the traditional learning. He notes:

> The year 1918 witnessed La Jeunesse fighting alone for the new literary and intellectual movement. But shortly after June, 1919, there have sprung up in all parts of China numerous periodicals edited in most cases by young students who have caught the new spirit.[3]

Undoubtedly the growing sense of national unity and the conviction that China would be freed only by her own efforts from the humiliating one-sided treaties which had been forced upon her was the most far-reaching and important effect of the World War upon that country.

The war came at a time when the long series of factional struggles which have been so unfortunate for the new Republic was just beginning. Essentially these factional struggles have arisen out of the inability of any one group to replace the centralized authority which characterized the former Empire. Sun Yat-sen and his followers in the Kuomintang were chiefly responsible for the establishment of the Republic, but they were not strong enough to resist the almost immediate reassertion of authority by the most powerful officials of the old regime. Temporarily, this authority became centered in Yuan Shih-k'ai. Had he lived, perhaps China would have been spared the anarchy which she has since suffered, but undoubtedly the Republic would have been sacrificed. Upon Yuan's death in 1916, no one emerged strong enough to take over the autocratic power he had wielded, but, instead, all central authority became

---

[1] Hu Suh (this is an earlier form which Hu Shih used for his name), "The Intellectual China in 1919," in *The Chinese Social and Political Science Review,* December 1919, pp. 345–67.

[2] *Ibid.* [3] *Ibid.*

divided among several factions. These factions were continually changing in composition and forming new combinations and alliances in order to further their own interests, with the result that Chinese politics became characterized by an extreme instability and emphasis upon the individual leader.

Superficially, this factional struggle seemed to resolve itself into a contest for the control of the Central Government between the Kuomintang and a coterie of military governors of the provinces north of the Yangtze Valley. It would, however, falsely oversimplify the situation to say that this struggle was between those who were striving to establish parliamentary forms of government in China against those who were chiefly concerned in perpetuating an irresponsible oligarchic control. Both of these major groups were shot through with factional and individual rivalries which were every bit as important to the individuals concerned as were the more general differences which divided the Kuomintang South from the Militarist North.

Under such chaotic internal conditions it was not to be expected that the Central Government could give any effective attention to China's relations with the belligerent Powers. When questions of importance did arise, such, for instance, as the question of China's entrance into the war, they were considered solely from the viewpoint of the bearing they would have upon the fortunes of the factions and individuals striving for power.

Consequently, when China was finally ranged on the side of the Allies, this course was adopted largely because it would strengthen the hold of the northern Military chiefs upon the Central Government and in the hope that the Allies would reciprocate by financial concessions which could be used to increase their personal armies and therefore their personal power.

The interests of the Chinese people seem rarely to have influenced the decisions of those who claimed to represent the Chinese government. In fact most of the decisions taken with regard to China's relationship to the war, including the decision to join the Allies, exhibited a callous indifference to the welfare of the Chinese people.

Even the open defiance with which the Chinese Delegation at Paris countered the Japanese claims seems to have been welcomed, if not actually permitted, by the Military clique in Peking because it offered a convenient means of diverting the anger of the Chinese people away from themselves rather than because they believed that the Chinese program had any hope of success.

If, however, the so-called leaders showed themselves to be indifferent to the true interests of the Chinese people, the same can be said of the Allies in the way they used China during the war to secure petty advantages for themselves. The chief reason for the Allies to induce the Military clique to declare war upon Germany was to enable the Allies to drive the Germans out of China and to cause their trade to fall into the hands of their own merchants.

Neither was President Wilson's championing of the Chinese claims at Paris undertaken solely in the interests of the Chinese people. His stand against Japan's Shantung claims was the logical outcome of the increasing conflict between the policies and interests of the United States and Japan in China, a conflict which the temporary withdrawal of the European powers from the Chinese scene threw sharply into the limelight.

Finally, largely through Allied propaganda which toward the end of the war was a potent agency for spreading the ideals of modern national democracy throughout the length and breadth of China, the Chinese people began to imbibe Western political ideology. The success of the student movement in Peking in shaking loose the grip of the Military leaders upon the government struck a new note in Chinese history. Public opinion at last had shaken the seats of the mighty.

Appendix

APPENDIX I

DOCUMENTS REGARDING JAPAN'S TWENTY-ONE DEMANDS OF 1915*

A. JAPAN'S ORIGINAL DEMANDS AS HANDED TO THE PRESIDENT, YUAN SHIH-K'AI, BY MR. HIOKI, THE JAPANESE MINISTER, JANUARY 18, 1915

(Japanese translation)

Group I

The Japanese Government and the Chinese Government, being desirous to maintain the general peace in the Far East and to strengthen the relations of amity and good neighborhood existing between the two countries, agree to the following articles:

ARTICLE I. The Chinese Government engage to give full assent to all matters that the Japanese Government may hereafter agree with the German Government respecting the disposition of all the rights, interests and concessions, which, in virtue of treaties or otherwise, Germany possesses *vis-à-vis* China in relation to the Province of Shantung.

ART. II. The Chinese Government engage that, within the Province of Shantung or along its coast, no territory or island will be ceded or leased to any other Power, under any pretext whatever.

ART. III. The Chinese Government agree to Japan's building a railway connecting Chefoo or Lungkow with the Kiaochou-Tsinanfu Railway.

ART. IV. The Chinese Government engage to open of their own accord, as soon as possible, certain important cities and towns in the Province of Shantung for the residence and commerce of foreigners. The places to be so opened shall be decided upon in a separate agreement.

Group II

The Japanese Government and the Chinese Government, in view of the fact that the Chinese Government has always recognized the predominant position of Japan in South Manchuria and Eastern Inner Mongolia, agree to the following articles:

ARTICLE I. The two Contracting Parties mutually agree that the term of the lease of Port Arthur and Dairen and the term respecting the South Manchuria Railway and the Antung-Mukden Railway shall be extended to a further period of 99 years respectively.

ART. II. The Japanese subjects shall be permitted in South Manchuria and Eastern Inner Mongolia to lease or own land required either for erecting buildings for various commercial and industrial uses or for farming.

ART. III. The Japanese subjects shall have liberty to enter, reside and

* *The Sino-Japanese Negotiations of 1915,* Japanese and Chinese Documents and Chinese Official Statement, Carnegie Endowment for International Peace, Division of International Law, Pamphlet No. 45.

travel in South Manchuria and Eastern Inner Mongolia, and to carry on business of various kinds—commercial, industrial and otherwise.

ART. IV. The Chinese Government grant to the Japanese subjects the right of mining in South Manchuria and Eastern Inner Mongolia. As regards the mines to be worked, they shall be decided upon in a separate agreement.

ART. V. The Chinese Government agree that the consent of the Japanese Government shall be obtained in advance, (1) whenever it is proposed to grant to other nationals the right of constructing a railway or to obtain from other nationals the supply of funds for constructing a railway in South Manchuria and Eastern Inner Mongolia, and (2) whenever a loan is to be made with any other Power, under security of the taxes of South Manchuria and Eastern Inner Mongolia.

ART. VI. The Chinese Government engage that whenever the Chinese Government need the service of political, financial or military advisers or instructors in South Manchuria or in Eastern Inner Mongolia, Japan shall first be consulted.

ART. VII. The Chinese Government agree that the control and management of the Kirin-Changchun Railway shall be handed over to Japan for a term of 99 years dating from the signing of this Treaty.

Group III

The Japanese Government and the Chinese Government, having regard to the close relations existing between Japanese capitalists and the Han-Yeh-Ping Company and desiring to promote the common interests of the two nations, agree to the following articles:

ARTICLE I. The two Contracting Parties mutually agree that when the opportune moment arrives the Han-Yeh-Ping Company shall be made a joint concern of the two nations, and that, without the consent of the Japanese Government, the Chinese Government shall not dispose or permit the Company to dispose of any right or property of the Company.

ART. II. The Chinese Government engage that, as a necessary measure for protection of the invested interests of Japanese capitalists, no mines in the neighbourhood of those owned by the Han-Yeh-Ping Company shall be permitted, without the consent of the said Company, to be worked by anyone other than the said Company; and further that whenever it is proposed to take any other measure which may likely affect the interests of the said Company directly or indirectly, the consent of the said Company shall first be obtained.

Group IV

The Japanese Government and the Chinese Government, with the object of effectively preserving the territorial integrity of China, agree to the following article:

The Chinese Government engage not to cede or lease to any other Power any harbour or bay on or any island along the coast of China.

Group V

1. The Chinese Central Government to engage influential Japanese as political, financial and military advisers;

2. The Chinese Government to grant the Japanese hospitals, temples and schools in the interior of China the right to own land;

3. In the face of many police disputes which have hitherto arisen between Japan and China, causing no little annoyance, the police in localities (in China), where such arrangements are necessary, to be placed under joint Japanese and Chinese administration, or Japanese to be employed in police offices in such localities, so as to help at the same time the improvement of the Chinese Police Service;

4. China to obtain from Japan supply of a certain quantity of arms, or to establish an arsenal in China under joint Japanese and Chinese management and to be supplied with experts and materials from Japan;

5. In order to help the development of the Nanchang-Kiukiang Railway, with which Japanese capitalists are so closely identified, and with due regard to the negotiations which have for years been pending between Japan and China in relation to the railway question in South China, China to agree to give to Japan the right of constructing a railway to connect Wuchang with the Kiukiang-Nanchang line, and also the railways between Nanchang and Hangchou and between Nanchang and Chaochou;

6. In view of the relations between the Province of Fukien and Formosa and of the agreement respecting the non-alienation of that province, Japan to be consulted first whenever foreign capital is needed in connection with the railways, mines and harbour works (including dockyards) in the Province of Fukien;

7. China to grant to Japanese subjects the right of preaching in China.

B. COUNTER-PROJECT OF THE CHINESE GOVERNMENT, HANDED TO MR. HIOKI
ON FEBRUARY 12, 1915

(Japanese translation)

Group I

The Governments of China and Japan, being sincerely desirous to maintain the general peace of the Far East and further strengthen the friendly relations and good neighborhood subsisting between the two countries, have concluded the following articles:

ARTICLE I. The Chinese Government declare that they will give full assent to the dispositions that may hereafter be agreed upon between the Japanese and German Governments in regard to all interests which Germany possesses in the Province of Shantung by virtue of treaties or recorded cases (excepting the provisions of Section I of the Convention for the Lease of Kiaochou to Germany).

The Japanese Government declare that, when the assent of the Chinese Government in regard to the interests above referred to has been given, Japan will restore Kiaochou to China, and they recognize the right of the Chinese Government to participate in the negotiations mentioned in the preceding clause between the Japanese and German Governments.

ART. II. The Japanese Government agree that they will be entirely responsible in regard to indemnification for losses of all kinds occasioned by Japan's military operations in Kiaochou; and although the Customs, telegraphs and posts within the leased territory of Kiaochou will, pending the restoration of Kiaochou, be administered for the present as heretofore, the military railways and telegraphs which were constructed for the use of the Japanese troops will be immediately removed; and the Japanese forces remaining outside the leased territory of Kiaochou will first be withdrawn and those remaining within the said territory will be completely withdrawn at the time of the restoration of Kiaochou to China.

ART. III. In case the Chinese Government propose themselves to construct a railway from Chefoo and Lungkou to connect with the Kiaochou-Tsinan Railway and raise a foreign loan for the purpose, they agree, provided Germany is willing to abandon the right to furnish capital for the Chefoo-Weihsien line, to negotiate first with Japanese capitalists.

ART. IV. The Chinese Government agree, for purposes of foreign trade, to select suitable places in the Province of Shantung and open them as marts; and the regulations relating to such marts will be determined by China herself.

Group II

The Japanese Government declare that they will always respect the complete sovereignty of China in the Three Eastern Provinces, and accordingly the Chinese and Japanese Governments have, with a view to the development of their commercial relations in the southern portion of the Three Eastern Provinces, agreed upon the following articles:

ARTICLE I. The Chinese Government agree that the term of lease of Port Arthur and Dairen shall be extended to ninety-nine years, expiring in the eighty-sixth year of the Republic or in the year 1997 of the Christian era, and that the time for the restoration of the entire South Manchuria Railway to China shall be extended to ninety-nine years, falling due in the ninetieth year of the Republic or in the year 2001 of the Christian era, and further that in all other matters the provisions of the respective original treaties shall be adhered to.

ART. II. The Chinese Government consent, upon the expiration of the term of the Japanese management of the Antung-Mukden Railway, to negotiate with Japan respecting the manner of extending the said term and to continue to carry into effect all other provisions according to Art. VI of the Annex to the Agreement relating to Manchuria concluded between Japan and China.

ART. III. The Chinese Government shall select places, in addition to the marts already opened, in the Three Eastern Provinces and of their own accord open them to trade, and after fixing the boundary lines, permit merchants of Japan and other countries freely to reside, trade, and carry on commercial and industrial business of all kinds, and also to rent land, after fair negotiation with the respective owners of such land with regard to rental, for the erection of buildings required for commercial and industrial purposes. Such merchants, however, shall equally pay taxes and contributions imposed upon them.

ART. IV. If, not later than one full year from the day on which the present Agreement is signed, any Japanese syndicate desires to engage in mining in the southern portion of the Three Eastern Provinces, the Chinese Government shall consent to grant to such syndicate for the term of one year only the privilege of prospecting mines in that region with the exception of those on which prospecting or mining has already been commenced. Of the mines which have been examined, permission shall be granted to work one-half the number according to the provisions of the Chinese Mining Law; and the remaining mines shall be disposed of by China herself.

ART. V. The Chinese Government agree that if it is found necessary hereafter to construct railways in the southern portion of the Three Eastern Provinces, they will construct them with capital provided by China herself; and if foreign capital is required, they will first negotiate for a loan with Japanese capitalists.

ART. VI. The Chinese Government declare that if it is proposed hereafter to employ foreign advisers in regard to political, financial, and military affairs of the southern portion of the Three Eastern Provinces, preference will be given to Japanese.

ART. VII. The existing treaties between China and Japan in regard to the Three Eastern Provinces shall remain in force as heretofore except as otherwise provided for in the present Agreement.

Group III

Notes to be Exchanged Respecting the Han-Yeh-Ping Company.

As the Han-Yeh-Ping Company, being a Chinese commercial concern, has undoubtedly, according to the laws of China, the right to preserve its property and conduct and supervise its business, the Chinese Government do not find it proper to take measure immediately in its behalf without first consulting the Company. If, however, the Company desires on a future occasion to come to agreement with Japanese capitalists for the joint management of its present business, the Chinese Government will give permission in so far as such step does not conflict with the laws of the country.

C. EXCHANGE OF NOTES BETWEEN CHINA AND JAPAN RESPECTING THE RESTO-
RATION OF THE LEASED TERRITORY OF KIAOCHOW BAY, OF MAY 25, 1915

[*Japanese text*]

PEKING, May 25, 1915

MONSIEUR LE MINISTRE:

In the name of the Imperial Government, I have the honour to make the following declaration to your Excellency's Government:

If, upon the conclusion of the present war, the Japanese Government should be given an absolutely free disposal of the leased territory of Kiaochou Bay, they will return the said leased territory to China subject to the following conditions:

1. Opening of the whole of Kiaochou as commercial port;
2. Establishment of a Japanese settlement in the locality to be designated by the Japanese Government;
3. Establishment, if desired by the Powers, of an international settlement;
4. Arrangements to be made, before the return of the said territory is effected, between the Japanese and Chinese Governments, with respect to the disposal of German public establishments and properties and with regard to the other conditions and procedures.

I avail, etc.

(*Signed*) EKI HIOKI

HIS EXCELLENCY
　　MR. LU CHENG-HSIENG,
　　　Minister of Foreign Affairs

[*Chinese text*]

PEKING, May 25, 1915

EXCELLENCY,

In the name of my Government I have the honour to make the following declaration to the Chinese Government:

When, after the termination of the present war, the leased territory of Kiaochow Bay is completely left to the free disposal of Japan, the Japanese Government will restore the said leased territory to China under the following conditions:

1. The whole of Kiaochow Bay to be opened as a Commercial Port.
2. A concession under the exclusive jurisdiction of Japan to be established at a place designated by the Japanese Government.
3. If the foreign Powers desire it, an international concession may be established.
4. As regards the disposal to be made of the buildings and properties of Germany and the conditions and procedure relating thereto, the Japanese Government and the Chinese Government shall arrange the matter by mutual agreement before the restoration.

I avail, etc.

(*Signed*) HIOKI EKI

HIS EXCELLENCY
　　LOU TSENG-TSIANG,
　　　Minister of Foreign Affairs

APPENDIX II

SINO-JAPANESE AGREEMENT OF SEPTEMBER 24, 1918, WITH REGARD TO SHANTUNG*

The Japanese Minister for Foreign Affairs (Goto) to the Chinese Minister in Japan (Chang Tsung-hsiang)

TOKYO, September 24, 1918

SIR: In view of the neighbourly feelings of friendship between our two countries, the Government of Japan, being desirous of arranging matters in a spirit of harmony, has drawn up an agreement which it regards as a satisfactory settlement of all outstanding questions relating to the Province of Shantung, and I now have the honour to bring this proposal to the notice of your Government. The terms of the proposed agreement are as follows:

1. All Japanese troops stationed along the Shantung Railway—with the exception of one Company which will be left at Tsinan—will be withdrawn to Tsingtao.

2. The Chinese Government may establish a Police Force which shall take over the duty of guarding the railway.

3. The Administration of the Shantung Railway shall set aside a sufficient sum to meet the expenses of the Police Force.

4. Japanese subjects are to be employed at the Headquarters of this Police Force and at all important stations and in the Police Training School.

5. Among the employes of the Shantung Railway posts shall be given to Chinese subjects also.

6. After it has been definitely decided to whom the Shantung Railway is to belong the railway is to be placed under the joint management of China and Japan.

7. The Civil Administration Offices now in existence are to be abolished.

I have the honour to request that you will communicate to me the views of your Government with regard to the above proposal.

I have (etc.) BARON GOTO

The Chinese Minister in Japan (Chang Tsung-hsiang) to the Japanese Minister for Foreign Affairs (Goto)

TOKYO, undated

SIR: I have the honour to acknowledge receipt of your letter couched in the following terms:

[Quotes in full letter from Minister for Foreign Affairs of September 24, 1918.]

I have the honour to inform you that the Government of China accepts with pleasure the proposal contained in the letter quoted above.

I have (etc.) SEAL OF CHANG TSUNG HSIANG

* *Foreign Relations of the United States, 1919,* Vol. I, pp. 571–72. [Included in the dispatch from the Minister in China (Reinsch) to the Acting Secretary of State, No. 2534, Peking, February 20, 1919.]

APPENDIX III

ANNOTATION OF THE MINUTES OF THE DISCUSSIONS OF THE SHANTUNG QUESTION, 1919*

August 13, 1919

(NOTE. Of the three articles of this Section, Article 158 was not offered with Articles 156 and 157. Article 158 stipulates for the transfer of documents, archives, records, etc., conforming to a principle applied to other sections on transfer of territory by Germany.)

The following statement of the Japanese claims was read by Baron Makino before the Council of Ten on January 27:

"The Japanese Government feels justified in claiming from the German Government the unconditional cession of:

"(a) The leased territory of Kiao-Chow, together with the railways and other rights possessed by Germany in respect of Shantung province.

"(b) All of the islands in German possession in the Pacific Ocean north of the Equator, together with the rights and properties in connection therewith."

(See notes of a conversation in M. Pichon's room at the Quai d'Orsay, January 27. BC-12.)

In this statement Baron Makino also mentioned the taking of the leased territory as well as the railway line connecting Tsingtau with Chinanfu, which the Germans used for military purposes, by Japanese forces, in conjunction with British contingents, after failure on the part of the German Government to reply to the notice to surrender the leased territory of the Kiaochow with a view to its restoration to China, such notice having been made by the Japanese Government, in consultation with the British Government conformably with the agreement of 1911. After other remarks, mainly with reference to the islands, he made the following termination of the statement:

"In conclusion, it may be stated that, in view of the extent of their efforts and achievements in destroying German bases in the Extreme Orient and the South Seas, and in safeguarding the important routes in the Pacific and Indian Oceans and the Mediterranean waters, to say nothing of their contribution in other respects the Japanese Government feel confident that the claims above advanced would be regarded as only just and fair."

He added that a documentary statement of the Japanese claims would be handed in by him at a later date.

Dr. Thomas Wang expressed the hope that the Great Powers would reserve decision until the views of China had been heard, and this was agreed to.

---

* Miller, David Hunter, *My Diary at the Conference of Paris with Documents,* Vol. XIX, pp. 171–201, Part IV, Section 8, Shantung (Articles 156 to 158), Annotations by H. C. Nixon. (Reprinted by permission).

Statement on behalf of China was made on the following day. (See notes of a Conversation in M. Pichon's room at the Quai d'Orsay, January 28. BC-13.)

Mr. Koo said the Chinese Delegation would ask the Peace Conference for restoration to China of the leased territory of Kiaochow, the railway in Shantung, and all other rights Germany possessed in that province before the war. The territories were an integral part of China, were part of a province containing 36 million inhabitants, Chinese in race, language and religion. The lease to Germany had been wrung out of China by force. If the Conference were to take a different view from restoration, were to transfer those territories to any other power, it would be, in the eyes of the Chinese Delegation, adding one wrong to another. The Shantung province was the cradle of Chinese civilization, the birthplace of Confucius and Mencius, and a Holy Land for the Chinese. The density of its population made it unsuitable for colonization; and the introduction of a foreign power could only lead to the exploitation of the inhabitants, not to genuine colonization. Strategically, Kiaochow commanded one of the main gateways of North China. China was cognizant of the services rendered to her by Japanese army and navy in rooting out German power from Shantung, was deeply indebted to Great Britain for helping in this task, and was not forgetful of the services rendered by other Allies whose troops in Europe held in check any enemy who might otherwise have sent reinforcements to the Far East. But the Chinese Delegation felt it false to their duty to China and to the world not to object to paying debts of gratitude by selling the birthright of their countrymen and thus sowing seeds of discord for the future. The Chinese Delegation trusted the Conference would give full weight to the rights of China, the rights of political sovereignty and territorial integrity, and her desire to serve the cause of universal peace.

Baron Makino at this point read the words of the Japanese ultimatum to Germany of 1914, and said since the occupation of Kiaochow, Japan had been in actual possession. In view of all that had passed between the Governments of China and Japan he thought China fully realized the import of Japanese occupation. A friendly interchange of views on this subject had been entered into, and Japan had agreed to restore Kiaochow as soon as Japan had free disposal of the place. Agreements had also been reached with regard to leased railways. As notes had been exchanged, he thought that a statement of these engagements might be worth the consideration of the members of the Council.

Asked by President Wilson whether he proposed to lay these notes before the Council, Baron Makino said he did not think the Japanese Government would object, but he would have to ask its permission. Asked by President Wilson if he would do likewise, Mr. Koo said the Chinese Government had no objection to raise.

M. Clemenceau asked both the Japanese and Chinese Delegates to state whether they would make known to the Council the conditions of restoration agreed between them.

Baron Makino said he would do so provided his Government would make no objection. He did not think it would. There was, however, one point he wished to make clear: Japan was in actual possession of the territory under consideration; it had taken it from Germany by conquest; before disposing of it to a third party it was necessary that Japan obtain the right of free disposal from Germany.

President Wilson pointed out that the Council was dealing with territories and cessions previously German without consulting Germany at all.

Baron Makino said the work now in hand was one of preparation for presentment of the case to Germany. It followed that the cession of Kiaochow would have to be agreed upon by Germany before it was carried out. What should take place thereafter had already been the subject of an interchange of views with China.

Mr. Koo said China did not hold quite the same view as Baron Makino regarding the restoration of Kiaochow. He was far from desiring to intimate that Japan after obtaining the leased territory and other rights in Shantung from Germany, would not return them to China, he had every confidence in Japan's assurances that she would not retain them herself; and he was glad to hear Baron Makino confirm these assurances before the Conference. But there was a choice between a direct and indirect restitution. Of the two, China would prefer the first.

As to arrangements referred to by the plenipotentiary from Japan, Mr. Koo presumed that reference was made to the treaties and notes in consequence of the negotiations on the twenty-one demands in 1915. The circumstances were, to say the least, disconcerting to the Chinese government, as the latter was constrained to agree to them only after an ultimatum from Japan. Apart from these circumstances, they were, in view of the Chinese Government, only provisional and temporary arrangements subject to the final review of this Conference, being questions arising from the war. Furthermore, if the treaties and notes had been entirely valid, the fact of China's declaration of war on Germany had altered the situation in such a way that on the principle of *rebus sic stantibus* they could not be enforced today. China had been made to agree that she would give full assent to whatever arrangements Japan might make with Germany on the disposal of Germany's rights, privileges and concessions in Shantung. But the provisions did not preclude China's joining the war, nor did it prevent China from participating in this Conference as a belligerent, nor did it prevent her from demanding from Germany direct restitution of her rights. In declaring war against Germany, China stated that all treaties and conventions concluded between China and Germany should be considered nullified by the state of war between them. If, then, the leased conventions had been terminated, the leased territory of Kiaochow and such other rights and privileges enjoyed by Germany in Shantung had all reverted to China as the territorial sovereign. Even if the lease had not been terminated by declaration of war, Germany would be incompetent to transfer it to another power.

(The meeting then adjourned.)

The question was touched again, April 15th, at a meeting of the Foreign Ministers. (See Notes of a Conversation in M. Pichon's room at the Quai d'Orsay, April 15th. F.M. 4.) With reference to Mr. Lansing's proposal for a "blanket" article of renunciation by Germany of territory and territorial rights outside her European frontiers (cf. Art. 118 of Treaty), Baron

Makino said the question of disposal of German territory in China could not be dealt with in a general clause of renunciation, since the territory in question was a leased territory and not a purely German one; and furthermore, in regard to the disposition of that territory, a treaty had been entered into between Japan and China. In consequence, he maintained, the question required special treatment. Upon mention by Mr. Lansing that China had prayed the Conference that the territory in question be restored to her, Baron Makino explained that the treaty between Japan and China to which he had referred dealt with the restitution of the territory to China, that it had been agreed the areas leased by Germany should positively be restored to China.

Mr. Lansing enquired in view of this statement as to restitution whether Japan would object to the Five Great Powers acting as trustees. (No answer is recorded in the minutes. M. Pichon said the discussion seemed to be getting away from the subject.)

In connection with additional discussion of the "blanket" article, at the same meeting, Baron Makino said if the proposal were adopted, it would be necessary to make reservation in the case of Kiaochow, which could not be included in a general clause.

At the next meeting of the Foreign Ministers, when the draft of the "blanket" article was read, Baron Makino insisted on the reservations by the Japanese Delegation with respect to Shantung and Kiaochow, saying that he had on a previous occasion drawn attention to the fact that Japan claimed all the rights acquired by Germany from China. (Notes of a Conversation in M. Pichon's room at the Quai d'Orsay, April 17th. F.M. 5.)

Mr. Lansing enquired whether these rights were claimed from Germany or from China.

Baron Makino replied that they were claimed from Germany.

Mr. Lansing said in the event of special treatment being required for Shantung, he would ask the Japanese Delegation to propose a special clause; with a precise text, it would be possible to debate on the reservation, the purport of which he was not aware.

Baron Makino referred to the fact that in January he had made a general statement of the Japanese claims (Meetings of Council of Ten cited above) and had stated that the claims would subsequently be presented in such form as to be introduced into the treaty. He proposed to bring forward a few articles embodying these claims. All he meant by recalling the reservations was to give notice that he proposed to put forward these articles.

Mr. Lansing observed that the Japanese statement had been made before the Council of Ten, and he thought it would be right that the Council of Ten should take this matter into consideration.

When it was pointed out that meetings of the Council of Ten had become rare and the procedure proposed might delay decision for some time, Baron Makino said that he was engaged in certain pourparlers which might, he thought, lead to an early settlement of the question.

Baron Makino agreed, with reservation previously stated, to the adoption of the "blanket" article of renunciation.

On April 22nd, Baron Makino offered two draft articles on the subject of Shantung, at a meeting of the Council of Four. (Notes of a meeting at

President Wilson's house, April 22nd, 11:30 A.M. I.C. 175C, British Index and Reference.) Those articles did not contain the expression, "free and clear of all charges and encumbrances," which occurs at the end of Art. 156 and Art. 157 of the Treaty and was added at the instance of the Japanese; otherwise there is no variation between the two draft articles submitted and the text of Art. 156 and 157 aside from such changes as may have been made by the Drafting Committee for the sake of uniformity. At this meeting, Baron Makino undertook to explain more fully the Japanese claims relating to the leased territory of Kiaochow and the rights in respect of Shantung province. After reviewing his statement made before the Council of Ten in January (quoted in part above), he made a statement on the negotiations between Japan and China.

Baron Makino said, in statement read at this meeting, that Japan approached China in January, 1915, with a view to reaching before the termination of the war, an agreement as to the basis of restitution to China of the leased territory of Kiaochow and of disposing of other German rights in relation to Shantung, so that Germany might find no pretext to refuse acquiescence in Japan's demands at the final Peace Conference and that she might not find it possible to recover her influence in China, thereby becoming again a grave menace to the peace of the Far East. He mentioned the treaty made between China and Japan in 1915 and summarized the exchange of notes that accompanied it, and said that early in 1917, Japan began, in conjunction with her Allied Powers to direct her efforts to induce China to sever relations with Germany and, if possible, declare war against her; that China's declaration of war against Germany came more than two years after the signing of the aforementioned treaty between Japan and China.

On the 24th of September, 1918, says Baron Makino's statement, the Chinese Minister at Tokio exchanged with the Minister of Foreign Affairs of Japan a series of notes, which provided, among other things, for the withdrawal of the Japanese civil administration, the management of the Tsingtao-Chinan Railway as a joint Sino-Japanese undertaking upon determination of its ownership and the guarding and policing of the railway. The Chinese Minister also solicited the aid of the Japanese Government in the matter of arranging loans for building two railway lines connecting with the Tsingtao-Chinan Railway and practically coinciding with the lines projected by Germany. To this the Japanese Government consented. The preliminary contract covering these loans was made between the Chinese Government and the Japanese bankers, and the Chinese Government actually received from the bankers an advance of twenty million yen according to the terms of the contract. It was contended:

First. That Japan has undertaken to restore Kiaochow to China on conditions, none of which can be regarded in any sense as unjust or unfair, considering the part Japan took in dislodging Germany from Shantung.

Secondly. That the declaration of war by China against Germany could have no relation whatever to the validity of the treaty and the appended agreement which were concluded between Japan and China more than two years prior to the declaration of war, nor could it alter or affect in any wise the situation in connection with which the aforesaid treaty and agreement were made.

Thirdly. That the arrangements of September, 1918, which were made more than one year after China's declaration of war, could not have been entered into without presupposing the existence and validity of the treaty of May, 1915. Some of the provisions of the former dealt with the subject-matters or furthered the claims, set forth in the latter. In fact, the arrangements of 1918 were intended to be, and are, a supplement and sequel to the treaty of 1915. It is to be noted that China has actually received the advance of twenty million yen according to the terms of the above arrangements.

To these summaries and deductions, I may add that as between Japan and China there is a well-defined course laid out, for effecting the restitution. Any other course could (would?) be against the definite arrangement which has been agreed to between the two Governments concerned. What Japan now seeks is to obtain from Germany the rights of free disposal of the leased territory and Germany's rights, privileges and concessions in relation to Shantung for carrying out the provisions of the treaty of 1915 as well as of the arrangements of 1918.

Baron Makino's statement opposed on the basis of international law the claim that the declaration of war abrogates *ipso facto* treaties of lease of territory, and said further, "I feel firmly convinced that full justice will be done to the claims of Japan based upon her sacrifices and achievement and upon the fact of actual occupation, involving the sense of national honor."

Baron Makino handed around the draft of clauses which the Japanese wished included in the Treaty with Germany. Upon question by President Wilson, he explained that the cables Tsingtao-Shanghai and Tsingtao-Chefoo, mentioned in Art. 1 (156 of Treaty) were German concessions, though not in the original concession. He said they were Government cables.

President Wilson said he had already described as well as he could to M. Clemenceau and Mr. Lloyd George what had happened in his conversation with Baron Makino and Viscount Chinda.

Mr. Lloyd George said that so far as Great Britain was concerned they were in the same position towards Japan as towards Italy. They had a definite engagement with Japan, as recorded in the note of the British Ambassador at Tokio, dated 16th February, 1917. (A copy of this letter is attached as Appendix II to I.C. 175C, the minutes of the meeting.) It conveys the message, "His Majesty's Government accede with pleasure to request of Japanese Government for assurance that they will support Japan's claims in regard to disposal of Germany's rights in Shantung and Islands North of Equator on occasion of Peace Conference, it being understood that Japanese Government will, in eventual peace settlement, treat in the same spirit Great Britain's claims to German Islands South of Equator." Hence, so far as Great Britain was concerned there was a definite engagement. The only doubt he felt was as to whether the ultimate destination of Kiaochow was a matter for inclusion in the Treaty with Germany.

In the case of other German possessions in the Far East the Japanese Government had undertaken to support the British claims south of the Equator, and the British Government had undertaken to support the Japanese claims in the islands north of the Equator. So far as Great Britain was concerned it was not proposed to press for the immediate allocation of the mandates for these islands, but only for their surrender to the Allied and Associated Powers. The allocation was left for settlement afterwards. When the time came, we should have to press the claims of Australia and New Zealand to the islands south of the Equator.

Baron Makino said that Japan had expressed her willingness to support the British claims.

Mr. Lloyd George said if Japanese claims for the surrender by Germany of Kiaochow were put in the Treaty, Australia and South Africa might demand the same treatment with reference to territorial claims. There was hardly time to settle all these details before the Treaty.

Viscount Chinda said if Mr. Lloyd George had in mind that Kiaochow should be placed on the basis of the mandatory system as the South Pacific Islands, the Japanese Delegation thought that Kiaochow ought to be on a definite basis. The mandatory system rested on the basis that these islands were in a state of civilization necessitating their being taken care of by other people. This did not apply in the case of Kiaochow.

Mr. Lloyd George said this was true.

Viscount Chinda said the Japanese Government had a duty to perform to China in this matter, and they could not carry out their obligation to China unless Kiaochow was handed over to them. The Japanese Delegates were under an express instruction from their Government that unless they were placed in a position to carry out Japan's obligation to China, they were not allowed to sign the Treaty. They had no power to agree to postponement of this question.

President Wilson asked if it would be possible for the Japanese Government more particularly to define the arrangements she would expect to maintain with China in Shantung province. In the paper he had been given, the statements were sufficiently explicit as regards the town of Kiaochow and the bay of Kiaochow, but not so explicit in regard to the railway and the administration.

Viscount Chinda said the notes explained that the railway administration would be a joint undertaking.

President Wilson said it was not very explicit. Some further definition was required of the term "joint administration." The document was explicit about the establishment of a police force by China towards the cost of which the railway would make a contribution. He understood that at each station, by which he supposed was meant, railway station, as well as at the training school, there would be Japanese. The document did not explain the position taken by these Japanese.

Upon remark by Viscount Chinda that they were only intended to be instructors, he thought, and that there were many foreign instructors in the Chinese administration; followed by remark by Mr. Lloyd George that there were, in the customs, for example; President Wilson said this was part of a series of things which had been imposed on China. With further remark by Mr. Lloyd George that they had asked for the Customs officials, President Wilson said they had done so after a certain experience. He was fairly clear about the railway concession. He asked if there were not included in the lease to Germany certain concessions about exploitation.

Viscount Chinda suggested mines.

Baron Makino said the mines were amalgamated into the railway.

Viscount Chinda said there were three mines.

Baron Makino said the mines had not paid, and had been amalgamated into the railway, mainly for the use of the railway. The coal was not of very good quality. Germany had given up their concessions. One of the mines was not of much value.

President Wilson asked if there were any great iron deposits.

Mr. Lloyd George suggested they had not been made much use of.

President Wilson agreed, not up to the present.

With remark by Mr. Lloyd George that if this arrangement were included in the Treaty, the question of mandatories would have to be settled and this might create delays and difficulties, President Wilson cited Viscount Chinda's statement about Kiaochow's being in a different condition from the islands. President Wilson asked Viscount Chinda if the railway was a joint enterprise with China.

Viscount Chinda replied in the affirmative.

Baron Makino said Japan had already worked joint enterprises very well with China. In the case of the Sino-Japanese Timber Company, for example, where Japan and China had the same number on the directorate and where dividends were paid in equal proportions. There were several similar concerns, the directorates always consisting of equal numbers of both nationals.

President Wilson asked if there were any restrictions on these railways. His interest was to keep open the door with China.

Baron Makino said there was nothing in the agreement with China against the open door.

President Wilson pointed out that, as had happened in many instances, he was the only one present whose judgment was independent. His colleagues (M. Clemenceau and Mr. Lloyd George) were both bound by treaties, although perhaps he might be entitled to question whether Great Britain and Japan had been justified in handing round the islands in the Pacific. This, however, was a private opinion.

Mr. Lloyd George pointed out that they were only the German islands.

President Wilson here made a statement that is given a summary of more than three hundred words in the minutes. He said he would like to repeat the point of view he had urged on the Japanese Delegation a few days before. Peace of the Far East centered upon China and Japan. He did not like to see complex engagements that fettered free determination. He was anxious that Japan show to the world as well as to China that she wanted to give the same independence to China as other nations possessed, that she did not want China to be held in manacles. . . . . What he feared was that Japan, by standing merely on her treaty rights, would create the impression that she was thinking more of her rights than of her duties to China. . . . . He wished to emphasize the importance in future that States should think primarily of their duties toward each other. The central idea of the League of Nations was that States must support each other even when their interests were not involved . . . . He would like to see Japan in the position of leader in the Far East standing out for these new ideas.

. . . . When he had seen the Japanese Delegates two days ago he had said that he was not proposing that Kiaochow should be detached from the treaty engagements but that it should be ceded to the powers as trustees with the understanding that all they were going to do was to ask how the treaties were to be carried out and to offer advice as to how this could be done by mutual agreement. . . . . What he was after was to attain a more detailed definition as to how Japan was going to help China as well as to afford an opportunity for investment in railways, etc. He had hoped that by pooling their interest the several nations that had gained a foothold in China (a foothold that was to the detriment of China's position in the world) might forego the special position they had acquired and that China might be put on the same footing as other nations. . . . . There was a lot of combustible material in China and if flames were put to it the fire could not be quenched for China had a population of four hundred million people. It was symptoms of that which filled him with anxiety. . . . . He did not wish to interfere with treaties . . . . The war had been partly undertaken to establish the sanctity of treaties. Although he yielded to no one in this sentiment there were cases he felt where treaties ought not to have been entered into.

Baron Makino, referring to President Wilson's remarks on the larger ideas of international relationship, said the best opinion in Japan favored that point of view. For China the best opinion in Japan wanted equal opportunities or the "open door." He was glad of it. He recalled, however, that international affairs in China had not always been conducted on very just lines. (Mr. Lloyd George interjected that this was undoubtedly the case.) Baron Makino shared the views of one of the Japanese elder statesmen who had remarked that Japan would have to enter into a good many joint undertakings with China and must be content to share equally, half in half, in them.

President Wilson said he was satisfied on that point. He wanted that principle, however, to be shown in a concrete way to China. Baron Makino, referring to remarks on Shantung, said that there, Japan had only entered into an agreement, whereas Germany had assumed almost complete sovereignty. All Germany's concessions over and above the agreement between Japan and China would now fall through. There remained only the concession mentioned in the treaty which had already been discussed. Reverting to the larger views expressed by President Wilson, he stated that the Minister of Foreign Affairs at the opening of the session (in January he thought) had said that the Japanese Government was ready to contribute towards anything just that was proposed in China. As regards more concrete matters, as extraterritoriality, maintenance of foreign troops, spheres of influence and the Boxer Indemnity, four principal points China had most at heart, he gathered from the speech of the Minister of Foreign Affairs that the Japanese Government was ready to discuss them with the Great Powers. Japan would be glad to discuss these questions. Extraterritoriality was a matter which would take some time. Japan had accomplished it and China could follow in her footsteps.

President Wilson asked what was the idea of Japan as to extraterritoriality in the settlement contemplated at Kiaochow.

Baron Makino said extraterritoriality was considered as an established principle all through China. If the principle changed, Kiaochow would form no exception.

President Wilson said he felt he realized the situation in fuller light than ever before. He asked whether the Japanese Delegates would prefer to draw the Chinese into conference. As China was a full member of the Peace Conference final judgment could not be passed without seeing them.

Baron Makino did not object to China being heard but did not want to enter into discussion with them. It was difficult to discuss with people who had preconceived ideas to dispel them in one or two conversations.

(After some further discussion, it was agreed that Japan would not exercise her right to be present and that the best plan would be for discussion with the Chinese to take place in their absence.)

Baron Makino said before the meeting ended he wished to say a word about the form of restitution of Kiaochow to Japan. The Japanese Government attached supreme importance to the form which had been submitted that morning (draft articles cited above). To-day fresh instructions had been received from the Government, and he could not too much stress the matter.

On the afternoon of April 22nd, the question of Shantung was discussed with the Chinese. (See Notes of a Meeting at President Wilson's house, April 22nd, 1919, at 4: 30 P.M., I.C. 175E.)

President Wilson mentioned the conference he had with the Japanese on the previous day and the meeting with the Japanese in the morning. Since last seeing Mr. Koo he had read the documents. He mentioned the exchange of notes between Japan and China, in which Japan had laid down certain conditions, which the Chinese Government had accepted. Great Britain and France (Mr. Lloyd George said this had occurred between the two exchanges of notes between China and Japan) had entered into a similar but not identical agreement with Japan that they would support the claims of the Japanese Government on the Continent and in the islands north of the Equator. In the case of the British Government it had been on the understanding that Japan supported her claims to German islands south of the Equator. Great Britain and France were much in the same position on the matter.

Mr. Lloyd George explained that at the time the submarine campaign was very formidable. There was a shortage of torpedo-boat-destroyers in the Mediterranean. Japanese help was urgently required, and Japanese had asked for this arrangement to be made. We had been hard pressed and had agreed.

President Wilson, after reading extracts from the notes exchanged between China and Japan, said the Chinese Delegation would see the embarrassing position which had been reached. Mr. Lloyd George and M. Clemenceau were bound to support the claims of Japan. Alongside of them the Chinese had their exchange of notes with Japan. Mr. Koo, before the Council of Ten, had maintained that the war cancelled the agreement with the German Government. It did not cancel the agreement between China and Japan, made before the war. He had urged upon the Japanese that the leased territory of Kiaochow, as in case of Pacific Islands, be settled by being put into the hands of the Five Powers as trustees. He did not suggest the breaking of treaties, but it might be possible to modify the treaty and bring about an agreement. He had also proposed that all Governments renounce the special rights they had acquired in China. The Japanese were not willing to have Kiaochow handed over to the Five Powers; British and French Governments were bound by treaties. Pressed for meaning of their agreement, the Japanese had replied that the exploitation of two coal mines and one iron mine, not proving successful, were now bound up with the railway; they stated that they would withdraw the civil administration, would maintain troops only on the termini of the railway, and if a general agreement was reached would withdraw their extraterritoriality. He said the Japanese had urged that they wanted a community of interest with the Chinese in the railway, and the only reserve they made was for a residential district in Kiaochow.

Mr. Koo explained that the Treaties of 1915 and the subsequent exchange of notes were the outcome of 21 demands which Japan had made on China and all were part and parcel of one transaction. He felt that the treaties and notes which had been exchanged after Japan had delivered an ultimatum stood outside of the regular procedure and course of treaties. They dealt with matters arising out of the war. . . . . On the 7th of May (1915) the Japanese sent China an ultimatum in regard to the majority of the demands giving China only 48 hours within which to accept. . . . . This caused absolute consternation to the Chinese Government which eventually had to submit to *force majeure.*

Mr. Lloyd George asked if they had not appealed to the United States.

President Wilson said they had and the United States had intervened in regard to the infringement of sovereignty and political independence. The whole transaction, however, had been kept extremely secret, and the United States only learned of it in a roundabout way.

Mr. Koo said secrecy had been imposed upon China by Japan under severe penalities. . . . . The Chinese Government felt that treaties and notes exchanged as a result of these 21 demands followed by an ultimatum were on a different footing from the ordinary. . . . . For the last four years since they had captured Kiaochow, Japanese troops had penetrated far into the province of Shantung. The Chinese Government had protested and asked Japan to withdraw her troops who were stationed 250 miles up the railway, but they had refused and had established civil administration bureaus in the interior of Shantung and extended their control even over the Chinese people by levying taxes on Chinese people and asserting judicial power over them. Feelings of Chinese people against extension of Japanese control were so strong that the Chinese Government was constrained to take some immediate step to induce Japan to withdraw troops and remove civil administration bureaus, to relieve the situation until final settlement at the Peace Conference.

Mr. Lloyd George said it looked that by the Treaty with China, Japan would get more than the Germans had had. He asked Mr. Koo which he would prefer, the Treaty with Japan or the transference to Japan of the German rights.

Mr. Koo said the situation was so difficult he must speak frankly. The Japanese position was so close to China, especially in Manchuria, where they occupied a railway which was connected with Peking, that to transfer the

German rights would create a serious situation. With the Japanese on the Manchurian railway and the Shantung railway, Peking would be, as it were, in pincers.

At this point, President Wilson remarked that the Japanese claimed that the administration of the railway would be a joint one and that they proposed to withdraw the Japanese administration. Further comment by him and by Mr. Lloyd George brought out that possibly Japan was claiming greater rights than Germany had exercised; that as the British and French Governments had to support the Japanese claims to what Germany had had, they wanted to know whether China would be better off according as Japan could exercise the rights that Germany had or those she obtained by her Treaty, whether the Treaty with Japan was better for China than Germany's rights.

Mr. Koo, after consulting his colleague, said he could make no choice, because both alternatives were unacceptable; he would merely compare them; the Treaty and Notes with Japan provided for the restoration of the leased territory to China on certain conditions, but such restoration would be only nominal. Between the two he thought that the German rights were more limited.

President Wilson, after emphasizing that he had put the Chinese case as well as he could to the Japanese Delegation, said what he asked now was only a means of getting out of a position that was extremely difficult. In this Conference the United States was the only Power entirely unbound. Great Britain, France, China and Japan were all bound by treaties; bound to keep these treaties because the war had largely been fought to show that treaties could not be violated.

Mr. Lloyd George said he would like to have the two positions examined by British, French and American experts.

M. Clemenceau said he had no objection.

President Wilson read extracts from the Treaty and from Groups IV and V of the 21 demands, recalling that there were demands designed to exclude other Powers from the commercial and industrial development. Then he asked if the following point of view would appeal to the Chinese plenipotentiaries: Hereafter, whatever arrangements were made both Japan and China would be members of the League of Nations, which would guarantee their territorial integrity and political independence. China would receive a kind of protection she had never had before and other nations would have a right they had never had before to intervene. He, himself, was prepared to advocate at the Council of the League of Nations and at the Body of Delegates that the special positions occupied by the various nations in China should be abandoned. Japan declared she would support this. There would be a forum for advocating these matters. The interests of China would not be overlooked. .... While there was doubt as to the Treaty and Notes between China and Japan, there was no doubt as to the agreements entered into by France and Great Britain. Even if the agreements between China and Japan were abandoned, these Governments were bound to support Japan in getting whatever rights in Shantung Germany had. The question for the Chinese to consider was, would they prefer to retain the rights secured by the latter in treaty with China or would they prefer Japan should inherit the German rights in Shantung.

Mr. Koo said the Chinese people were at the parting of the ways. The policy of the Chinese Government was one of co-operation with Europe and the United States as well as with Japan. If, however, they did not get justice, China might be driven into the arms of Japan. There was a small section of China which believed in Asia for the Asiatics and wanted the closest co-operation with Japan. If the Government, believing the justice of the West and that their future lay there, failed to get justice there, the consequential reaction might be very great. Further he wished to say the validity of the arrangements was questionable, since they had arisen out of the war, which China subsequently entered, and since new principles had now been adopted by all nations as the basis of peace and the agreements with Japan appeared to be in conflict with them.

President Wilson said these were serious considerations, but he would not like Mr. Koo to entertain idea that there was injustice in an arrangement based on treaties which Japan had entered into. He emphasized the sacredness of treaties, and said the unjust treatment of China in the past had not by any means been confined to Japan. He hoped the quandary in which the Powers were would be stated to the Chinese people, that it would be shown to them that the undoing of the trouble depended on China uniting in reality with other nations, including western nations. The heart of the world went out to China's 400 millions of people. Any statesmen who ignored their fortunes were playing a dangerous game. But it would not do to identify justice with unfortunate engagements that had been entered into.

M. Koo thought it would be better to undo unfortunate engagements now if they endangered the permanence of the future peace.

Mr. Lloyd George said that the object of the war was not that. It had been fought as much for the East as for the West, China had been protected by the victory that had been won, the doctrine of the mailed fist had been propounded in relation to China. The engagements had been entered into with Japan at a time when support of that country was urgently needed..... Kiaochow could not have been captured without Japanese support. It was a solemn treaty and Great Britain could not turn around and say the treaty was a bad one and should not be carried out. Within treaties he would go to the utmost limits to protect the position of China. On the League of Nations he would always be prepared to stand up for China against oppression, if there was oppression. It would be of no service to herself for China to regard treaties as mere scraps of paper.

M. Clemenceau said M. Koo could take every word Mr. Lloyd George had said as if he had said it also.

No decision was recorded at this meeting. M. Koo made an additional remark that the engagements just considered had been made to meet a world situation, not one in the Far East, while President Wilson and Mr. Lloyd George emphasized idea that they were to meet a world situation, to prevent German domination of the Far East as well as to save Europe. Mr. Lloyd George wished to consider further, and President Wilson asked the Chinese to consider the question further and expressed the hope it would be taken up again soon.

In compliance with suggestions made at the afternoon meeting on

April 22nd at President Wilson's house, the Shantung situation was examined by M. Joan Gout, Mr. E. T. Williams and Mr. Macleay, who were directed to express an opinion as to whether it would be more advantageous for China if Japan were merely to inherit the rights possessed by Germany in Shantung and Kiaochow or if she were to accept the position created by the Sino-Japanese Treaties and Agreements of 1915 and 1918. (See Report of Committee on Shantung and Kiaochow. Appendix II to Notes of a Meeting at President Wilson's house April 24th, at 4 P.M., I.C. 176C.) They found that either alternative presented serious disadvantages for China. But they were of opinion that it would be more advantageous for China to accept the first alternative and to agree to Japan succeeding to the rights and the position which Germany possessed in Kiaochow and the province of Shantung in 1914 on the outbreak of the war, provided that Japan's rights, both in the leased territory and in the province, were confined strictly to those secured to Germany by the Treaty of March 6, 1898, and by subsequent Sino-German agreements in regard to mines and railways. They noted that those treaties and agreements did not confer right to establish outside the leased territory any form of civil administration in the province of Shantung, or maintain troops in any district or town in the province, or to employ German troops or police to guard the Kiaochow Tsinanfu Railway. They noted further that by terms of agreement between Germany and China on the 31st December, 1913, the two railways in province of Shantung, which Germany obtained concessions to build in place of lines originally contemplated in the 1898 Convention, were to be constructed as Chinese Government railways, would become property of the Chinese State, not of the concessionaries. No comment on this report was recorded in the minutes to which it was attached as Appendix II.

(This report was also attached as Appendix III, to I.C. 176F, notes of a meeting at President Wilson's house, April 25th.)

A Chinese statement was before the Council of Four at the meeting at President Wilson's house April 25th, 6:30 P.M. (See I.C. 176F, and Appendix IV.) This summarized the remarks made in previous meetings by the Chinese; and as to the question which alternative China would prefer, the Treaty with Japan or the transfer to Japan of the German rights, the Chinese found neither acceptable because of the difficulties in both. Following the review of the difficulties, the Chinese Delegates here submitted the following four propositions as a settlement:

I. Germany renounces to the Five Allied and Associated Powers her holdings, rights and privileges in Shantung for restoration to China.

II. Japan, being in possession of the said holding, rights and privileges, engages to effect the said restoration to China within one year after the signature of the Treaty of Peace with Germany.

III. China agrees to make a pecuniary compensation to Japan for the military expenses incurred in the capture of Tsingtao, the amount of the said compensation to be determined by the Council of Four.

IV. China agrees to open the whole of Kiaochow Bay as a commercial port, and to provide a special quarter, if desired, for the residence of the citizens and subjects of the Treaty Powers.

This report, prepared on April 23rd, and the report of the committee on

Shantung and Kiaochow (just cited above) led to additional discussion of the question by the Council of Four (more particularly of three at the time) at the meeting of the 25th.

President Wilson, after calling attention to the reports, asked Mr. Lloyd George if the British and French were bound to transfer Kiaochow and Shantung to Japan.

Mr. Lloyd George said that sooner or later they were.

M. Clemenceau agreed.

Mr. Lloyd George had discussed the question with Mr. Balfour, who had suggested that we talk over the terms on which Japan would hand the German rights in Shantung and Kiaochow back to China. That would meet the Japanese sentiments of pride, which compelled them to insist on the transfer of Kiaochow and Shantung to them and not to the Allied and Associated Powers. There was something to be said for Japan in this respect, since the Far East was the only sphere in which Japan was greatly concerned. Mr. Balfour thought the Japanese might accept the Chinese suggestion except for their first proposal. Mr. Lloyd George said we ought to discuss with Japan the conditions in which she would cede the territory back to China.

There was other discussion, particularly on the role Japan had played in the war.

President Wilson, commenting on Mr. Lloyd George's suggestion that the best plan would be for some one to sound the Japanese before they saw the Supreme Council, said they should be told that the Allied and Associated Powers could not consent to the return of Kiaochow and Shantung on the terms on which they had agreed with China. He suggested that Mr. Lloyd George and Mr. Balfour should see Baron Makino and Viscount Chinda.

(Mr. Lloyd George undertook that Mr. Balfour should see the Japanese representatives.)

A summary by Mr. Balfour of the results of this conversation with the Japanese as arranged was before the Council at a meeting at President Wilson's house, April 28th, 11 A.M.; it was discussed at this meeting, at which Mr. Balfour was present, with supplementary remarks; and Mr. Balfour was instructed to write a letter to Baron Makino, according to Mr. Balfour's own suggestion. (See Notes of a Meeting at President Wilson's house, April 28th, I.C. 177A and letters attached, Appendix VI and Appendix VII.)

Mr. Balfour stated that the Japanese denied that they intended to modify in their own favor the conditions which the Germans had imposed upon the Chinese in connection with the Shantung Peninsula, or that their treaties with China would have that effect; they said they proposed surrendering all military control over the Peninsula, that it was their intention fully to restore Chinese sovereignty in the leased territory; the provisions in the Treaty of 1918, with regard to maintaining a garrison at Tsinan and guarding the railway with Japanese troops were purely provisional, referring only to the period of transition after peace; they intended to make this period as short as possible but named no date for termination of this transitory arrangement. The Japanese proposed to retain German rights of an economic character consisting in: (1) A right to claim a concession at Tsingtau, not excluding the right also for other countries to organize an international concession if desired; (2) The

German rights in the railways already built and the mines associated with them, the railways were built on land which is in full Chinese sovereignty; (3) Concessions granted to the Germans for building two other railways, to be built with Japanese capital, concerning which negotiations were in process between the Chinese Government and the Japanese capitalists; the Chinese Government would be able to secure the same position in regard to these two railways as it has over other railways constructed by foreign capital. The Japanese, for reasons of national dignity, were unwilling to modify the letter of treaties with China, but were ready, Mr. Balfour understood, to give complicit assurances; (a) That any concession given them by China at Tsingtau would not exclude other foreign enterprise from the port; (b) That the economic control of the railway, which the possession of the majority of the shares give them, would be used in any way to discriminate between trade facilities of different nations. (It was stated by Mr. Lloyd George that Baron Makino, on behalf of the Japanese, had accepted Mr. Balfour's memorandum, just summarized in this paragraph.)

President Wilson, in connection with the Balfour memorandum of conversation with the Japanese, asked what would be the effect of saying to the Japanese: "We transfer to you the German rights but we do not confirm any arrangement you made with the Chinese earlier in the war and we do this provided that you give a definite assurance that you will not exercise your provisional rights for employing military forces in Shantung." There was nothing on which public opinion of the United States was firmer than on this question that China should not be oppressed by Japan. Public opinion expected him to take the same line for Japan as he had taken for Italy. There was some difference between the two cases inasmuch as there was a definite understanding by China to transfer territory to Japan.

(After an interval devoted to other subjects, Mr. Balfour was introduced and reviewed the circumstances of the memorandum and of a conversation had with the Japanese after the one dealt with in the memorandum.)

Mr. Balfour said Baron Makino had come again to see him on Sunday evening. With great delicacy but perfect clearness he had indicated that Japan wanted a decision on the Japanese claims as a whole, had pointed out that Japan was asked to agree to the League of Nations although she could not obtain recognition of her claims for equality of treatment. He had said that public opinion in Japan was much concerned on this question, that if Japan was to receive one check as regards Shantung and another check as regards the League of Nations the position would be very serious. Consequently, it was very important to obtain a decision on the question of Shantung before the Plenary Meeting to be held the same afternoon on the subject of the League of Nations. He understood that if Japan received what she wanted in regard to Shantung, her representatives at the Plenary Meeting would content themselves with a survey of the inequality of races and move some abstract resolution which would probably be rejected. Japan would then merely make a protest. If, however, she regarded herself as ill-treated over Shantung, he was unable to say what line the Japanese Delegates might take.

President Wilson could not abandon China, he had told the United States Delegation, "If Japan will return Kiaochow and Shantung to China and relinquish all sovereign rights and will reduce her claims to mere economic concessions foregoing all military rights, I would regard it as returning these possessions to China on better terms than Germany had held them."

Mr. Balfour said there was no doubt Japan was doing this. (President Wilson said his experts did not agree.)

President Wilson drew attention to the fact that Japan had retained the right to keep troops in Shantung, while Germany had had no such rights, even temporarily; and said if the Japanese would concede all military rights and make their agreement a purely economic one, he would agree to what they desired. He referred to mention by himself at previous meetings that when the League of Nations was set up he would make a proposal for the cession by all the Powers concerned, including Japan, of their rights of extraterritoriality.

Mr. Balfour thought the present Japanese Government more liberal than that of 1915, said the Japanese had made it clear that the right to keep troops in Shantung was only to be exercised temporarily, and felt the Japanese would be willing to limit themselves to purely economic claims.

(At Mr. Balfour's suggestion it was agreed that he write a letter to Baron Makino according to the discussion as to the line it should take. It was also agreed that Japanese representatives should be asked to meet the Council on the following day.)

In Mr. Balfour's letter to Baron Makino dated April 28th (attached as Appendix VII to I.C. 177*A*), he stated that the Council was satisfied as to the permanent arrangements come to between Japan and China on the subject of Shantung, accepting the view as represented by Mr. Balfour in his memorandum of conversation with Baron Makino and Mr. Balfour's remarks supplementary to it. These arrangements were for Japan to hand back to China the whole of the leased territory in complete sovereignty after cession by Germany, retaining only the economic rights enumerated in the Balfour memorandum, and carrying out the policy of the open door in spirit and letter. It was stated that anxiety was expressed on the temporary arrangements with regard to guarding the line and garrisoning Tsinan. These were interferences with Chinese sovereignty in excess of anything the Germans could claim under their Shantung arrangements. "They hoped you would consent to discuss this relatively unimportant aspect of the Shantung question to-morrow at 11 o'clock. They quite recognize, and greatly regret, the inconvenience to which you may have been put owing to the fact that the Plenary Conference (on the League of Nations) will, under this arrangement, precede the Shantung discussion. . . . but hope you will forgive the inevitable postponement."

On April 29th, the question was again discussed, with Japanese present. (See Notes of a Meeting at President Wilson's house, April 29th, at 11 A.M., I.C. 177*B*, revised.) Most of the discussion hinged on the question of police for the guarding of the railway. President Wilson made strong objections to any arrangements by which the Japanese Government might exercise any such rights as being in excess of rights exercised by Germany and being an infringement of Chinese sovereignty. It was difficult for him to face public opinion in the United States on the question, and it would greatly increase his difficulty if the transfer of rights to Japan was greater than those exercised by Germany; he was not willing to admit the right of the Japanese Government to exercise supervision over the police force. After extensive discussion, Mr. Balfour made proposals which were amended and given to the Japanese for consideration. These provided in substance that it be the declared policy of Japan to hand back to China in full sovereignty the Shantung Peninsula, retaining only the economic privileges possessed by Germany; that the intention of the clauses relating to police on the railway was only to give the owners security for traffic; such Japanese instructors as may be required to assist in policing the railway may be selected by the Company. President Wilson made the following proposal: "Surrender to China of all right of sovereignty and retention with regard to the railway and the mines only of the economic rights of a concessionaire, retaining, however, the privilege of establishing a non-exclusive settlement at Singtau." The Japanese undertook to consider these formulae and report as soon as possible.

The Japanese were at the meeting of the Council on April 30th. (See Notes of a Meeting at President Wilson's house, April 30th, 12:30 P.M., I.C. 177F–revised.) In reply to question by President Wilson, the Japanese Delegates declared that:

The policy of Japan is to hand back the Shantung Peninsula in full sovereignty to China retaining only the economic privileges granted to Germany and the right to establish a settlement under the usual conditions at Tsingtao.

The owners of the railway will use special police only to ensure security for traffic. They will be used for no other purpose.

The police force will be composed of Chinese, and such Japanese instructors as the directors of the railway may select will be appointed by the Chinese Government.

At this point there was a prolonged conversation between President Wilson and the Japanese which developed into a general discussion. The Japanese attached validity to the arrangements with China, and wanted the policy here declared before the Council of Four to appear clearly as the voluntary expression of the Japanese Delegates' interpretation of the policy of their Government, that no impression be given that this decision was forced. This last expression came as a result of a remark by President Wilson that he supposed, as the Japanese representatives proposed to make public the policy declared at the outset of the meeting, he was at liberty to use that part of it which most concerned him. President Wilson said frankly he must insist that nothing he said should be construed as any admission of the recognition of the Notes exchanged between Japan and China. At another part of the conversation, he pointed out that the League of Nations would provide means of mediation in the case of issues between Japan and China that might arise, when the Japanese mentioned the possibility of friction in Shantung.

Upon question by Sir Maurice Hankey as to what he was to send to the Drafting Committee, Viscount Chinda produced a draft of clauses to be inserted in the Treaty, including alterations agreed on the previous day. As to Articles 156 and 157 of the Treaty, the two articles here submitted contain at their ends the phrase, "free of all charges and encumbrances." Viscount Chinda said the modifications of the draft previously submitted were added because "instructions from the Japanese Government state expressly that surrender of the German public property should be unconditional and without compensation." The articles were approved and directed to be forwarded for information of the Drafting Committee.

These articles (156 and 157 of Treaty) were not changed between May 7th and June 28th; but (2) of the Protocol, signed on June 28th, deals with Article 156. The Germans made a criticism of these articles. (See Comments by the German Delegation on the Conditions of Peace, Second Part, II, 11, Kiaochow.) The Allied reply stated that though holding the railway and mines to be public property they "would be prepared, in event of Germany adducing proof to the contrary to apply to such private rights as German nationals may be able to establish in the matter, the general principles laid down in the conditions of peace in respect of compensation of this character." (Approved by Council on June 12th, at President Wilson's house. See C.F. 62 and Appendix IV.) For an additional discussion see Notes of Meetings at President Wilson's House on June 21 (C.F. 76 and C.F. 80).

APPENDIX IV

BIBLIOGRAPHY

GOVERNMENT SOURCES

GREAT BRITAIN. Foreign Office. *An Agreement between the British and German Governments concerning Combatant Prisoners of War and Civilians*. London, His Majesty's Stationery Office, 1918, [Cd. 9147] (Parliamentary Papers, Commons, 1918, Vol. XXVI).

————. *British Documents on the Origins of the War, 1898–1914* (edited by G. P. GOOCH and HAROLD W. V. TEMPERLEY), Vol. XI. London, His Majesty's Stationery Office, 1926.

————. *British and Foreign State Papers, 1915,* Vol. 109. London, His Majesty's Stationery Office, 1915.

GREAT BRITAIN. *Parliamentary Debates,* Fifth Series, 1915, Vol. 70. London, His Majesty's Stationery Office, [1915].

————. *Parliamentary Debates,* Fifth Series, 1918, Vol. 110. London, His Majesty's Stationery Office, 1918.

FRANCE. Ministères de la Guerre et des Affaires Etrangères. *Bulletin périodique de la presse chinoise.* Paris, 1917–1923.

————. *Bulletin périodique de la presse japonaise.* Paris, 1917–1923.

UNITED STATES. *Conference on the Limitation of Armament, Subcommittees, Washington, November 12, 1921—February 6, 1922* . . . . Washington, D.C., Government Printing Office, 1922.

————. *Papers Relating to the Foreign Relations of the United States, 1910–1919.* Washington, D.C., Government Printing Office, 1915–1934.

————. *Senate Documents* 66 Cong., 1 sess., No. 106, Vol. 10. Washington, D.C., Government Printing Office, 1919.

————. *Senate Documents* 66 Cong., 1 sess., No. 76, Vol. 13. Washington, D.C., Government Printing Office, 1919.

OTHER DOCUMENTARY SOURCES

CARNEGIE ENDOWMENT FOR INTERNATIONAL PEACE. Division of Intercourse and Education. *The Imperial Japanese Mission, 1917* (Publication No. 15). Washington, D.C., [Press of B. S. Adams], 1918.

————. Division of International Law. *The Consortium* (Pamphlet Series, No. 40). Washington, D.C., The Endowment, 1921.

————. Division of International Law. *Shantung, Treaties and Agreements* (Pamphlet Series No. 42). Washington, D.C., The Endowment, 1921.

————. Division of International Law. *The Sino-Japanese Negotiations of 1915, Japanese and Chinese Documents and Chinese Official Statement* (Pamphlet Series No. 45). Washington, D.C., The Endowment, 1921.

COCKS, F. SEYMOUR, ed. *The Secret Treaties and Understandings.* London, Union of Democratic Control, 1918.

KAUTSKY, KARL. *Outbreak of the World War* (German documents collected by Karl Kautsky and edited by Max Montgelas and Walter Schücking, translated by Carnegie Endowment for International Peace, Division of International Law). New York, Oxford University Press, 1924.

MACMURRAY, JOHN V. A., comp. and ed. *Treaties and Agreements with and concerning China, 1894–1919* . . . . (Publication of Carnegie Endowment for International Peace, Division of International Law). 2 vols. New York, Oxford University Press, 1921.

MILLER, DAVID HUNTER. *The Drafting of the Covenant.* 2 vols. London, 1928. New York and London, G. P. Putnam's Sons, 1928.

————. *My Diary at the Conference of Paris, with Documents.* 21 vols. (Vols. II–XX, documentary material). New York, 1924.

PARIS, PEACE CONFERENCE, 1919. China: . . . . *The claim of China submitting for abrogation by the Peace conference the treaties and notes . . .*, *between China and Japan on May 25, 1915* . . . . (Delegation propaganda: China). [Paris, Impr. de Vaugirard, 1919.]

————. China: *Telegrams received by the Chinese delegation in support of their stand on the Shantung question* (Delegation propaganda: China). [Paris, Impr. de Vaugirard, 1919.]

————. Japan: *Quelques Observations sur le memorandum chinois demandant la restitution directe du territoire cédé à Bail de Kiaotchéou ...* (Delegation propaganda: Japan). [Paris, 1919.]

————. *Supreme Council, Council of Five (Foreign Ministers)*, Secretary's notes of meetings . . . . (F.M. . . . .) mimeographed.

————. *Supreme Council, Council of Heads of Delegations*, Secretary's notes of meetings . . . . (H.D. . . . .) mimeographed.

————. *Supreme Council, Council of Ten*, Secretary's notes of meetings . . . . (B.C. . . . .) mimeographed.

RUSSIA. (R.S.F.S.R.). *Un livre noir, diplomatie d'avant guerre et de guerre d'après les documents des archives russes (1910–1917*). Paris, Librairie du travail, [1927–1931].

SIEBERT, B. DE, and SCHREINER, G. A. *Entente Diplomacy and the World; Matrix of the History of Europe, 1909–1914* . . . . (collected, edited, and translated by Benno de Siebert; English edition arranged and annotated by George A. Schreiner). New York and London, G. P. Putnam's Sons, 1921.

YEARBOOK

BELL, H. T. MONTAGUE, and WOODHEAD, H. G. W., comps. *China Yearbook, 1913.* London, G. Routledge & Sons, Ltd., [1914].

NEWSPAPERS AND PERIODICALS

Far Eastern Review, 1914–1920, Shanghai.
Japan Times, Weekly edition, 1913–1920.
Japan Weekly Mail, 1914–1919. Tokyo.
New York Times, 1914–1931, New York.
North China Herald, 1914–1920, Shanghai.

The Peking Leader, 1914–1919, Peking.
The Times (London), 1914, London.
Utro Rossii, January 18, 1918, Harbin.

SPECIAL STUDIES

Hu Suh (Hu Shih). "The Intellectual China in 1919," *The Chinese Social and Political Science Review*, December 1919, p. 345.

Reinsch, Paul S. "Secret Diplomacy and the Twenty-One Demands," *Asia*, Vol. XXI (November 1921), p. 937.

Tegengren, Felix. "The Iron Ores and Iron Industry of China," *The Geological Survey of China, Memoirs*. Ser. A, No. 2. Peking, 1921–1924.

Timperley, H. J. "Japan in Manchukuo," *Foreign Affairs*, Vol. XII (January 1934), p. 294.

Williams, E. T. "Japan's Interest in Manchuria," *University of California Chronicle*, Vol. XXXIV (January 1932).

GENERAL BOOKS

Ariga, Nagao. *La Chine et la Grande Guerre Européenne au point de vue du droit international d'après les documents officiels du gouvernement chinois*. Paris, A. Pedone, 1920.

————. *La Guerre Russo-Japonaise au point de vue continental et le droit international* ... Paris, A. Pedone, 1908.

Baker, Ray Stannard. *Woodrow Wilson and World Settlement*. 3 vols. Garden City, New York, Doubleday, Page & Company, 1922.

Clyde, Paul. *International Rivalries in Manchuria, 1689–1922*. Columbus, Ohio, Ohio State University Press, 1926.

Frothingham, T. G. *The Naval History of the World War, 1914–1915*. 3 vols. Cambridge, Harvard University Press, 1924–1926.

Graves, William S., Gen. *America's Siberian Adventure, 1918–1920*. New York, J. Cape & H. Smith, 1931.

Grey, Viscount (Edward) of Fallodon. *Twenty-Five Years, 1892–1916*. 2 vols. New York, Frederick A. Stokes Company, 1925.

Grondijs, Ludovic H. *La Guerre en Russie et en Sibérie*. Paris, Editions Bossard, 1922.

Houang, Tchang-sin. ... *Le Problème du Chemin de fer Chinois de l'Est* ... Paris, Les écrivains réunis, 1927.

Ishii, Kikujiro, Viscount. *Diplomatic Commentaries* (translated by W. R. Langdon). Baltimore, 1936.

Ito, Masunori. *Kato Takaaki Den* (a biography of Count Takaaki Kato, in Japanese).

Lansing, Robert. *The Peace Negotiations, a Personal Narrative*. Boston and New York, Houghton Mifflin Company, 1921.

Price, Ernest B. *The Russo-Japanese Treaties of 1907–1916 concerning Manchuria and Mongolia*. Baltimore, Johns Hopkins Press, 1933.

Reinsch, Paul S. *An American Diplomat in China*. New York, Doubleday, Page & Co., 1922.

T'ang Liang-li. *The Inner History of the Chinese Revolution.* London, G. Routledge & Sons, Ltd., 1930.

Trotsky, Leon. *The Lessons of October, 1917* (translated by S. Lawrence and I. Olshan). London, Labour Publishing Company, Ltd., 1925.

Weale, B. L. P. *The Fight for the Republic in China.* New York, Dodd, Mead, & Co., 1917.

Young, A. Morgan. *Japan under Taisho Tenno, 1912–1926.* London, G. Allen & Unwin, Ltd., 1928.

Young, C. Walter. *The International Relations of Manchuria.* Chicago, University of Chicago Press, 1929.

—————. *Japan's Special Position in Manchuria.* Baltimore, Johns Hopkins Press, 1931.

Index

INDEX

Allied Powers: action of, in Manchuria, 160–66; and China's entrance into war, 83–84, 93–95, 100, 102–3, 106, 108, 113, 144; and China's participation in war, 142; and Chinese Eastern Railway, 166, 171–72; and deportation of Germans, 148, 149, 153–57; and enemy vessels in Chinese waters, 150–51; and secret treaties with Japan, 95 ff., 197–98, 206–7, 215, 217

American commissioners to the Peace Conference, and the Shantung question, 222

American interests in China, 118 ff.

Anglo-Japanese Alliance, 108; and Japan's entrance into the war, 7 ff., 13

"Athos" (ship), 98

Balfour, Rt. Hon. Arthur J. (Foreign Secretary and member of British Delegation to Paris Peace Conference), 222–24

Bethlehem Steel Corporation, 41, 62, 118–19

"Blanket" clause in the Treaty of Versailles, 211–12

Bolshevik Revolution, 142, 159; effect in Manchuria, 159 ff.

Boycott, anti-Japanese, 78, 234

British Dominions: representation of, 190–91; territorial demands of, 193

Bryan, William Jennings (U.S. Secretary of State, 1913–1915), 63, 74

Cecil, Lord Robert (member of British Delegation to Paris Peace Conference), 207–9

Chang Hsün, General, 107

Chang Tso-lin (military governor of Fengtien, inspector-general of Manchuria), 141

China: entrance into World War, 78 ff., 83–84, 86, 89, 93, 99–100, 104, 105, 108, 113, 140, 144, 152 ff.; financial assistance to government, 110 ff., 123 ff., 146; measures against German subjects and property, 100, 104, 147–48, 150 ff.; participation in World War, 140 ff.; protest to Germany, 90; *White Book*, 156 (*see also* Entrance into World War; Politics, internal)

Chinda, Viscount Sutemi (Japanese Delegate to Paris Peace Conference), 208, 210, 213, 227–28

Chinese Delegation to Paris Peace Conference of 1919, 4, 175, 178 ff.; attempts to include reservations in treaty, 229 and note; before the Council of Four (Three), 216 ff.; program of, 183–84, 206; relations with the American Mission, 182–83, 204

Chinese Eastern Railway, 159–60, 166, 168; Allied control of, 166, 171–72; American proposals regarding, 169–72; Japanese - American differences concerning control, 170 ff.; Russo-Japanese Agreement on Chang-chun portions, 166–67

Clemenceau, Georges (Premier of France and head of French Delegation to Paris Peace Conference), 213

Consortium, 29, 82, 84, 102, 112, 123–24, 142, 146; Manchuria and the, 30, 36–37

Council of Foreign Ministers, 212

Council of Four (Three): Chinese Delegation and, 216 ff.; Shantung question before, 213 ff., 221–22, 229 n., 230

Council of Ten, Shantung question before, 194 ff.

Cruiser squadron, Far Eastern, 18

Czechoslovak troops in Siberia, 169 and note

273

C₂